AMERICA'S BUSINESS LEADERS PRAISE

CONCEPTUAL SELLING

"Unlike other sales training programs . . . *Conceptual Selling* is a non-manipulative process that makes the sale almost automatic."
   —Donald R. Keough, President and Chief Operating Officer, The Coca-Cola Company

"*Conceptual Selling* is the only help available to a sales professional to . . . learn his customer's values and attitudes (and) know where the customer is in his buying process . . ."
       —John Knopp, Regional Development Manager, Hewlett-Packard

"*Conceptual Selling* talks about the other things that make the 'close' almost automatic. . . . If you practice the *Conceptual Selling* principles . . . the quality of that 'close' is a thousand-fold improved."
       —Henry J. Cockerill, Senior Vice President, Coca-Cola, U.S.A.

"*Conceptual Selling* has taught us there are no bad buyers, just poor sellers."   **—Dan Pratt, President, Marketing Corporation of America**

"The entire focus is upon customer satisfaction long term . . . *Conceptual Selling* is an easy, logical, natural sequence to follow."
       —Ralph Jacobsen, Manager, Sales Training (Retired), Kimberly-Clark Corporation

"It helps tremendously. . . . Unlike other training, *Conceptual Selling* focuses upon the buyer's behavior. . . . Because it helps plan, analyze and critique, things happen a lot faster."
               —Jerry Barnes, Vice President, Bank of California

"THE BEST BOOKS I HAVE READ ON SELLING ARE *STRATEGIC SELLING* AND *CONCEPTUAL SELLING*."
               —Scott DeGarmo, *Success*

Robert B. Miller rose from associate to Vice-President-General Manager for North American operations at Kepner-Tregoe, Inc., which offers consulting services for senior management of Fortune 500 corporations and the federal and state governments. He personally consulted with such companies as Ford, General Motors, Citicorp, and Rolls-Royce. In 1974, he founded Robert B. Miller & Associates, where he began developing the innovative sales systems and other programs that have made Miller Heiman & Associates one of America's top sales consulting firms.

Stephen E. Heiman rose in nineteen years from National Account Salesman for IBM (where he increased sales in all product areas by more than 35 percent and was in the top 5 percent for total sales and percentage quota) to Director of Marketing at Kepner-Tregoe, to Executive Vice-President of North American Van Lines, where he increased sales and profits by 36 percent in four years. In 1978, he joined Robert Miller as co-principal and full partner in what became Miller Heiman & Associates Inc. and has since helped train thousands of sales management executives from top corporations across the country.

Tad Tuleja has twenty successful books to his credit, including *Strategic Selling* and *Beyond the Bottom Line,* named by *Library Journal* as one of the best business books of 1985.

CONCEPTUAL SELLING

The Revolutionary
System For
Face-To-Face Selling
Used By America's
Best Companies

Robert B. Miller and Stephen E. Heiman

with Tad Tuleja

WARNER BOOKS

A Warner Communications Company

Warner Books Edition

Copyright © 1987 by Miller-Heiman, Inc.
All rights reserved.
This Warner Books edition is published by arrangement with
Miller-Heiman, Inc., 1990 North California Blvd., Suite 940
Walnut Creek, CA 94596

Warner Books, Inc., 666 Fifth Avenue, New York, NY 10103

W A Warner Communications Company

Printed in the United States of America
First Warner Books Printing: March 1989
10 9 8 7 6 5 4 3

Library of Congress Cataloging-in-Publication Data

Miller, Robert B. (Robert Bruce), 1931-
   Conceptual selling.

   Reprint. Originally published: Berkeley, Calif. :
Miller-Heiman, c1987.
   1. Selling. I. Heiman, Stephen E. II. Tuleja,
Tad, 1944-   . III. Title.
[HF5438.25.M566   1989]   658.8'5   88-17324
   ISBN 0-446-38906-4 (pbk.) (U.S.A.)
   ISBN 0-446-38907-2 (pbk.) (Canada)

FOREWORD

CONCEPTUAL SELLING places the emphasis squarely where it belongs; upon the customer. The principles in conceptual selling are a constant reminder to all of us that ultimately we win only if our customers win.

We have long held that one of the commandments for losing in business is to concentrate on the competitor rather than the customer. *Conceptual Selling* is a practical guide for putting the customer first on a daily basis.

Unlike other sales training programs which provide tricks for closing the deal, *Conceptual Selling* is a non-manipulative process that makes the sale almost automatic, and furthers the long term buyer-seller relationship.

One of the appeals of *Conceptual Selling* is that its principles transcend different cultures. Since The Coca-Cola Company is a worldwide enterprise selling products in over 155 countries, we find that the concepts give us a common language for communicating with each other and a common set of principles to guide day-to-day selling efforts.

Mr. Robert W. Woodruff, the late patriarch of The Coca-Cola Company, once said, "The world belongs to the discontented." Everlasting dissatisfaction with what we are doing is part of our continuing spirit of winning. As The Coca-Cola Company begins its second century, we know that whatever made us successful yesterday simply will not be good enough to keep us there tomorrow. We must listen to our customers as their needs change in this dynamic world. We cannot afford to be blissfully content with the way we are doing things now.

Conceptual Selling is one of the proven and effective tools that we have found to help us in those efforts.

> Donald R. Keough
> President and Chief Operating Officer
> The Coca-Cola Company

CONTENTS

"I ZIGGED WHEN I SHOULD HAVE ZAGGED"

Why the Best Sales Professionals in the World Asked for a Face-to-Face Selling System

Gentleman Jim Corbett's boxing students used to say that sparring with him was like participating in a fight between the past and the future: your punches always landed in places he had vacated long before.

Anybody in business today will have a pretty good idea of how they felt. The rate of change in today's markets is so rapid, the concept of product loyalty has become so shaky, and competitors have become so sophisticated and aggressive, it seems you have to run twice as fast every day just to keep up with the changing needs of your present customers, and punch twice as hard as you ever did to nail down every piece of new business. Even then the targets keep moving.

We don't know anybody in business, for example, who hasn't gone out one fine morning to discover that one of his oldest and most secure customers has suddenly been snatched away by the competition. "In the old days," a twenty-year sales veteran lamented to us recently, "when you tied down a sale it stayed tied. In today's haywire markets, you can't count on anything lasting for ten minutes." Everybody in sales knows that's true.

In this climate of constant flux, the one thing every business needs is an articulate method for ensuring steady and predictable growth—growth that lasts not only through the changes that are already threatening your own and your clients' businesses, but through changes nobody has even thought of yet, and that are bound to threaten most dramatically those businesses without a reliable system for anticipating them.

The hit-and-miss "pitch" techniques that were the mainstay of selling in calmer years can't even begin to address the problem of slipping sales in today's superheated markets. Anybody who continues to rely on those blind techniques is increasingly likely to wind up like the French generals who built the Maginot Line in the 1930s: when Hitler's tanks arrived, they discovered that their once impregnable defense had been set up for a type of warfare that no longer existed. Today, as the cornerstone of all business success, you need a method of managing the personal sales call that is as far beyond the traditional techniques as the blitzkrieg was beyond trench warfare. You need a systematic approach that puts your work and your company's sales base beyond what one of our colleagues calls "the mercy of the next day," when your competitor can always waltz in, address a customer need you haven't identified, and pull the rug out from under you.

This radically new and completely systematic approach to selling—the only approach that can ensure steady growth in today's volatile markets—is exactly what we teach at Miller Heiman.

Our first book, *Strategic Selling,* made widely available to the sales profession—the largest profession in the world— one of several programs we have been delivering for ten years exclusively to America's most successful corporations. It placed at the disposal of far more sales professionals than our corporate programs could reach our thoroughly tested, repeatable system for planning overall account strategies—strategies that are valid for every account you deal with, and that you must have to put yourself in the right place, at the right time, in front of the right people, to achieve every specific sales goal.

What more could anyone want? Once you've learned to plan your strategy so you consistently position yourself in perfect face-to-face selling situations, isn't that enough? Once actually in the right door, shouldn't any sales rep worth the name be able to manage the one-on-one encounter to a successful outcome?

The answer we've gotten to that question from over 95 percent of our clients—companies that comprise a profile of corporate excellence in America—is short and to the point: Strategic Selling is an astonishingly effective program that gets solid, bottom-line results; but when it comes to maintaining your competitive edge in today's cutthroat, haywire markets, it's only half the game plan.

In a very real sense, we developed the Miller Heiman Conceptual Selling program in response to popular demand for the "second half" of the game plan: the half that provides the complementary, step-by-step, repeatable system for managing every sale *after* you've got the right person in the right place at the right time—in other words, once you're actually *in there.*

Managing the face-to-face sales encounter is often called sales "tactics," and in the late 1970s, many of our clients were telling us something very surprising about tactics: exactly those people who should be the best at planning their selling tactics—including highly experienced sales professionals who have already learned to plan their overall account strategy—in reality don't plan tactics at all. When they finally get to their most critical meetings, rather than relying on a tactical system that's as effective as the strategy that got them there, even the best of them rely instead on the two things salespeople have relied on since the Phoenicians were trading with the Egyptians: their superior product knowledge and the personal, gift-of-gab techniques they mastered over quieter years. Once you're in the ring with a client, the common assumption still goes, the lightning speed of your footwork should be enough to dazzle him into signing.

To use another boxing illustration, that was exactly the sort of blind assumption that got heavyweight contender Jack Roper knocked flat on his back, and out of contention, after he had battled his way to a 1939 title bout with Joe Louis. The strategy Roper used to get to that bout had been fine. Having carried him through years of hard work, and past the toughest competition in the world, his strategy had finally put him in exactly the right position for the biggest win of his career. Yet once in there, he learned a painful lesson: strategy wasn't enough. His fancy footwork proved tactically useless, and he ended up a footnote to boxing history, remembered only for his classic post-knockout admission: "I zigged when I should have zagged."

There probably isn't a sales representative alive who hasn't had the sales equivalent of Roper's experience; and, as things stand now, when you find yourself tactically KO'd in a sales call, often you are no more enlightened than he was about where, or why, you went wrong. With order forms blank and contracts unsigned, you can only trudge home dazed and confused, wondering where you zigged when you should have zagged.

Because at Miller-Heiman we always practice what we teach; and because one of the things we teach is how to listen—really listen—to your clients; and finally because over the years our clients' suggestions have consistently helped us to improve our programs, we took very seriously what they were asking us to do.

"Look," they were saying in effect. "We're delighted to have the reliable discipline and the repeatable structure you taught us to put in place for our strategy. We're now able, with complete predictability, to position ourselves effectively even with our most complicated accounts. But then you leave us hanging. At the crucial moment when we come face to face with a client or prospect and it's time to *carry out* the strategy, we have to fall back on traditional, trial-and-error techniques. We're like the general who gets his troops in perfect field position and then realizes that the only weapons he has to give them are slingshots. What we need now is a *tactical* system that is as reliable and repeatable as your strategic system—one we can use to manage each face-to-face sales call to the best possible conclusion, so it works for us and our clients too."

Conceptual Selling was, and is, our answer to that request. It's a system that recognizes at the outset two related facts that most salespeople are completely unaware of, but that our clients are constantly pointing out to us:

1. When sales representatives prepare at all for an individual sales call, they usually concentrate on just one thing: the polished and supposedly all-important "product pitch."
2. In recent years, rapid change has become the only sales constant, the pitch is not merely the least important part of a sales call; often it works *against* your success.

Conceptual Selling shows you, step by step and using your own selling situations as live, working models, how to replace the increasingly unreliable pitch techniques with a unique face-to-face selling *system*. That system is built on the previously unidentified fact that what happens in every quality sales call is a clearly definable *process* that makes you and your customer partners in each others' business success.

We emphasize the uniqueness of Conceptual Selling for two reasons. First, looking inward for a moment, Conceptual Selling is a totally different program from, and stands independent of, our own Strategic Selling program, and of every other program we offer. Many of our clients take only our Conceptual Selling program; others begin their association with Miller Heiman by taking Conceptual Selling, and then go on to participate in Strategic Selling, our Large Account Management Program (LAMP) program, or one of our other programs.

Second, looking outward, Conceptual Selling is so completely different from everything *else* on the market that it can be, and frequently has been, seen as nothing short of revolutionary. No other program, anywhere, gives you a proven method, laid out in a series of steps anyone can understand and implement, for replacing the unreliable and untestable sales pitches with a completely reliable, completely tested process—a process that makes it possible for you to manage every face-to-face sales call to a profitable conclusion.

Conceptual Selling is the only program that shows you precisely how to work with your customer to discover the real reasons your product or service will—or won't—result in business that's good for you both. It's the only program whose object is to guide you not only through the satisfactory close of a single sale, but through long-term partnerships with your customers—partnerships cemented by the knowledge that you are selling, *and they are buying,* for solid reasons everyone understands. Finally, and most importantly, Conceptual Selling is the only program that allows those partnerships to be as dynamic as they must be to weather the market turmoil that is the hallmark of business today.

The system we offer here, then, is literally a 180-degree turnaround from the idea that selling means getting your tail in the door and pitching the hell out of the product. It's a system, as we've proved over and over, that is far more valuable than even the most "sophisticated" pitch techniques.

But its value isn't just that it's different. The ultimate value of anything in business is that it delivers consistent, bottom-line results, no matter how turbulent the conditions in your own or your clients' markets. Conceptual Selling does that. It's a system that creates satisfied customers who are with you, as real partners, in every buy they make. It's a system that leads, predictably, to the enthusiastic referrals and re-orders on which long-term sales growth depends. And—getting back to the bottom line—it's a system that consistently produces the most important result of all: increased income all around.

That last point, increased income, is worth a bit more attention to make a very specific point about the value of Conceptual Selling in today's rapidly shifting markets. Obviously we can't predict how much your bottom line is going to improve when you put Conceptual Selling in place. But we can give you some indication by sharing what one of our clients achieved when he plugged the Conceptual Selling tactical program into the already effective use of Strategic Selling.

Shade Information Systems is a Midwest-based sales leader in the field of computer peripherals. Last year, one of their top sales executives wrote to tell us that, when they implemented not only our system for planning overall account strategy, but in addition the tactical planning system that makes up Conceptual Selling, they were "*able to go from a $20 million company to a $46 million company in just two years with no new products.*"

Aside from the fact that this already successful company more than doubled its business in two years with no new products, Shade's experience also underscores the value of Conceptual Selling in other ways. Shade is in the computer forms business—one of today's most hotly competitive fields not only in terms of the number of companies involved, but also because customers here are extremely sophisticated, and because the rate of change in both technological development and marketing here is so intense. In all of these respects, Shade is not the exception, but in fact operates under the *typical* conditions in which business is carried out today, and will continue to be carried out as we streak toward the end of the twentieth century.

Conceptual Selling is the only program specifically designed to ensure long-term success in precisely these conditions. And it is the only program that has already been successfully tested in these conditions by scores of highly varied industry leaders—companies whose management and sales personnel have been forward-looking enough to realize that the people who buy from them, like all customers today, are better informed, more demanding, and more quality-conscious than ever before in history.

These sales leaders have recognized a fundamental fact. They know, because the people who are buying have changed, that selling must change too. They realize, in fact, that the vanguard has already changed—has already left razzle-dazzle and the product pitch behind. Every sales leader today knows that the customers he's calling on require a lot more asking, learning, explaining, discussing, and sharing of reliable information than ever before. Conceptual Selling meets that requirement by showing you how to develop and use a very specific buyer/seller communication process that leads, predictably and consistently, to quality sales.

The object here is not only to free both you and your customers from the gimmickry of blind "techniques." It's to make it second nature for you to zero in on the actual process by which every buying decision is made. Nobody else teaches that process, because nobody else has ever identified it. Conceptual Selling not only identifies this critical factor in sales success. It gives you a solid, proven method for managing the process so that, no matter what unforeseen changes tomorrow may bring to your markets, and no matter how dramatic and threatening those changes may seem to others, you will never become one of the Jack Ropers of the sales world, wondering where you zigged when you should have zagged.

We've said that Conceptual Selling is totally different from Strategic Selling, and totally independent of it and of all the other programs we offer. That's true. The entire process, and all of the new terms and planning procedures that you will use in this book, are unique to Conceptual Selling.

But of course there are similarities between Conceptual Selling and our other programs.

The most important one is our concept, which is also our philosophy and our commitment, of "Win-Win." Win-Win is our shorthand for saying that, in any truly successful sale, both the customer and the salesman should "Win"—that is, each one should come out of the sale knowing that his or her best interests have been served.

We realize this statement may surprise you, because we've been using boxing and military metaphors throughout this introduction. But we use them for two good reasons. One, we know that sales reps readily understand them, because they reflect the way most salespeople have been trained. Two, the metaphors highlight the fact that, if you don't manage your sales calls effectively, you can get hurt, and hurt badly. We do *not* mean to imply by our use of these confrontational images that we think of the customer as the enemy. In fact, nothing could be further from the truth. Our entire system rests on our belief that selling can no longer be viewed as a series of one-on-one confrontations.

The reason is entirely pragmatic. The constant change that everyone must cope with today is threatening enough in itself; the last thing any of your clients wants is a sales rep with the old "Let the buyer beware" attitude: the kind of Sam Slick character who comes across with platitudes and buzzwords and smiles, but who is really only interested in the order—even if he has to burn you to get it. Our Win-Win approach is exactly the opposite of Sam Slick's, and we developed it for the most practical of reasons: it's the only approach to your accounts that will get you not just today's order but consistent, and increasing, future business.

Another similarity between Conceptual Selling and our other programs is, as we've already mentioned, that we take a hands-on approach to *your* problems. There are no canned case studies in any of our programs, and you won't find any here. Instead, like the professionals who attend our programs in person, in this book you'll use a series of Personal Workshops; just as they do, you'll use them to plan effective tactics for your own upcoming sales calls. Because of this hands-on, pragmatic method, you will begin to notice a difference in your face-to-face selling encounters even before you finish the program. From the experience of thousands of clients, we know that once you start to apply even the first steps of Conceptual Selling to your own situations, you will immediately begin to understand—with much greater precision than you now imagine possible—exactly what you need to do in every individual sales call to bring it to a Win-Win conclusion.

A third similarity is our audience: the professional salesmen and saleswomen who come to us, year after year, to sharpen their selling skills. Our clients are not sows' ears. They are highly successful sales professionals who ask us to make them still more successful. We do that.

But it's clearly a two-way street, and in fact nothing better exemplifies our Win-Win philosophy in action than the fact that our corporate clients have also helped us to be more successful. We have already mentioned that it was in response to our clients' urgings that we developed Conceptual Selling in the first place. That is only one example of how the people to whom we deliver our programs have been as valuable a resource for us as we have been for them.

The corporate sales representatives and managers who have participated in one or more of our programs now number in the tens of thousands. Obviously we can't thank them all individually, but we can identify and thank their companies. We happily do so here, by dedicating this book to them.

This is more than a gesture on our part. In a real sense these companies— sales leaders all—have helped us create Conceptual Selling by proving its value in the toughest crucible of all: today's turbulent arena of revolutionary market change. Our appreciation, therefore, to:

Acme Resin Corp.
Airborne Freight
Airwick Industries, Inc.
Alexander & Alexander
Allen-Bradley Company
Ambassador Cards
American Bank
  Stationery Company

American Can Company
American Cyanamid Co.
American Microsystems
American Satellite
Apollo Computer, Inc.
Applied Magnetics
ARA Services, Inc.

Arkwright-Boston
  Insurance
Avis, Inc.
Bank of America
The Bank of California
Bekins Company
Beloit Corporation
Beverage Management
Booz•Allen & Hamilton
Bourns, Inc.
R. E. Burrell
Burroughs Corporation
Bussman Manufacturing
C. F. Mueller Company
CMP Publications
Caldwell Partners
Central Paper Company
Central Rigging and
  Contracting
Cincom Systems, Inc.
Citation Computers
The Coca-Cola Company
Cognos, Inc.
Coleman Company
Comshare, Inc.
Container Corporation of
  America
Continental Can Company
Control Data Corporation
Creative Establishment
daka Corporation
Datachecker/DTS
Data Documents, Inc.
Decker Communications
De Luxe Check Printers
Dow Chemical Company
Ebasco Services
  Incorporated
Emery Worldwide

Eutectic Castolin
Exxon Office Systems
First National Bank of
  Chicago
Fisher Controls
Floating Point Systems
Frito-Lay, Inc.
General Electric
  Company
Genstar
Geometric Data
Frank B. Hall & Co., Inc.
Hallmark Cards
Harris-Lanier Corporation
Hercules Incorporated
The Hertz Corporation
Hewlett-Packard Co.
Honeywell, Inc.
IBM
ICI Americas, Inc.
Information Systems of
  America
International Chemical
The International Forum
ITT Dialcom, Inc.
James River Graphics, Inc.
Jerrold Electronics Corp.
Johnson & Johnson
Kimberly-Clark
KLA Instruments
Lockheed Georgia
  Company
Lockheed-California
  Company
Management
  Compensation Group
Marketing Corporation of
  America

Massachusetts Mutual Life
   Insurance Co.
Marriott Corporation
McDonnell Douglas
McGraw Edison Company
Medstat Systems
Memorex Corporation
National Advanced
   Systems
National Semiconductor
NBI, Inc.
NCR Corporation
NL Industries
Owens-Corning Fiberglass
Pacific Mutual Life
   Insurance Company
Pallm Inc.
Pansophic System, Inc.
Pepsico, Inc.
Periphonics Corporation
Pitman Company
Policy Management
   Systems Corp.
R. R. Donnelley & Sons Co.
Racal-Milgo, Inc.
RCA
Research Cottrell, Inc.

Reynolds Metals
Ricoh of America, Inc.
Rockwell International
Ryder/P.I.E. Nationwide
Saga Corporation
G. D. Searle Laboratories
The Seven-Up Company
Shade Information
   Systems
Shared Medical Systems
Sweda International, Inc.
Synergex Corporation
Szabo Food Service
Tandem Computers
Taylor Instruments
Technicon Instruments
Tektronix, Inc.
Teradyne, Inc.
Thermatool, Inc.
Times Fibre
   Communications
TRW Electronic
   Components Group
W.T.C. Airfreight
Warner Jenkinson Co.
Wilson Sporting Goods
Zehntel, Inc.

   In addition, we owe a special debt of gratitude to our
wives, Diane and Rosalie; and to Cathi Gregory, Ralph
"Jake" Jacobsen, Lila Karpf, John Knopp, Larry Lowery,
David Miller, David Shick, Barry Trailer, and Tad Tuleja.
Without them this book would not have become a reality.

                                             R.B.M.
                                             S.E.H.

Berkeley, California
1986

Conceptual Selling:

Basic Principles

▲

▶ 1 ◀

WHY PEOPLE REALLY BUY

Three years ago a major American manufacturer, experiencing problems with the food service company that was managing its dozens of employee cafeterias around the country, went looking for a replacement. On orders from the top, the vice-president in charge of operations invited the incumbent's four major competitors to the manufacturer's Chicago headquarters. Each candidate for the replacement contract, the invitation letter stipulated, would be given ninety minutes to present its case to a selection committee composed of finance, operations, and employee service managers. The presentation date was one month away.

Because this multiple-site food service contract involved potential income of several million dollars a year, all four of the invited vendors expressed strong interest. Their sales managers designated top people to handle the new account presentation and made it painfully clear that their pitches had better be perfect. The four individuals who were chosen—all top-notch, experienced professionals—understood that the Chicago sales call would be one of the most important calls they would ever make. So they spared no effort in preparing.

But they didn't all prepare the same way.

Three of the four prepared in the sales rep's time-honored manner. They crammed their heads full of product and service specs and burned a month's worth of midnight oil memorizing their companies' capabilities. They boned up on the presentation techniques that had worked for them over the years. And they prepared perfectly timed, brilliantly written pitches that made their individual service packages look like offers no sane person could refuse.

The pitches all had catchy anecdotal openings (for establishing "rapport" with the committee), plenty of arguments and counterarguments (for deflecting the inevitable objections), and a copious supply of trial closes. Not to mention the usual supportive material: among the three of them, these candidates had put together enough spread sheets, statistical abstracts, overheads, diagrams, and colored slides to keep a congressional committee in session for a year.

If you've ever presented a product or service to a potentially major new client, you'll probably recognize what we're describing here as the traditional "dog and pony show." The circus metaphor is appropriate because the idea behind such sales presentations is essentially the same one behind big top performances: you are the ringmaster in charge of the show, and your job is to keep the action moving—to keep the customer's attention constantly engaged, so he can't be distracted or bored. Trot out enough dancing dogs and prancing ponies, and the customer will be so dazzled by your staging that the ink will dry on his check before he knows what's hit him.

The man sent in by the fourth candidate—we'll call him Gene—didn't buy this traditional wisdom. A few months before the manufacturer sent out its invitations, Gene had attended one of our two-day programs on Conceptual Selling. In those two days we had taught him a method for managing his face-to-face sales calls that completely reversed everything he had done in presentations before—and that went to the heart of the issue posed by the title of this chapter: why people really buy.

We'll be talking about why people buy throughout this book, and demonstrating to you, as we demonstrated to Gene, how understanding *your customers' buying process* makes you a much smarter and more successful seller than you can possibly be if you limit yourself to a three-ring display of your product, hoping one of the acts will hit home. The first step in understanding that process is to remember a seemingly simple message we gave Gene:

> *People buy for their own reasons,*
> *not for yours.*

The message is critical because until you know your customers' reasons for wanting—or not wanting—to buy, you're selling with blinders on. No matter how many reasons you may have for believing your product or service is a great buy, they will mean nothing unless each customer has solid reasons of his own for wanting to do business with you.

Difficult though it can be to find out what those reasons are, sales success today depends on doing just that—and on staying in touch with each customer's reasons when they change (as they often do) from one sales call to another. In this era of accelerated change, when even your long-time customers face new problems every day that can radically alter the way they see your product or service, taking a customer's views for granted, even for a minute, can doom the most "secure" account. In fact, that's just what had happened in the Chicago contract: the incumbent was on the way out because he had failed to keep on top of the manufacturer's altered view of his service needs.

We consider understanding your customers' needs so important that we make this understanding, along with the product knowledge every professional has to have, part of a sales success "equation":

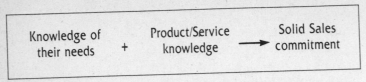

As the arrangement of factors here implies, we believe that every solid sale must *begin* with the customer: with his needs, his problems, and his range of reasons for buying.

The Most Obvious Fact in the World

Obvious? To anybody involved in selling as a profession, the fact that people buy for their own reasons—and that until you know those reasons you're selling blind—ought to be the most obvious fact in the world.

But it isn't. To judge from the way most salespeople approach their customers, in fact, what's really obvious is that they've not only missed this truth, but that they've been encouraged, even trained, to ignore it. That was certainly evident in the way Gene's competitors prepared for the Chicago call. All their statistics and slide shows and zippy phrases boiled down to a message, hidden though it was, that could be translated simply: "Here are *my* reasons that you guys ought to want to buy."

In the month before the Chicago presentation, as his competitors were planning floor shows that would have done Las Vegas proud, Gene kept "the most obvious fact in the world" firmly in mind. He prepared no dog and pony show, no list of objections to be overcome, no letter-perfect ninety-minute spiel. Instead he focussed on what he had to *find out* to determine whether, in fact, his company could provide a solution the manufacturer could use.

In searching for the customer's reasons for wanting to buy, he did some background work on the manufacturer's capabilities and problems: he talked to people who had done business with the manufacturer before; he visited one of their plant sites to get a first-hand look at their current cafeteria operations; he tried to learn as much as he could about *why* they were so dissatisfied.

He didn't get all the answers, of course; and so, as he had learned and practiced in our Conceptual Selling program, he started making a list—not of statements he would make to the committee, but of some very specific *questions* to ask before he began. That list of questions became the basis for Gene's entire presentation.

Did his seemingly maverick planning work? Did the question-intensive, client-centered preparation for this call—the pivotal sales call of his career—turn out to be more effective than the traditional circus acts?

After he had nailed down the contract and pocketed a six-figure commission, Gene explained just how well it had worked. "It was almost too easy," he said. "I didn't have to say more than fifty words. I introduced myself, told them I understood they were having difficulties with their food service operation, and asked them to tell me what they were.

"For most of the next hour I could barely get a word in edgewise. They fell all over themselves helping me to pinpoint their problems. About every ten minutes there would be a lull, I would question them about an area where there was still a gap in my information, and the whole thing would start up again. Following your format for first getting the missing information that was vital for my understanding of the buying process, most of what I had to do in the presentation was to draw them out and take notes.

"When they finally wound down, I just scanned the notes and gave it back to them. 'It seems like you're having trouble in this area, and this, and this. Here's what we can fix, and here's how I think we can do it.' It became the most natural thing in the world for me to give them a quick, no-bull rundown of how our Unique Strengths could address their problems. By that time we were in the sale together—we really had become partners in the process. I didn't even have to quote them a price; they begged me to get the contract work moving.

"As I was walking out," Gene finished, "and making mental notes for our lawyers, I passed the next guy coming in. He was lugging all these portfolios and projectors, and I just grinned inside."

In the several years we have been introducing professionals like Gene to Conceptual Selling, we have heard stories like his hundreds of times. The storytellers always mention the same things: first, the outright surprise their customers feel in meeting a salesperson who keeps his mouth shut; and second, the eagerness with which their customers cooperate with a salesperson who spends more time asking then telling.

In one way or another, all Conceptual Selling success stories include the same basic revelation. Gene puts that revelation well. "That call proved again," he told us, "what I've been discovering over and over since I started selling 'conceptually'. I didn't have to *sell* these guys. They already had a thousand reasons for wanting to buy. I just had to find out what those reasons were, and let them know there were specific ways I could help them with their specific needs and problems."

Most salespeople never get to this revelation. Trained to think of their business as the art of persuasion, they're convinced they *have* to "sell the guy" by giving him reasons to buy. So they try to stay in control of the sale at all times, pushing hot buttons and rattling off features and benefits until even the most reluctant prospect (so the theory goes) is talked into saying "Yes, I'll buy."

Increasingly, in these days of smarter and more demanding customers, this theory is falling to pieces. In fact—as Gene's competitors found out in Chicago—it is often the salesperson's very desire to stay in complete control of the sale that sends the sale spinning wildly out of his control. Far from being accidental, this is the inevitable outcome of the still widely popular assumption that the expert salesperson is always a ringmaster-type, "take charge" guy.

The Myths of Selling

That erroneous assumption underlies most of the given wisdom of our profession. Consider four common examples of this given wisdom—beliefs that can quite accurately be called the myths of selling:

Myth 1: push the Slinky Sphinx. Scene from a recent television sitcom: A novice shoe salesperson, after fitting a customer for a pair of "Elite Petite" sandals, is called aside by the store manager. "I told you to move the Slinky Sphinx models, didn't I? Why are you showing her the Elite Petites?"

"She said she liked them, boss."

"I don't *care* what she likes. We make four bucks a pair on the Elite Petites and five and a quarter on the Sphinx. Do what I tell you: push the Slinky Sphinx!"

Allowing for comic hyperbole, this isn't an uncommon situation. It happens in sales every day, and not just in retailing: we see it constantly in corporate sales. The underlying assumption is that good selling is always "salesperson-driven." If, for any one of a thousand different reasons, you (or your boss) want the Slinky Sphinx pushed, your job is to take charge, stay in charge, and convince each and every customer that the Slinky Sphinx is what *she* wants too.

The idea that this kind of "product push" is good selling is the oldest, the most durable, and probably the most costly of selling myths. It goes hand in hand with the old idea that selling has to be a numbers game: that is, the more money you pocket each time out, the better off you will be. According to the numbers game philosophy, the customer's needs or wants become important only if they don't happen to tie in with what you're pushing; when that's the case, given the fact that your first consideration is always volume, your job is to change the customer's mind. How? Push the Slinky Sphinx.

The "product push" mentality explains better than any other single thing why salespeople so often shoot themselves in the foot. But it certainly isn't the only myth spawned by the ringmaster attitude toward selling.

Myth 2: Use anything that works. If your major concern is not satisfying the customer, but getting as much of his money as you can in your pocket, it often follows that you're not going to worry too much about how you accomplish the goal. You're allowed to do anything—including lie, plead, cajole, intimidate, and embarrass the customer— as long as you get his agreement to buy. All dollars are alike; therefore, any sale is worth making.

At its worst, this attitude leads to the pernicious game of Beat the Buyer, popular with snake oil salesmen and the less scrupulous door-to-door drummers. But you don't have to have it in for your customers to fall for the "anything that works" myth. Plenty of quite ethical salespersons walk into their face-to-face calls with nothing but a bag of selling "techniques"; and so, just like the hit-and-run artists, they are forced to keep on pushing buttons blindly in the hope that, sooner or later, something will work. Because they have no idea *what* will work, even when they succeed in making a sale, they have no method for repeating their success. With this trial and error approach, you start every new sales call at Square One.

Myth 3: Keep him on the track. In the pseudo-methodology called "track selling," the salesperson memorizes a script (usually designed by his company's "buyer psychology" experts) and delivers it orally, verbatim, to every customer he meets. Typically the track selling script begins with a friendly and/or zippy "grabber," proceeds through a maze of "If . . . then" directions designed to answer every possible objection, and ends with a grab bag of trial closes. According to track selling theory, the salesperson should stick to this game plan, whatever the individual prospect has to say, because at the end of the script is the commission. You can see why they call it track selling: just like an engineer keeps his locomotive on the main line, the track seller is supposed to steer the customer away from any "sidings," and drive the sale straight to the close.

The problem with this kind of prescripted pitch technique is that it assumes your customers are stupid and/or infinitely malleable: it assumes they'll let you take charge because they've been to the same sales training program you have. That seldom happens. In fact track selling, which promises you so much control, really fosters a kind of tunnel vision that can easily alienate the customer and kill the sale. Often the gung-ho track seller, putting on steam so he can get to the light at the end of the tunnel, finds out it's the headlight of an oncoming train.

Myth 4: Do more legwork. If you've bought in to Myths 1 to 3, you know that, no matter what your monthly numbers are right now, your ultimate success is spelled out in just one word: more. So if you're pulling out all the stops on every call and you're still not meeting your quota, what do you do?

If you subscribe to the given wisdom of selling, you don't try to analyze what you might be doing wrong in terms of customer contact or in terms of whether or not there's a real match between your customers' needs and your product. You continue to assume your techniques are fine; you're just not working them hard enough. Because you've been told over and over that selling is only a numbers game, you have to reason by the numbers. You know a certain percentage of your prospects will never buy your product, no matter how great your floor show. But a certain percentage will. So the answer is simple. Even though your "kill ratio" may stay exactly where it is, if you make more sales calls you're going to pull in more money. Simple logic, right?

It's more like simple-*minded* logic. Nothing better illustrates why than a story Tom Peters and Bob Waterman tell in their book *In Search of Excellence.* They quote a General Instruments sales executive who stayed especially "close to the customer" one year and came in at 195 percent of quota—tops in his division:

> *A fellow at corporate called me and said, "Good job, to be sure, but you average 1.2 sales calls a day and the company averages*

*4.6. Just think of what you could sell if you
could get your average up to par." You can
guess my response, after I came down off the
ceiling; I said, "Just think what the rest could
sell if they could get their calls down to 1.2."*

The point we underline here is not that you should make
fewer or more sales calls than you're making now. The
essential thing to sales success isn't numbers at all. It's
having a system for ensuring that, however many calls you
make, every one is managed as effectively and predictably
as possible; you achieve that kind of management only by
stepping beyond the kill ratio malarkey and focusing on
the many different reasons your many different customers
may have for wanting what you have to sell. The General
Instruments executive understood that. He knew that
success has everything to do with getting to know the
individual customer, and nearly nothing to do with how
many doorbells you ring.

Myth 5: You gotta believe! You're committed to pushing
the Slinky Sphinx, you're pulling out every hat trick you
know to get the order, you're doing it a hundred times a
week, and you're *still* not Salesperson of the Year. You know
what your problem is? You don't have the right attitude.
The reason you don't make those sales is that you don't
believe you can make them. What you need is Positive
Thinking.

Urged on by the one-note philosophies of various preach-
ers, pop psychologists, and sales "motivators," millions of
people now believe that, whatever you want in life, if you
only believe in it hard enough, sooner or later you will get
it. It's all inside you, goes the line. Change your way of
thinking, and you can change the world.

Yes, we need confidence in what we're doing. We need
the conviction that we can go that extra mile or put in that
extra effort for the once-in-a-lifetime presentation. But if
positive thinking was what made the difference, racetracks
would be churning out millionaires faster than McDonald's
does hamburgers. The rah-rah, motivational approach to

selling leads nowhere in today's frenzied, competitive economy, because it lacks the same thing the other myths of selling lack: a solid, verifiable system for going beyond trial and error, and transforming desire into results.

Correcting the Myths: Focussing on Decision-Making Process

We provide that system by shifting the focus away from tricks the salesman is supposed to perform—that is, away from false promises of "control"—and toward the one thing that remains predictable and stable from customer to customer, and from sales call to sales call: *the customer's decision-making process.*

The program we present in Conceptual Selling is a roadmap to your customers' decision-making process. As a preview of what you'll learn about the process, here are the main principles we'll develop:

1. "Buying" is a special case of *decision-making.*
2. Every time one of your customers makes a buying decision, he does so in a series of *predictable and logical steps.*
3. The steps of the decision-making process take place in an equally predictable and logical *sequence* that can be identified and tracked by the seller.
4. By systematically following this sequence, and helping your customer to follow it, you discover one of two things. Either (a) there is a solid fit between his needs and the solution you can offer, which can lead to a quality sale; or (b) there is no such fit, and you shouldn't be doing business together in this particular situation. Both discoveries give you valuable information about how to proceed with the customer, and about how best to use your valuable, and limited, selling time.
5. By ignoring or working against the customer's decision-making process, you ensure confusion, resentment, and—sooner or later—lost sales.

Obviously, our focus on the decision-making process makes Conceptual Selling a "customer-driven," not a "seller-driven" system. We realize this may make you nervous. Many newcomers to our system express the fear that allowing the client's decision-making process to direct the course of the sale will take things out of their hands—will cause them to lose control. They soon find out that exactly the opposite happens. When you start to work *with* your customers—when you act as a facilitator of the buying process—you always end up with more control, both in the individual sales call and in terms of future business, than you had when you relied on "techniques."

There's a sound reason for this. When you help someone to do what he already wanted to do—make a wise buying decision—he knows he has actively *bought* your solution and not been passively *sold* it by force feeding or manipulation. Someone who knows that buys much more than your current product or service; he buys into a partnership with you that is the linchpin of predictable, long-term sales success.

Tactical Planning:
The Three Phases of the Sales Call

To manage each one of your sales calls so that your customers do know that doing business with you is a mutually satisfying, Win-Win enterprise, you need to do exactly what Gene did in preparation for his Chicago call: *tactical planning.*

By tactical planning, we mean something very specific. We mean consciously thinking through in advance how you are going to handle the *three key phases* of the sales call.

We hinted at those phases earlier, when we presented the sales "equation" linking your product knowledge, your knowledge of your customer's needs, and solid sales commitment. That equation can also be expressed visually, in the form of a diagram:

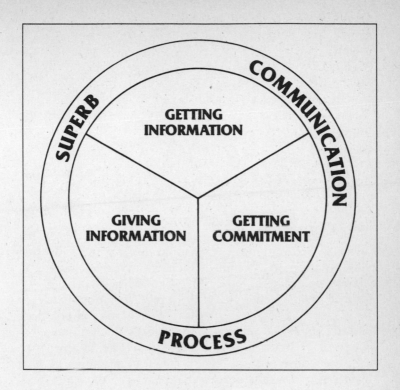

In this diagram, the three pieces of the "pie" correspond to the three key phases of the sales call; the outer rim, labelled Superb Communication Process, stands for a dynamic tactical element we will explain in detail in future chapters.

Phase One of the sales call—Getting Information—involves understanding what *you need to know* about your customer's current situation so you can effectively tell your story. In other words, it's finding out the client's reasons for being interested in doing business with you. Contrary to the given wisdom, this is where every good sales call *begins.*

Phase Two—Giving Information—involves describing and possibly demonstrating your product or service in relationship to the needs of the customer. In other words, it means giving him or her the information *he or she needs* to make a sound buying decision. We show you how to give information that goes beyond the "features and benefits" of your product, and that effectively differentiates you from everybody else who is giving your prospects information.

Phase Three—Getting Commitment—means resolving any of the uncertainties that might prevent your potential client from buying, even though the fit between his needs and your solution is right. We don't mean "overcoming the customer's objections." We mean working with him so that the two of you *share* Commitment to the selling process, at every step of the way.

One caution. When we speak of the three phases of the sales call, we don't mean you should think of them like the phases of the moon, coming in the same invariable sequence every time. There is *no set order* to these phases; we number them merely to make the distinction between them clear. Every sales call is a dynamic interaction between buyer and seller, and that means that you must be able to move freely from one phase to another at any time, not in response to some hypothetical, ideal sequence, but in response to what's actually happening in the call. Tactical planning enables you to do that. When you use the three-phase framework we'll be explaining, you always know three things with precision at any given moment in the call: you understand exactly where *you* are, exactly where your *customer* is, and exactly *what still needs to be done* to move the sale toward a Win-Win conclusion.

In our tactical selling programs, our corporate clients plan their actual sales calls in a series of hands-on workshops. Because we intend to make Conceptual Selling as immediately useful to you as our two-day programs are to them, you'll do the same thing here, in a series of specially designed Personal Workshops based on the live program format. In preparation for the first of these Personal Workshops—presented at the end of the next chapter—you'll need to get some pencils and a notebook, and to do one other thing: choose three or four upcoming sales calls, with specific customers, to serve as the models for your planning.

You'll be planning face-to-face tactics for these calls in all your Personal Workshops, and because we want that planning to pay off as quickly and handsomely as possible, we recommend that you choose not necessarily "typical" customers in "typical" encounters, but calls that are significant to you, for whatever reason, and about which, again for whatever reason, you are uneasy or uncertain. Planning tactics for meetings with difficult customers, or those who are hard to figure, is the best and fastest way we know of highlighting the buying process and of bringing predictability into your most significant selling situations.

In our two-day corporate programs, our clients do intensive planning for sales calls they know they will make very soon—usually a day or two after the programs end. Since you'll probably be spending more than two days on Conceptual Selling, it's not practical for you to do quite the same thing. We suggest you choose sales calls that are scheduled a few days, a week, or even a month or so from today. This will give you time to learn and practice all the Conceptual Selling principles before implementing them face to face.

If you're one of the thousands of sales professionals who work behind a counter, on a selling floor, or in another situation where customers usually come to you, you can't pick specific upcoming encounters; you'll have to choose "typical" encounters. We recommend you pick some recent situations with "tough sell" customers—situations where perhaps you didn't make the sale, or where making it was a fight all the way. For you no less than for our corporate clients, our tactical selling system can help to move such difficult sales forward.

Once you turn the final page of *Conceptual Selling,* of course, you will be able to apply our principles to encounters with all your prospects, and in every face-to-face situation. The tactical planning you'll do here, on your chosen selling encounters, will provide the live, working model for all your future planning efforts.

To prepare you for the first Personal Workshop, we will introduce an idea that takes our explanation of why people really buy one step further, and that lays the necessary groundwork for managing the three phases of the sales call. It's an idea that is exclusive to the Conceptual Selling program, and in fact gives the program its name: the idea of customer "Concept."

▸ 2 ◂

LIFE BEYOND THE PRODUCT PITCH

Why doesn't everybody own a Ginsu knife? They'll hack through copper pipe and keep their edge. You can beat them with a hammer and they won't break. You can slice a tomato so thin that, as Woody Guthrie once quipped, "even a politician could see through it." And, compared to other high-quality kitchen knives, they're relatively inexpensive. The Ginsu knife, in short, is one terrific product.

So why doesn't everybody own one?

The answer has nothing to do with the product. If Ginsu knives could be sold exclusively on their merits, they'd probably be in every kitchen in America. It has to do with the way these excellent products, like many excellent products, are presented to the potential consumer—in other words, with the way they are sold. The failure of the Ginsu company to capture the entire kitchen utensil market—in spite of a good product, intensive television advertising, and the fastest-talking pitchmen in the business—points to a fundamental misperception about *why people really buy.*

We said in the last chapter that people buy for their *own* reasons, not for yours. The Ginsu case illustrates the point well. The company has been very good at telling its potential customers about its products—that is, in giving them the *company's* reasons that they should buy. But the media blitz method they have used by its very nature has prevented them from asking individual customers what they were looking for in a knife. As a result, Ginsu has connected with only a fraction of its possible buyers—and as of this writing is rumored to be in some financial difficulty.

The same lesson applies to any business. Of course some customers will respond to being *told* why they should buy a given product. But the *vast majority will not.* The vast majority of potential customers in any market have to be reached through their own needs and interests; they cannot be moved to spend their money because of the "obvious" or "objective" benefits of a product—no matter how great that product is. Any seller who relies on the Product Pitch alone, therefore, is inevitably going to miss out on business.

As the Ginsu case shows, that's true even when you're used to tolerating the 5 or 10 percent response rate that is common in saturation advertising. It's even more dramatically true in the world of face-to-face selling: in that world, a 5 or 10 percent close ratio would spell only sudden death. That's why, if you go one-on-one with your customers, you need something much more reliable than a good product, a head full of features and benefits, and a snappy demonstration. You've got to be able to zero in on each *individual* customer's reasons for wanting, or not wanting, to buy. In today's face-to-face selling environment it's essential to get beyond the old-fashioned Product Pitch.

The fundamental reason that it's essential can be stated in the form of a seemingly crazy proposition: *Nobody has ever sold a product.*

Nobody Buys a Product Per Se

This isn't as crazy as it might sound, and you can prove that to yourself very easily. Think about the last time *you* bought something. Whether it was something as minor and disposable as a newspaper or as major and durable as a car, what you paid money for was not really the physical, tangible purchase itself, but the *expectation of what that purchase would do for you.* In a sense all buyers are futures traders: when we buy, we anticipate the satisfaction of certain needs from the purchase, and it's really the idea of "X need satisfied" that we're paying for. If we've just put down a quarter for a paper, for example, we expect to be informed about the day's events. If we shell out several thousand dollars for a car, we expect a certain level of performance, prestige, or convenience. The people who sent in their checks to the Ginsu company did so not because the knives are objectively "good" but because they anticipated that the knives would fill a need that they personally had for them—whether it was slicing tomatoes paper-thin or hacking through pipe to impress their friends. In every purchase the expectation of satisfied needs is the key.

We can put this in the form of an adage that underlies the entire Miller-Heiman approach to selling:

No one buys a product per se. *What is bought is what the customer* thinks *the product or service will* do *for him or her.*

This idea—this notion of what the prospective client thinks the product or service will be able to do—is what we call *Concept.* A customer's Concept is his "mindset" or his "solution image" of what he wants to get done. Today, more than ever before, selling to the customer's Concept is the beginning of all good selling. To define this critical idea a little more precisely:

1. The Concept is *already in place.* That is, even before you meet a prospective client, it's reasonable to assume that he or she has already formed some idea

about you, your company, and your products or services. That idea will be based on the customer's *past experiences,* and it may be totally off base as far as you are concerned. But it's likely that prospects hold Concepts about you and your product even before you meet them—and it's deadly to ignore these preconceptions.

2. The Concept is absolutely *personal* for each individual. It is *subjective* and *different* for every customer you deal with. No two people ever buy (or refuse to buy) a given product or service for precisely the same reasons. So in Conceptual Selling we insist that it's never the product or service that makes or breaks the sale, but the individual customer's subjective view of what the product or service can do for him.

3. Your customer's Concept is linked to his or her individual *values and attitudes.* We'll be talking more about values and attitudes later in the book. The basic point is to broaden the traditional salesperson's emphasis on "product specs" and point out again that people buy for *their* reasons. Those reasons are always subjective and internal.

No Assumptions

If good selling begins with understanding the prospect's Concept—that is, with understanding a pre-established, personal, and value-laden idea about you and your product—it stands to reason that you have to enter each selling situation with an open mind, ready to listen rather than speak. Unless you're a mind-reader, there's no way you're going to be able to understand anybody's Concept by intuition; and since the human mind changes notoriously and dramatically from day to day, there's no way you're going to be able to understand even your oldest, most "reliable" customers' Concepts at the beginning of a given sales encounter, unless you do more asking than telling.

Because you can so easily mislead yourself about what your potential customer is thinking, we advise all the sales professionals we deal with to follow an elegantly simple rule.   Whenever you sit down with someone, whether you've known him five minutes or five years, make *no assumptions* about what he's thinking.   Treat every sales call as if it were your *first* call on this customer.   No matter how long you've been doing business with "good old Joe," the fact is that his Concept can always change between one call and the next, in response to factors about which you may be ignorant, and over which you have no control. The client's Concept, therefore, is something you have to identify, and reidentify, on every call.

Identifying the Concept

First, to clear up a confusion that we encounter constantly when we introduce customer Concept to sales professionals, especially those in high-level marketing positions. It's very common for people who have spent a lot of time developing and "pre-selling" a product to say something like this: "I'm really glad you're focussing on this. We've been trying to get our customers to understand the concepts behind our products for years, and we haven't had much luck in getting it across."

No, we say, and you probably never will. Because what a salesperson or selling organization usually means by "the concept behind the product" may have absolutely nothing to do with the *customer's* Concept of the product. To people in sales, "concept" often signifies a kind of pre-production blueprint—the theory underneath the product that the marketing and R & D people had in mind before the product became a reality. To some prospective accounts, of course, that "concept" *will* be significant, but it's a fallacy to assume that it will be equally significant to all potential buyers—or that it's ever going to be as significant to the client as his or her *own* ideas.

An example. You've seen the free glass promotions put on by fast food restaurant chains, where the customer who purchases a certain soft drink gets to keep the container. Typically the free glasses are donated by the soft drink supplier, which initiates the promotion as a way of boosting fountain sales; the restaurants are happy to participate, because their own sales also go up.   In most cases, then, these promotions provide an ideal fit between the soda seller's promotional "concept" and the restaurant customer's Concept.

But there is one major fast food chain that has never accepted these promotions. We once asked one of their divisional managers why. His answer illustrates very well that there is no *necessary* similarity between the seller's and the customer's "concept."

"Sure, we'd sell more soda," he acknowledged. "But I'd have a mutiny on my hands in half my restaurants. You've seen our floor space. We pride ourself on space efficiency, but that's because we *have* to be efficient: we've got half as much space in a typical unit as our competitors. That's why we always say no to the promotions. When I see a salesman trying to hand me giveaway glasses, you know what I *really* see? A twelve-cubic-foot box of kitchen stock that's going to get in everybody's way."

This customer's Concept, in other words, was a mental picture of potential clutter. No matter how great the seller's "concept," there was no way it was going to mesh well with the client's feeling of being cramped.

Trying to sell your company's "concept" of a product, therefore, is ultimately going to be no easier—and in many cases may actually be harder—than trying to sell the product itself. Selling *your* concept of the product is really only a sophisticated form of product cramming, and it very seldom gets you good results. It may, in fact, lead to negative results, because it can tend to distract you from the one thing that is going to make the sale work or not work: what your *customer* is thinking.

Since every sale and every potential buyer is different, we obviously cannot tell you for an individual selling situation what your customer is likely to be thinking. This book, however, will show you how to find that out, every time you sit down face to face. Right now we'll confine ourselves to a few guidelines, or general "clues" to look for when you're discovering your customer's Concept.

Focus on Results: Three Clues

We've said that the Concept is the potential buyer's expectation of what you and/or your product will be able to *do* for him. Another way of saying that is to point out that customers, just like you and just like everyone in business, are always looking for *results*. Only if they think you can provide them with the results they need will they want to hear about your product.

To be more specific, we have found that the Conceptual results a customer expects always relate to one or more of three basic areas:

1. Discrepancy. By discrepancy we mean a perceived gap in the prospect's mind (not your mind) between where he is right now and where he wants to be. Unless someone perceives such a gap between his current situation and an ideal—and unless he believes that you can help him bridge that gap—you can pretty much forget about making a sale.

You know the old joke about how hard it is to buy something for the guy who has everything. It's ten times as hard to *sell* that guy something. This ties in with the relationship between Concept and desired results. If your potential customer is perfectly content with his current situation, there's no way he'll expect you to deliver results that can improve it. In short: no discrepancy, no sale.

For example. Say I'm currently driving a five-year-old automobile with 90,000 miles on it. It has most of the options I want—except for a cassette tape player—and looks fairly good for its age. If I'm completely satisfied with it as is, there's no discrepancy and therefore no point in your trying to sell me a new car. But if the neighbor's stares are getting me down, or if the rust on the left rear fender is beginning to embarrass me, there is an obvious gap between where I am and where I would like to be.

Discrepancy has changed my Concept of "new car" so that I am more open to a possible sale.

2. *Importance*. In addressing the customer's Concept, you always need to be alert to the level of importance he or she assigns to a given task to be accomplished. Take the car-minus-cassette scenario. If I'm just vaguely dissatisfied with the lack of a cassette because I'd like some music as I drive, then the discrepancy is low, the importance is low, and there's not much chance of a sale. But say I'm on the road twenty or thirty hours a week, I've got to review taped material frequently, and I want to optimize the use of my road time. Then the importance level may rise, and a salesperson who addresses my Concept about a tape player—that is, my expectation that it will improve my road time—will have a good chance of selling me one, or of selling me a car with one in it.

3. *Solving a problem*. We've mentioned that a synonym for "Concept" is "solution image." If your customer has an urgent problem, the discrepancy level is by definition going to be high. If you can provide something that dovetails with the ideal solution he has in mind, your chances of making the sale are very good.

That's obvious enough. What's not so obvious is that, even if your customer's problem is not staring him in the face at the moment, you might *still* be able to sell to his "solution image" by demonstrating that your solution can help him *avoid* a problem in the future.

Take the car with the 90,000 miles. Let's face it, at that mileage the maintenance and repair bills are probably going to be running you a couple of hundred dollars a month in the near future, so you may be faced with the classic "trouble avoidance" option of "Pay me now or pay me later." If my Concept about a new car is that it will free me from the anxiety over the old one breaking down, then your chances of selling me one will be good—*if* you pick up on my Concept and focus on your maintenance-free models.

To sum it up: Picking up on the customer's Concept is not incidental to good selling. It's the basis on which all long-term success is built, because it's the only thing that ties in directly to what the buyer believes needs to get done.

"Customerized" Selling

What we're talking about here can be described as customized, or more accurately, "customerized" selling. In a highly competitive environment, where buyers have a vast array of choices, "customerizing" the sale is the only way the seller can survive, long-term. We can illustrate this with two examples.

First, an example of how *not* to customize a sale.

A friend of ours recently drove his road-worn sports car up to a car showroom, got out, and was met at the curb by an eager young floor salesman. Since our friend had driven up in a sports car, the salesman made the ostensibly reasonable assumption that he probably wanted a replacement. So, once inside, the youngster fell all over himself pointing out the compression ratios and zero-to-sixty speeds of the sports models they had on display.

But his assumption was unreasonable—and fatal. In fact our friend and his wife had just had their second child, and had reluctantly decided that it was time to trade in the sports car of his wild oats youth for a more practical model. His Concept of "new car," in other words, was built around his need for more room—not for an Indy 500 ride. Because he didn't find this out up front, the young salesman wasted our friend's time, and his own, and eventually assumed himself right out of a commission.

The second example. Another friend of ours entered a men's clothing store intending to buy a blazer. He asked the sales clerk for assistance, and instead of giving him the usual "Size 39s over there, Sir," he said, "Why don't we sit down for a couple of minutes, and you can tell me about your wardrobe." For ten minutes they talked about the colors he liked, the styles he preferred, the kind of functions he attended. "It was amazing," he told us later. "He actually took notes about color schemes. I walked out of there with two jackets, two pairs of slacks, a sweater, and three ties."

That was customerized selling. It was selling that made no assumptions; that began not with the product but with the customer's individualized interests and values and needs; and that demonstrated once again the basic truth that good selling always starts with the Concept.

Your Two Essential Selling Tasks

Haven't we forgotten about the product? Aren't we focussing so much on intangibles like values and expectations that we've made the product (or service) itself seem irrelevant?

Not at all. We're not saying that *all* you have to do is to make the Concept Sale. And we're not saying that product information is unimportant. Knowing your product or service intimately has always been essential to good selling, and that's no less true today. But we're now living in a world where competition is more intense than ever, where customers have become extremely sophisticated, and where the choices that they are being offered are wider than ever before in history. In that world, concentrating on product alone is a way of digging yourself into a hole. Yes, you have to sell the product. But that's only one of your tasks.

Every time you sit down with a customer today, you need to perform two distinct but interrelated selling tasks. We call those tasks the *Concept Sale* and the *Product Sale.*

We can define the Concept Sale as the process of identifying what your customer thinks your product or service can do for him. The Product Sale, by contrast, *relates* the product or service to the identified Concept—just as the men's store clerk related his particular product line to our friend's Concept about "clothing." In making the Product Sale, you provide the nuts and bolts information that most salespeople are so eager to give out. You provide, for example product specifications, technologies, implementation, and so forth.   Other examples are given in the chart below. (By "Buying Influence" in this chart we mean the person on whom you are calling.)

Your Two Selling Tasks

CONCEPT SALE defined

- No one buys a product per se. What **is** bought is what that product is thought to do for the Buying Influence.

- What the Buying Influence "thinks" the product will do, is a **concept.** It is a generalized idea built upon past experiences.

- Different Buying Influences buy different concepts.

PRODUCT SALE defined

The Product Sale comes second and **relates** your product/service to the concept. It provides product:

- description
- specifications
- demonstration
- packaging
- technologies
- capabilities
- bells & whistles
- implementation

You'll notice in this chart that what you provide in the Product Sale is essentially the "features and benefits" of your product.   There's nothing wrong with doing that—in fact, it's one of your two essential tasks.   The reason we have been playing down the Product Sale up to this point is that it is so often *overplayed*. In traditional sales training the salesperson is asked to unscrew the top of his head, stuff his skull full of terms and pictures and figures, and then go out and throw all this stuff in the customer's lap. There are two related mistakes that often follow from this emphasis on product knowledge:

- The salesperson forgets about the customer's Concept entirely, and tries to make *only* the Product Sale.
- The salesperson talks about the customer's Concept, but only *after* he has trotted out the bells and whistles.

The bad effects of the first mistake we've already pointed out, in the sports-car scenario above. But it can be just as deadly to put the Concept on hold until you've done the more familiar and comfortable work of describing what your product can do.

The Seller's Most Common Mistake

In fact, *trying to make the Product Sale first is probably the single most common mistake made in selling.* It follows from the traditional view of selling as product-pushing; it is perpetuated by the fact that it's more comfortable for most salespeople to tell rather than ask; and it is aggravated by the common "track" style of presentation technique, in which you're supposed to begin your spiel with a "grabber" about the product: "This car can do 130 miles per hour," for example, or "Watch me slice through this steak like it's butter."

Such product-oriented teasers work fine *if you happen to be talking to the right person.* But what if you come out with the 130 miles per hour come-on with someone who thinks 55 miles per hour is still too fast? What if you're putting on the steak-slicing show for somebody who turns out to be a vegetarian? What's very likely going to happen is that your bells and whistles are going to blow up in your face.

There's a kind of Boomerang Effect that operates in a lot of product selling, where the seller with superior product knowledge tells the customer more than he ever wanted to know about his product, and ends up submerging him— and the sale—in useless data. Sure, knowing your product inside out can help you make certain sales to certain people. But you can also kill a potentially good sale with product specs, if you lay them out in front of a customer whose Concept cannot relate to such data.

We see this happen all the time in high-tech selling, where the field representatives are often engineers who have been selected as sales reps precisely because they know the products so well. It's a very common error for such "field engineers" to try to sell the vice-president or general manager of a major corporation as if he or she were also an engineer. That almost never works—as a field engineer from one of the major computer companies confirmed in a story he told us recently.

"In my first major corporate sale," he said, "the customer was a big textile firm that had been having inventory problems. Their data processing people, who had asked us for a presentation, ate up everything I told them. But then I had to make a pitch to the general manager, a crusty old guy who had to approve the deal because it was going to top 500 grand. I was giving him the whole nine yards— all the ROM and RAM, bit and byte stuff the DP people had loved—when he cut me off in mid-sentence. 'Son,' he said, 'the only bites I give a damn about are the ones I take at dinner. Can this son of a bitch keep track of 400,000 yards of sixteen different fabrics every month and tell me exactly where they are, or can't it?'

"I just gulped and said 'Yes sir, it sure can.' "

" 'Good,' he said. 'Now you show me exactly how'."

He ended up making the sale, but only after he had put the bit and byte fandango behind him and begun to concentrate on what the general manager wanted to know— on his very specific and personal understanding of what the new computer system might *do* for him and his organization.

Notice that the two things the manager asked of the salesperson link up directly to the two essential selling tasks.

- First, he wanted to know whether or not the new computer system could solve his problem—could provide an answer to his "solution image." Addressing that concern, first, was making the Concept Sale.

- Then, once he was assured that the sales rep was interested in solving his problem, the manager wanted to know *how* he proposed to do it: he wanted the sales rep to move to the Product Sale.

The lesson is that *both* selling tasks are important, but that the *Concept Sale must always come first.*

Further Advantages

Avoiding the Boomerang Effect is only the most obvious advantage of making the Concept Sales first. There are many others. When we follow up on the salespeople who have been through our Conceptual Selling program, we ask them to tell us what benefits they have noticed in their own businesses from starting each face-to-face encounter with the Concept Sale. A handful of responses recur again and again:

1. Making the Concept Sale first allows you to *learn more about your customer* than you could possibly learn if you started off with the Product Sale. Even the most product-oriented seller will acknowledge that the more you know about your individual customers, the better your long-term chances of keeping them on board. Making the Concept Sale first is preeminently a "close to the customer" approach.

2. By drawing out the customer's current interests and concerns, the Concept Sale enables you to *focus on*

results that he or she really wants to get accomplished—not just the results *you* think your product can or should deliver. This in turn makes it possible for you to highlight the specific objectives you can address, and to tailor your presentations accordingly.

3. Because making the Concept Sale first is so rare in today's environment, you are *unlikely to be pigeonholed with the competition,* as "just one more product-pusher," by a customer you approach in this manner. As we illustrated with the story of the Chicago presentation in Chapter 1, the very oddity of the "question first" style gives the questioning salesperson a unique advantage over all those competitors who concentrate mostly on telling.

4. Making the Concept Sale first *minimizes the importance of price competition.* It lets the customer know that you are interested in delivering value—value that he specifically needs—and therefore it puts you several steps ahead of those competitors who are merely playing low-bid games.

5. In the majority of corporate sales, although several or many Yesses are necessary for the sale to go through, there is always one person's Yes that counts as final approval. Making the Concept Sale first is an ideal way to *position yourself with the person who makes the final decision.* As we pointed out in the anecdote about the general manager who didn't care to hear about bits and bytes, such final-approval decision-makers are typically less interested in nuts and bolts than they are in what you can do for their organization. With such people, focussing on Concept is critical.

6. Finally, focussing on Concept first enables you to spot, early in the selling cycle, those customers or situations where you simply cannot come out Win-Win. Let's face it, not everybody in the business world *wants* to play Win-Win: in terms of values

and attitudes, some people are constitutionally unable or unwilling to let you Win—they thrive on making others Lose. In addition, there are plenty of business situations where, even with the best of intentions, the seller and the buyer simply cannot forge a deal that will let both of them feel that they've Won. Focussing on Concept first enables you not only to spot good opportunities, but also to identify, early in the selling cycle, sales you should not pursue.

We realize this last point may strike you as anathema. Most salespeople are still being taught that selling is a numbers game, that you should go for every piece of business every time, and that there's no such thing as a bad sale. Throughout this book, and especially in the chapter on Joint Venture selling, we'll be insisting on exactly the opposite proposition. In our combined fifty years in selling, we've seen plenty of bad sales—from the defective bedroom suite that had to be returned to the factory three days after shipment, to the computer installation that was sold to a company just south of the Arctic Circle, and that turned out to be just slightly difficult to service when the temperature was 40 degrees below zero. You know it's true. *Everybody* in sales has written business that turned out to cost him more than it was worth. We'll be showing you throughout this book how focussing on the Concept Sale can keep you clear of that kind of business, so that every one of your sales ends up, over the long term, as Win-Win.

Personal Workshop:
Concept/Product

In this first Personal Workshop, you'll have the opportunity to apply our idea of customer Concept to your own real-life situations. You should write the heading "Concept/Product" at the top of a notebook page, and set aside about thirty minutes to go through the following two-part exercise.

Part A: When You're the Buyer

Step 1: Select a significant purchase. To clarify the notion of customer Concept, begin by thinking about a situation where you yourself were the customer. Select a recent, significant purchase you have made—not an impulse buy, but a major product or service purchase, where the buying decision had to be well thought out. Examples might be a new car, a television, a business suit, or an extended vacation. Choose one such purchase that was important to you, personally, and write down the item purchased in your notebook.

Step 2: Record your pre-purchase thoughts. Now, thinking back to just before you made this purchase, list in your notebook the expectations and considerations that went into your decision-making process. We've said that the pre-purchase Concept in any customer's mind relates to:

a) a feeling of *discrepancy* between where the customer is and where he or she wants to be;

b) the desire to accomplish something of *importance;* and/or

c) the need to solve a more or less urgent *problem.*

Using those three criteria as guidelines, write down what you felt the selected purchase was likely to *accomplish* for you. Remember that the same item can be bought for any number of reasons. One customer will buy a second color TV because he wants to be able to watch Sunday football undisturbed; another customer will buy exactly the same TV for the prestige value alone. What we want you to write down here are the pre-purchase considerations that were important to you, personally. These considerations— these personal reasons for looking around for a TV or VCR or vacation spot in the first place—comprise your "mental picture" or Concept of the purchase.

Step 3: Identify your reasons for the specific purchase. No matter what your general Concept was before buying, you had to make a very specific decision at the time when you laid the money down. You had to have a reason or reasons to buy *this* particular TV from *this* particular store at *this* particular time. In other words, you had to decide to buy a *specific* product or service. Write down here the reasons that you made that specific choice. Then, looking at the pre-purchase thoughts you just wrote down, notice the relationship between your original mental picture of the purchase and attributes of the specific product or service you selected.

Step 4: Record your after-purchase thoughts. Finally, write down a brief description of how you felt after making the purchase, and after you had used the product or service for a while. Specifically, record how you felt with regard to:

- Utility: How well did the product work?
- Value: Was its performance worth the price that you paid?
- Satisfaction: How happy were you with the purchase?

Once you've written down these after-purchase thoughts, you should have a pretty good idea of how well the specific product or service you bought satisfied the requirements established by your original "solution image." In other words, you'll know more clearly how well the Product tied in with the Concept.

Part B: When You're the Seller

Now that you've examined the idea of customer Concept as it relates to your own buying decisions, we'd like you to perform the same exercise with the shoe on the other foot. We asked you in the previous chapter to select a few sales calls that you could use as working models in this book. In this and in all subsequent Personal Workshops, we will be giving you directions to plan tactics for one of those selected model calls at a time. We encourage you, however, to perform the Personal Workshop exercises for two or three of your upcoming calls, so that the applicability of the Conceptual Selling format becomes all the more immediate and vivid.

Begin by choosing your most important upcoming call, and write down the following information:

- The name of the *account;*
- The name of the *person* you'll be calling on; and
- Your *single sales objective* for this account.

Briefly, by "single sales objective," we mean whatever you're trying to accomplish in this account that isn't happening right now. A good single sales objective is a specific description of *what* you want to sell to the account, *how much* of it you expect to sell, and *when* you want to accomplish this objective. For example: "Sell the Xanadu Corporation one dozen Alpha model digitalizers by June 1."

Once you've identified your sales objective, and you know whom you're going to be speaking to, we want you to put yourself in *that person's place* and then, as if with his "mindset," focus on *his* thoughts about the sale.

Step 5: Is this purchase significant? Imagining yourself to be your customer, ask yourself whether or not the single sales objective described above is *significant* to you or not. Do you, as an officer (or purchasing agent, or line operator, or whatever) of the Xanadu Corporation, really want or need the Alpha models? Can they make an impact on your operation, on your profit picture, or on your level of personal satisfaction? If you don't know the answer that your prospect would give to these questions, write down simply, "Don't know."

Step 6: Record your customer's pre-purchase thoughts. We're asking you in this Step to write down what your *customer* may be thinking with regard to the Alpha model sale. What expectations and considerations are entering into his mental picture? Is the Alpha sale likely to:

a) overcome a feeling of *discrepancy* between where he is and where he wants to get to?

b) accomplish something of *importance* to him?

c) help him to solve an urgent *problem*?

If the answer to any of these questions is Yes, specify: Write down which discrepancy, what importance, which problem. If the answer is No, write that down. What you're trying to get here is an understanding of what your *customer* thinks your product or service can *do* for him. You're trying to pin down your potential buyer's Concept.

We realize this isn't likely to be easy, and in fact that's one of the principal reasons that we're asking you to perform this exercise. When we have our program participants do the same exercise, and then ask them as a group what they've learned, invariably someone shakes his head and says, "I've learned that it's a hell of a lot easier to understand your own Concept for buying something than it is to understand somebody else's." To which we respond: "Terrific. That's exactly what we hoped it would show you." If this exercise does nothing more than make you aware that your customer's mental picture is fuzzy or even hidden from you, that's great. Since good selling always begins with his Concept, it's extremely valuable to realize, early in the selling cycle, that often you *don't* understand what he's thinking. The entire Conceptual Selling sales call process, which we'll be moving to in the next chapter, is designed to help you pin down the areas where you're missing information about Concept—and then to help you get that information, in the most efficient manner possible.

That completes the Personal Workshop exercise, and we realize you may be asking yourself why we asked you in Part B to repeat only the first two Steps of Part A. The answer reinforces what we just said about understanding your customer's Concept first. The third Step of Part A showed you how the specific product or service you purchased tied in with your pre-purchase Concept. You can't perform that exercise for your customer yet, because until you understand his Concept more fully, you don't know whether your particular product or service—the one you're trying to sell him—ties in with his Concept at all. And you can't gauge your customer's level of satisfaction with the sale, as you did for yourself in Step 4, because you haven't made the sale yet.

We'll be showing you later in the book how to relate your specific product or service to the prospective buyer's Concept, and how to determine his or her level of satisfaction.

"Developing" the Customer's Concept

One final point. Your customer's Concept isn't static. Like everything else in selling, it *evolves*, in response to new experiences and new information—including the information you bring him or her. In fact, no matter how you as a salesman handle the sale, the Concept is *inevitably* going to change over time. There are three ways in which this can happen:

1. The Concept can evolve *internally*, in response to the customer's own personal perceptions and expectations.
2. It can evolve in response to information that the customer gets from your *competition*.
3. It can evolve with *you*, as you work *with* your customer to refine and shape the Concept to your mutual advantage.

It's obvious which is the best case scenario here. It's always preferable for you to manage the evolution of a client's Concept *with* him, rather than allow it to be shaped by him alone or, worse yet, by him with your competition.

Because you can strongly influence the way someone thinks about doing business with you, we speak of the customer's Concept not so much as something you have to "discover" as something you can help "develop." The most successful salespeople we know think of their work as a process of continuous refinement. They approach each individual sales call with the understanding that the call begins, but never ends, with the preconceived Concept.

Gradually, building on a series of sales calls, they evolve a Concept of mutual success with every person they contact.

But it all begins with the initial Concept. With that cluster of impressions and past experiences—successes and aggravations, satisfactions and gripes—that your customer has in his mind when you first walk into his office. *Your first task is always to find out what that initial Concept is.* In other words, it's to get the *information you need* to understand your own and the customer's position.

There are effective ways and ineffective ways to seek out this essential information. We're going to introduce you to the most effective ways now.

THE THREE PHASES OF THE SALES CALL

▸ 3 ◂

PHASE ONE: GETTING INFORMATION

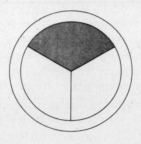

Contrary to popular opinion, the great salesperson is very seldom the person with the fastest mouth in the West. In the vast majority of cases, selling success begins with the ability to *ask good questions* and then listen—really listen—to the answers.

There are plenty of reasons for asking good questions on a sales call. To mention only the most important:

1. Good questioning allows you to *identify* clearly, and to *qualify* early in the selling process, not only the individual people you deal with, but also their companies; it helps you get a handle at the outset on whether or not a given company is an appropriate prospect at all.

2. It helps you to understand the *current* customer situation. Good questions can uncover the fact, for example, that a given customer, although a good

bet in general, is not an appropriate prospect at the present time, or for your current proposal. Therefore, good questioning helps you to schedule your calls more effectively.

3. Good questioning, at the outset of a sales call, helps to establish the rapport that is so helpful in fostering fluid communication between buyer and seller: it helps to establish a "comfort level" between the two that is critical to all interactive selling.

4. Good questioning lets you determine where you do, and where you do not, understand the *decision-making process* of a given corporate customer. It helps you avoid the all too common selling error of wasting your own and your customers' time by making the perfect presentation to the wrong person, in the wrong place, or at the wrong time.

5. It enables you to identify significant differences between your own capabilities and those of your competition. Good questioning can help you uncover your competitors' weaknesses and highlight your own strengths.

6. Good questioning can reinforce your *credibility* with a customer by demonstrating to him or her that you are in fact interested in his or her needs and opinions, and not just in pushing your product.

7. Finally, and arguably most important, good questioning can motivate and sustain your customer's interest, stimulate his thinking, and modify his attitudes—his Concept—regarding you and your product or service. In other words, it can generate a *fluid communication process* that gives both you *and* your customer the information that needs to be laid on the table to get you to a Win-Win conclusion.

Given these obvious advantages of good questioning, you'd think that sales professionals would typically spend the bulk of their time developing good questions, learning how to phrase questions properly, and in general focussing on Getting Information. But that isn't what happens.

In fact, just the opposite occurs.

The 80 Percent Syndrome

Our observation and experience with thousands of sales professionals tells us that on most sales calls, there is a kind of "80 Percent Syndrome" at work.

Imagine popping your head in at random on any given hundred sales calls. The focus of the call might be a thirty-dollar pair of shoes or a 3 million dollar computer system. The call might be an opening call on a new prospect or the salesperson might be two minutes from getting the contract. Whatever the situation, we'll bet that 80 percent of the time, the person who's going to be talking when you pop in will be not the customer but the salesperson. That's a typical pattern in sales calls: four out of every five minutes the seller and the buyer are together, it's the seller's gums that will be flapping.

Moreover, 80 percent of the time that the seller is talking, guess what he's going to be saying? Is he going to be focussing on the customer, or asking questions to uncover his Concept? Not on your life. The pattern we've found is very clear: 80 percent of the time the seller is talking, he is *telling* the customer something—in other words, he's making statements, not asking questions.

It gets worse. To take the 80 Percent Syndrome to its last fatal step, we'll make this observation: 80 percent of the time, the statements the seller is making have to do not with the customer's interests or needs, but with the virtues of the seller's product or service. It's usually the Product Pitch with a vengeance: the seller spends the bulk of his or her time pointing to bells and whistles. Whether or not the prospect wants to see them.

What does this mean in terms of the average sales call? Suppose you have an hour to spend with a given customer, and you fall into the common 80 Percent Syndrome with him. In that precious hour, your time will be divided in the following way:

- About *thirty-one* minutes will be spent in telling the customer about your product or service.

- Another *eight* minutes will be spent in telling him something else—that is, in making other statements.

- About *nine* minutes will be spent in asking him questions.

- The remaining *twelve* minutes will be spent in listening to the customer talk.

We can illustrate this in the form of a diagram. The pie chart here indicates the total sixty minutes in our hypothetical sales call, and the breakdown indicates how much time, according to the 80 Percent Syndrome, that the average salesman will spend on each activity.

Now, on calls that last *less* than an hour, the situation gets

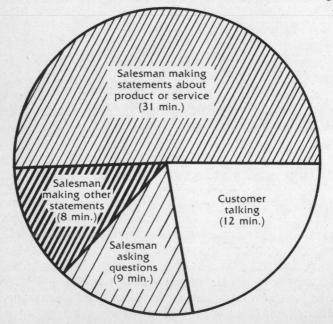

even worse. If fact, the less time the average salesperson has to spend with the prospect or client, the greater chance there will be that he will spend the *bulk* of that time talking. If you've only got twenty minutes to tell your story and you've got a head full of data to deliver, the natural temptation is to talk nonstop, to be sure you get it all in.

The result of this can be disastrous. If you only allow a customer one minute out of every five to get a word in edgewise, the information you get from him is naturally going to be inferior to what you would be able to get if you said less and listened more. Why? Because it's a physiological fact that you cannot talk and listen at the same time. You may be able to vaguely "hear" background noise; you may convince yourself that you're picking up on body language and nonverbal cues; but if you're honest with yourself you'll admit that you can't really *listen* intelligently when you're trying for the Motor Mouth trophy. If you doubt that, ask a friend to read you a newspaper article while you're reading him or her another one. The only words that either one of you will hear will be those that sneak through when you pause for breath. It's inevitable, therefore, when you fall into the 80 Percent Syndrome, that you will miss out on information that you need in order to make the sale work. Good selling begins not with Show and Tell, but with Getting Information—in other words, with *learning.* And you cannot learn effectively when you're talking.

Why Do Salespeople Talk So Much?

Our experience shows incontrovertibly that the 80 Percent Syndrome is extremely common, and that it is invariably damaging to good business. Why do sales professionals, whom you would expect to know better, indulge themselves so frequently in this counterproductive sales habit?

There are a variety of answers to that question. When we ask the question in our Conceptual Selling programs, we get answers like the following:

- "I feel more comfortable being in control."

Many salespeople fall into the trap of assuming that, when they're talking, they are in control of the sale. As we'll emphasize throughout the book, this equation of "talking" with "control" is almost always an illusion. It's a *comforting* illusion, however, and therefore a very common one.

- "It's my job to tell him about the product."

In other words, it's my job to engage in Product Pitch— whoever the prospective client and no matter what his or her real need for what I might have to sell. The fatal assumption here is that everybody has a need for your product, and that if you only tell him about the product, he'll understand that need and rush to buy.

- "Talking is what the customer usually wants you to do."

We hear this chestnut all the time. It's one of the most common excuses of all for not finding out what the prospect is thinking. There is a tradition, we admit, of letting the seller do the talking, and there are many customers who are guilty of contributing to the 80 Percent Syndrome themselves. Customers have to be educated, just like salesmen, to avoid the bad effects of the syndrome. We recognize that, so we're sympathetic with this response. We'll be explaining later in the book how to get your Mute Melvins to open up. Here we'll just make the basic point: no matter what he says and no matter how sympathetic he may seem to your jabbering, *no customer ever really wants the seller to do all the talking.* If your quiet client didn't have anything else to say to you, after all, you'd already have his order in your pocket.

- "Talking takes less planning."

This is certainly true, and we're always gratified to hear this "explanation" from a program participant: it means he's already begun to think about planning his sales tactics in advance, and has begun to realize that planning a sound questioning process *does* usually take more work than reviewing your product specs one more time. Many salepeople avoid questioning for this reason: it's much easier to run down the same old product line with every customer than it is to "customize" a new set of questions for every sales call. We're not saying that learning how to question is easier than learning how to make statements—only that it's ultimately more effective as a way of getting you to Win-Win.

- "Sometimes you're afraid to hear the answers."

This very honest response goes back to the seller's comfort level and to the illusion of control we just mentioned. It's true that, when you ask a question, you might get an answer you don't want to hear. But the solution to this unpleasant possibility should never be "Don't ask the question." It should be to establish a *questioning process* that enables you to use *whatever* answers you get to better understand the situation.

The Questioning Process

We say questioning "process" rather than questioning "techniques." The distinction is crucial. Every sales training program you've ever seen teaches what the trainers call "questioning." *But it's not really questioning at all.* The "questioning skills" that most programs teach are really only a series of manipulative techniques designed to make statements *sound* like questions, and to get the customer's name on the dotted line no matter what he says or thinks or needs.

You know the kind of "questions" we're talking about. The rhetorical come-ons like "Wouldn't you agree that's a good deal, Mr. Jones?"—where the only acceptable answer is Yes. The false-choice trial closes like "Would you like to sign the contract today or this Friday?" And the whole game of "asking" for the order—which isn't asking at all, but only a sophisticated form of manipulation. In traditional "questioning" training, you learn how to *force answers*. That's the last thing we want to encourage.

The point of asking good questions, as we define them, is never to "rephrase" a client's resistance or to "redirect" the course of an interview or to put the customer in a position where he's only allowed to say Yes. It's for you, the seller, to *find out something that you don't already know*. Rather than showing you techniques for tricking the buyer, we give you a field-tested process for getting the information you need to bring your sales to mutually satisfying conclusions.

There's an irony here. Salespeople who are primarily interested in "asking for the order" often find that getting the Yes answer they want is an uphill battle all the way. On the other hand, when you use an effective questioning process, you often *don't even have to ask for the order:* the order happens almost automatically as a result of the *other* questions you've asked.

Our questioning process enables you to maximize your understanding of the customer's situation *as he or she perceives it*. This understanding, as we've said before, is always the critical first step in any good Concept Sale. Working with this understanding, and using the questioning process we'll outline, you will be able to do something that the traditional "go for the order" type of questioning actually *prevents* you from doing: you will be able to create a fluid communication process between you and each of your customers, so that both of you always have the information you need to get yourselves, mutually, to Win-Win.

Personal Workshop: Identifying Missing Information

The beginning of our questioning process is to identify those areas of the sale where you are currently lacking information. There are a number of areas that are typically "information poor" for sellers, and we'll present them to you here, as an informal "laundry list" that you can use as a reference point throughout the rest of the book. In our programs we find that this exercise in "surfacing the gaps" provides a helpful starting point for people unfamiliar with our kind of questioning. So set aside about ten or fifteen minutes, and ask yourself the questions we indicate here, to see where more information would be useful in managing your upcoming sales calls. We suggest that you use as your models the same typical and/or significant sales calls that you selected in Chapter 1, and that you analyzed with regard to customer Concept in the Personal Workshop in Chapter 2. You might want to write down brief comments to yourself, under a heading "Missing Information."

Step 1: Do I need information about Buying Influences? When we use the term Buying Influence, we mean something quite precise. In Conceptual Selling a Buying Influence is defined as *anyone* who can have a positive or negative impact on your selling—whatever his position, whatever his company, and whatever his role in a given sale. The person you're calling on is one, but only one, Buying Influence. To determine whether you know all the Buying Influences for the sales call you're working with as a model, ask yourself:

- Who has *final approval* authority for the proposal I'm currently presenting?
- What person or persons in the buying organization will *use* the product or service I'm selling, on their actual jobs?
- Who will be *judging* my proposal?
- Do I have a *guide*—that is, someone who can provide me with reliable information—for this sale?
- With regard to the person I'm going to be calling on next: what is this person's degree of *influence* in the sale?

Step 2: Do I need information about buyer needs? Each of the various people involved in a sale will, of course, have

his or her own needs and desires regarding your proposal.
With regard to the person you're going to be calling on in
your next sales call, ask:

- What are the specific, measureable, tangible *results*
  that he or she expects to gain from what I'm selling?
- What are his or her personal *values and attitudes*
  regarding my current proposal? In other words,
  how does this person *feel* about what I'm trying to
  do?
- What is this person's perceived degree of *risk*
  involved?

**Step 3: Do I need information about the customer's buying
procedures?** Since the purchasing structures and individual buying procedures of different companies vary dramatically, and since they may even change from time to time
within the same company, you need to find out as much as
you can up front about how decisions are being made, right
now. Ask yourself, therefore, what information you need
to find out about:

- the *money* that needs to be allocated for your sale
- the *urgency* of your proposal to the company or
  customer—that is, whether or not your *timing* is
  right
- "political" factors in the buying organization
- any other factors that may be currently beyond
  your control

Step 4: Do I need information about possible new players?
In *Strategic Selling* we identified several typical "Red Flag,"
or extreme danger, areas in sales. One of these danger
areas in which lack of information can always undermine
a seller's chances of success is the appearance of new
players, or the rearrangement of existing players. To identify potential problems here, ask:

- Have there been any recent *changes* in the Buying
  Influences for this sale?

- Is there a *new face* on the scene, and if so, do I understand his or her possible influence on the sale?
- Has there been *reorganization* recently in the buying organization—no matter how seemingly "trivial" or "irrelevant" to my proposal?
- Am I certain that the person giving *final* approval for this sale has not changed?

Step 5: Do I need information about the competition? Since you don't sell in a vacuum, and since as we said earlier your customer's Concept can always be influenced by your competition, you need to ask:

- *Who* are the competitors for this sale?
- What are their primary *strengths* and *weaknesses*?
- What is the *price* differential—and is price a major factor to the customer?
- What is the *availability* of the principal competitors' products?
- What are their post-sale *service* capabilities?
- How are they positioned with the customer: Are they new players, running neck and neck with me, or firmly entrenched?

Step 6: Do I need information about customer "resistance"? We put resistance in quotation marks because we have found over and over that, as one business executive put it to us, "People don't resist their own ideas." They only resist ideas that somebody else is trying to foist on them— ideas that they don't "own." If you're experiencing resistance, you need to ask:

- Is this person *confused* about what I'm trying to do? Does he have a clear and accurate picture of my capabilities?
- If I'm being deluged with "objections," is there an identifiable *reason* for the customer's contentiousness? Is his disagreement personal, product-related, or both?
- Is it *realistic* to suppose that I can turn around this person at this time?

Step 7: Do I need information about my own uncertainties or worries? One of the sales professional's most deadly errors is to ignore the "grey areas" in a sales picture or presentation in the vain hope that the problems will go away if you don't think about them too much. We ask you to be particularly attentive to "surfacing gaps" in this area. If you're feeling at all uncertain or worried about an upcoming sales call, ask yourself:

- Is there an *uncovered base* here? That is, is there a Buying Influence for this sale that I haven't identified, or about whom I feel uncomfortable?

- Does the sales picture include a strong, antagonistic *anti-sponsor*?

- What's my *credibility* level with the buying organization, and with the Buying Influence I'll meet in my next call?

- What's the *real* fit, not the one I'd like, between my product or service and the customer's needs?

- What are the areas in the sale where I could profit from having more information? Or, to put it negatively, in what areas is my *lack of information* contributing to my uncertainty?

To a certain degree, this last question that we're suggesting you ask yourself sums up the whole enterprise. The whole point of going through a laundry list like this one, and in doing so before every sales call, is to make clear to yourself where you are *missing* the information you need in order to manage the sale well. The first order of business on every sales call should be to seek out that information.

You do that, naturally enough, by asking your customer questions.

Developing Questions: Three Guidelines

But not just any questions. In developing questions to be asked on an upcoming sales call, we have found that you should work from three basic guidelines. That is, there are three criteria to be met when you're sitting down before the sales call and trying to figure out what to ask Mr. Jones. The questions you ask him must:

1. *Get you answers to the things you need to find out.* We mean the most urgent and important things. Obviously, Mr. Jones is not going to have the time or the interest or probably the expertise to fill in every gap on your "laundry list" himself—at least not in a single sales call. That's why we suggest that, as you're focussing on what you need to find out, you narrow the laundry list "gaps" down to a manageable five or six. Choose pieces of missing information that you can reasonably expect to get from Mr. Jones, and pieces that are urgent in terms of the way you perceive the sale to be going.

2. *Be phrased in an effective manner.* You can identify very precisely and very rationally exactly what you need to find out about a given area, but you'll still fail to get that information if you phrase your questions badly. In developing questions it's important to phrase them so that you don't get loaded, self-serving, or defensive answers.

3. *Be presented in an appropriate sequence.* The best way to illustrate the importance of sequence is a negative one: What would happen in a sales call if the *first* question you presented to Mr. Jones was "How about signing this order?" Or if the last one was "How do you do?" No matter how appropriate your questions, and no matter how well they are phrased, you can still come up dry on the needed information if you ask the questions in the wrong order.

We urge you, whenever you're developing questions to be asked on a sales call, to keep these three criteria constantly in mind. We've found that you can improve the quality of your calls 100 percent just by spending five minutes before each call thinking about these three points.

The laundry list we presented in this chapter will help you think in a more focussed manner about the first point: that is, it will serve as a tool to help you identify the general areas where you're missing information. In the following chapter we'll zero in much more closely on those areas, and provide a detailed explanation of how to use the second and third criteria. We'll show you a) how to select the most appropriate questions for a given sales call, b) how to phrase those questions most effectively, and c) how to arrange them in a sequence that will create a positive flow of information between you and each of your customers.

▸ 4 ◂

THE QUESTIONING
PROCESS

Since good selling means not just "cramming product," but searching for a fit between your product or service and the customer's Concept, your principal attitude in a sales call should really be that of an *interviewer*—of a specialist in the art of asking questions.

In Conceptual Selling we define *four* distinct types of questions that should be asked in every sales call interview. Each type has its own distinctive *purpose;* that is, each one is designed to elicit a unique and specific type of information. Each type is phrased in a specific manner, using distinctive *key words.* And, as you put the four types of questions together into an effective interviewing process, you also need to give some attention to their *sequence.*

Before we go into detail regarding the purpose, phrasing, and sequencing of the four question types, here are some thumbnail definitions.

1. *Confirmation Questions:* These are questions that validate your data or that point out inaccuracies in what you thought was true.
2. *New Information Questions:* These are questions that force you to listen and accept the reality of current data; they also tell you the explicit business results that the customer expects.
3. *Attitude Questions:* These are questions that identify the customer's personal needs, values, and attitudes, and thus the urgency that he feels about meeting his needs.
4. *Commitment Questions:* These are questions that help you locate your current position in the sale.

With these brief definitions in mind, we begin with the one type of question that should always be asked near the beginning of a sales call, but that very few salespeople ever ask at all—the Confirmation Question.

Confirmation Questions

As our thumbnail definition illustrates, Confirmation Questions have a dual *purpose.* They help you to verify information you already have—or think you have—and they help you to reveal inaccuracies you may not have identified before. The answer you get to a Confirmation Question, therefore, can either validate or invalidate the data you think you have as you enter the sales call. But whether they validate *or* invalidate, these questions still provide you with the up-to-date picture you need to be able to proceed effectively with the call.

As an example of a good Confirmation Question, think back to the story we told in the first chapter about our friend Gene—the food service sales representative who nailed down a multimillion dollar contract in Chicago by doing more asking than telling. Going into the initial sales call for that deal, he knew that the potential client had been having trouble with its current food service supplier, and was looking for a replacement. That was his basic entry data. To check its validity, he began the sales call by asking: "Do I understand correctly that you're currently dissatisfied with the way your food service operation is being run?"

As it happened, the answer he got to that question confirmed what he already believed. The answer might have invalidated it, too. In a different scenario, Gene might have heard from the customer, "Hell no, we don't have any real problems with the service—we're just looking for a more competitive price." But that invalidation, just like the confirmation he actually got, would also have told him, right at the outset, what he was dealing with.

The point is that, *whatever* answers you get to your Confirmation Questions, they will always give you better quality information—and more up-to-date information— about the sale than you could possibly have *without* asking for confirmation. That is why it is foolish to avoid Confirmation Questions, and why it is usually appropriate to begin the sales call interview by asking one.

A summary of what we've been saying, with some sample Confirmation Questions, is presented in the box:

CONFIRMATION QUESTIONS

Purpose:
- To verify: What I think I know
             Results needed or problems
             Data accurate; up-to-date
- To reveal discrepancies in your information

Examples:
"Are you still having trouble with the delivery schedule?"

"Is Pete remaining as your boss in the reorganization?"

"Do you continue to use 20,000 units per week?"

Phrasing Confirmation Questions. If you look at the Confirmation Question Gene used in his presentation call, and at the sample Confirmation Questions given in the box above, you'll see that the focus of this first type of question is always the *current* situation. What you're trying to find out by asking a Confirmation Question is what's happening right now—and by implication, whether what's happening now is *different* from what was happening a week or a month ago.

We recommend two phrasing techniques to ensure that your Confirmation Questions do in fact focus on current reality. First, always phrase your Confirmation Questions *in the present tense.* Second, use *key words* that signal to the customer that you are asking for information about the present. "Does inventory *continue* to be a problem?" "Are you *still* using the X4000 models?" Other key words that are useful in phrasing Confirmation Questions are *remain, as usual, now, currently,* and *at the present time.*

A properly phrased Confirmation Question should be answerable by a simple Yes or No. We realize this may sound like heresy to you, if you've been trained never to take No for an answer. Sometimes that answer is exactly what you need to hear, however, to get your data straight. When you ask a Confirmation Question, you already have an idea in your mind about what the current situation is. Either that idea is correct, or it isn't. So a Yes or No answer is entirely appropriate.

One tip. Many times, when you're having trouble phrasing an appropriate Confirmation Question, you can shift to a statement-question combination, by first making a statement that you believe to be true about the past situation, and then asking, "Is this still the case?" If Mr. Johnson has been having inventory control problems, for example, you could begin the sales call by saying, "The last time I was here, you were experiencing database problems with the inventory system. Has that situation changed at all?" Again, the point to emphasize is that you want as accurate information as you can get about possible discrepancies between your view of the situation, and what that situation actually is, right now.

When to use Confirmation Questions. We've been emphasizing the value of Confirmation Questions early in the sales call, and have even suggested that you may want to open most sales calls by asking this type of question. We realize that to salespeople who have been trained to open with polite chit-chat in order to establish "rapport," this may sound iconoclastic.

There's nothing wrong with establishing rapport, and we're not saying that you should avoid the customary "How's your wife and kids?" exchanges. In some parts of the country, in fact—this is especially true in the South— jumping into the "real business" of the sales call without making these conversational overtures will turn your customer immediately into Stonewall Jackson. If you're comfortable by beginning your calls with this kind of pleasantry, fine; we don't advise you to drop anything that makes you or your clients feel comfortable.

Just remember that the chit-chat is *preliminary*. It's not part of the sales call proper. Breaking the ice is fine. But the sales call really begins only *after* you've broken the ice, and are ready to get down to business. Once the business starts, you've got to check out your information quickly. Never assume that because you've established rapport with Mr. Johnson, you can jump safely into a product demonstration, and slip the data confirmation. A lot of sellers make this mistake, because they think that people buy from them out of friendship. "I got that contract," you'll hear again and again, "for a simple reason: they like me."

Bull. Nobody buys anything from a salesperson simply because he's "well liked." Willy Loman found that out, and so does every other seller who relies solely upon "How's your golf game these days?" as a reliable opener. Our advice remains firm. Begin the conversation if you wish with the chit-chat that makes you both relaxed. But a) keep it short, because your time is valuable, and so is your customer's. And b) once you begin the substantive part of the sales call—once the emphasis shifts from the social niceties to the business at hand—always consider beginning your questioning with a Confirmation Question. One of the best ways of doing this, at the beginning of a sales call, is to state the *purpose of the meeting,* as you understand it, in the form of a Confirmation Question: "As I understand it, Jim, what we had planned to do today is assess your Finance Committee's reaction to my last presentation. Is that your understanding?"

You should also use Confirmation Questions *immediately before presenting any new product or service data* to the customer. This will maximize the chances that there actually is a possible fit between the product or service you're going to describe and the real needs of the customer, as he or she sees them. This goes back to what we said about *always making the Concept Sale first.*

Confirmation Questions are also valuable when you are *building a foundation for a close.* As you get closer to taking a customer's order, two things happen. One, your own confidence begins to rise. Two, your vulnerability rises, precisely *because* you're becoming more confident. As you proceed through all the complexities of a drawn-out selling process, and it looks as though the order is a certainty, the seller's tendency is always to start *assuming* things that may or may not be so. And the basic assumption a salesperson makes is that the customer's needs have not substantially changed since he began the selling process. Since customers' needs are in fact changing all the time, that can be a fatal assumption. One of the best ways we know to guard against it—and to keep you in touch with reality—is to ask Confirmation Questions as early in the sales call as possible, no matter how "certain" the close.

A summary of the key words to use, and of the best times to use, Confirmation Questions is given below on page 83.

New Information Questions

The second type of question to be asked on every sales call is the New Information Question. Often, these questions

KEY WORDS
Always ask in the present tense:
Still, remain, continue, as always,
now, currently.

WHEN USED:
- It is generally safe to start a sales call with a confirmation question.
- Ask before presenting any new product or service data; this will maximize chances you are describing a product that fits needs of the customer.
- When there is a need to build a foundation for a close.

follow up and build on Confirmation Questions, by asking for more detail on issues raised by Confirmation Questions.

The *purpose* of New Information Questions is threefold. It is to *update* your information, to *resolve your perceived information discrepancies* by filling in the gaps, and to get the customer to give you more detail about his or her required *results*. To give an example from the Chicago food service sale, Gene followed up his Confirmation Question with the following New Information Questions: "What's been happening in your current operation that you'd like to see not happening?" And, putting the same point less negatively, "I'd appreciate hearing a little more about what a *good* food service contract would look like to you." Other examples of New Information Questions are given in the box on page 84.

Phrasing New Information Questions. Novice journalists are often advised to observe the "Five W" rule in writing

NEW INFORMATION QUESTIONS

Purpose:

- To update information; fill in gaps
- To resolve perceived discrepancies
- To get "Results" information

Examples:

"How do you intend to approach
that problem?

"When do you envision
this happening?"

"Where must you do this?"

lead paragraphs to stories: as close to the beginning of the story as possible, they are advised to give the *who, what, when, where,* and *why* of the situation. In formulating New Information Questions, we advise you to use the same key words—with one important exception. Instead of asking "why," we say you should ask "how" or "how much" or "how many." "Why" can be useful as a kind of second-level probe, to follow up on an insufficiently answered New Information Question; but as an opening New Information Question, it tends to be confrontational, and seldom gets you the information you need.

New Information Questions that begin with the key words *who, what, when, where,* and *how* comprise only one subset of this question type, however. They are what we call *explicit* questions, since they ask the customer to provide very specific new information: "Where will the new plant be sited?" "How many units are processed per month?"

Comprising a second subset of New Information Questions are what we call *exploratory* questions. They invite the customer to explore, at his or her own level of detail, a general area where you need more information. Exploratory questions begin with key words like *tell, explain, demonstrate,* and *show.* Just like explicit questions, these questions seek for further information; but they do so in a more open, expansive manner. You can see the distinction between the two subsets of New Information Question by looking at the two questions Gene asked the food service selection committee. The first example ("*What*'s been happening . . . ?") is an explicit question which begins with one of the "journalist's opening" key words. The second example ("I'd appreciate hearing a little more . . . ") is an exploratory question that begins with a modified form of the key words *explain* or *show me.*

Since people are sometimes resistant to being told "Show me," we suggest using a grammatical technique that makes exploratory New Information Questions sound less confrontational. You can mute the perceived aggressiveness of a question—and this goes for any question, not just New Information Questions—by phrasing it in an indirect or subjunctive mode, that is, by employing such syntactical structures as "I'd like to . . . " or "I'd appreciate it if you would . . . " or simply "Could you . . . ?" Gene's second question here is an example. To a customer who is sensitive to being told to do something, the expression "I'd appreciate hearing more" may get you better results than the direct "Tell me more."

When to use New Information Questions. You use a New Information Question whenever you discover you are *missing specific information* regarding the current status of the sale. Obviously this can occur at any point in the sales call. We've already emphasized that New Information Questions can be valuable in following up on Confirmation Questions, and this is especially so when you get an unexpected answer to the Confirmation Question. For example, if you've just asked your client whether or not she's still using 1400 units a week, and you find out she's upped it to 2000, it's time for you to get New Information: the follow-up question might be something like "What's happened since the last time I saw you?" or "Could you tell me some more about the reasons for the increase?" Whenever you discover that the data you thought you had is now inaccurate, it's time to ask a New Information Question.

New Information Questions are also appropriate whenever you want to *encourage the customer to explore* the situation freely, on his or her own terms. As we've emphasized earlier, contrary to popular opinion, customers generally *want* to talk, and will do so at length if you give them the opportunity. Because this is so, asking New Information Questions often gives you an added benefit in addition to the missing information: it tends to put people more at ease. And someone who is at ease with you is more likely to *keep* giving you information.

In short, it is appropriate to ask a New Information Question at *any point* that you feel you have "surfaced a gap" in your information. Your prospect's pen may be poised above the contract, but if he says something at that point that isn't crystal clear to you, ask a New Information Question fast, or expect trouble down the line.

A concrete example. A friend of ours recently was literally seconds away from having a major customer sign a contract for a multimillion dollar industrial sale. The customer was a regional development manager, and as he was putting pen to paper he casually mentioned, "Now this just has to go to Division for the rubber stamp, and we're set." At that point our colleague *should* have said, "Just a second, Jim. Who do you mean by Division, and could you tell me some more about the 'rubber stamp' mechanism?" He didn't. He let Jim sign the paper and send it on to Division—and he never saw a commission. By failing to ask a New Information Question at a point where he obviously lacked a crucial piece of information, the sales rep simply assumed his way into a lost sale.

The key words and usage of New Information Questions are profiled below on page 87.

KEY WORDS:

What, where, when, how, how much, how many, explain, tell, show, demonstrate.

Caution: "Why" is a second-level probe; use as a follow-up question.

WHEN USED:

- When specific information is missing
- When you get an unexpected response to a Confirmation Question
- When you want to encourage the Buying Influence to explore freely with little guidance

Attitude Questions

While New Information Questions focus chiefly on the customer's desired results, Attitude Questions focus on how he personally *feels* about those results, and about what you can do for him and his company. The *purpose* of an Attitude Question is to get the customer to reveal personal information—information about how he or she, individually, will "Win" or "Lose" in this sale. Such questions seek to discover the individual customer's *values and attitudes* which are so important in determining Concept. And, because they get at those values and attitudes, they also frequently serve to uncover unidentified personal issues that a more "objective" New Information Question won't uncover.

Many traditionally trained salespeople are resistant to asking Attitude Questions, because they believe that what a client *feels* is none of their business, or is irrelevant to the sale. Many of them take Jack Webb's old line, "Just the facts, ma'am," as an unwritten motto. Big mistake. In today's selling, there is no single fact that is more important than what your customer is feeling, personally, about what you're trying to sell him. Personal feelings are what comprise his or her Concept, and if you do not understand the Concept, you really understand nothing at all. That's one reason that Attitude Questions are so important: they surface gaps in your information about *the one thing that drives the sale* — the client's mental picture of what buying from you can do for him. Remember that if results define *what* he buys, values and attitudes define *why.*

There's a second, related reason—one that also overturns the given wisdom about feelings. In our experience with thousands of selling situations, the vast majority of customers *want* to talk about their feelings. They welcome the opportunity to react personally with regard to a sales proposal, and the salesperson who gives them that opportunity has an immediate and enormous advantage over the competition.

We don't mean that people want you to psychoanalyze them, and we're well aware that some people *are* reluctant to tell you anything but "the facts." But when we advise you to ask Attitude Questions, we're not talking about indepth psychology or about the old "I'm your pal, Joe, you can level with me" malarky that sellers sometimes use as part of a "Get him to like me" approach. We mean simply that you should take a customer's attitudes about your product or service as a critical factor in the sale— perhaps as *the* critical factor—and that you should no more ignore them than you would ignore your own product specs or servicing capabilities.

It's especially important to remember this when you sense an *uneasiness or reluctance* that your New Information Questions have not been able to explain. A good example of this occurred in Gene's food service call in Chicago.

Typically, employee food service programs are partially subsidized by the corporation: they are often considered part of an employee benefit program that must be borne, as a cost, by the company. "When we started talking about subsidies," Gene told us after his Chicago call, "the committee just grimaced, and I realized it was time for an Attitude Question. I asked them how they felt about having to subsidize the food service operation. What I got was amazing. They went on for fifteen minutes expressing their resentment at the subsidy structure, and that gave me a lot of information about the operation that I hadn't even asked for. In the course of their gripe session, for example, all kinds of new information surfaced about the pricing schedule, the in-house supervision arrangement, employee relations—I obviously had tapped a nerve, and it turned into an information bonanza for me."

Gene's description illustrates two points that we have found to be typical in selling situations. Not only do Attitude Questions often open out the discussion with regard to the customer's feelings, but they also bring the salesperson a great deal of "hard," "nonsubjective" information that the Attitude Question didn't even ask for. So, by using New Information Questions and Attitude Questions in tandem, as it were, you can generate an enormous amount of information in a relatively short period of time.

A summary of the purpose of Attitude Questions, and a few typical phrasings, appear in the box on page 90.

Phrasing Attitude Questions. Since the goal of Attitude Questions is to surface information about personal values and attitudes, these questions typically use key words like *what, which, why,* and *how* in conjunction with phrasing that solicits a *judgment:* "*What* is your *opinion* about . . . ?" "*How* did John in Finance *react* to the prospectus?" And, most commonly, *"How* do you *feel* . . . ?"

New Information Questions and Attitude Questions, therefore, both use the "journalist's openers." But the Attitude Question uses these key words to *set up a probe for a value judgment.* As we said, it's not appropriate to use the key word *why* to solicit New Information; but it's entirely appropriate to use it in phrasing an Attitude Question.

ATTITUDE QUESTIONS

Purpose:

- To learn how this individual "Wins" or loses

- To discover previously unidentified issues

- To discover attitudes and values

Examples:

"What is your opinion?"

"Why is that best?"

"How do you feel about _____ ?"

One proviso, however. When you use "why" in forming an Attitude Question, remember that you are soliciting the person's judgment, *not* challenging or questioning it. As any parent of a three-year-old will tell you, this little word can be one of the most aggravating sounds in the language if it is overused or if it is used in a teasing, interrogative manner. In Conceptual Selling we begin with the premise that every good sale starts with your customer's Concept. The last thing you want to do with a "Why?" question is to give anyone the message that you think his Concept is invalid, or that he has "no good reason" for his opinion. Therefore, we caution you to use the "why" format sparingly, and to make it clear by your tone of voice that you are trying to *understand,* not criticize.

When to use Attitude Questions. You use an Attitude Question whenever you need a better understanding of *how your customer feels* about your being there, and about what you're trying to sell him. You can also use Attitude

Questions to solicit information about the personal feelings of other people in the buying organization who might influence your sale. Obviously, however, asking one person's opinion of another person's opinion is a task that is open to uncertainty, and whenever possible we suggest that you ask each Buying Influence *directly* about his or her feelings about the proposed sale.

Attitude Questions are important specifically when you need to identify *how a given individual will "Win" or "Lose"* with your sale. Since in a complicated corporate sale there may be several or many Buying Influences involved, and since no two of those Buying Influences will "Win" in the same way, it's very important to keep on top of each player's *personal* reasons for wanting, or not wanting, to buy. Attitude Questions to each one help you to do that.

Attitude Questions also help you determine what's *behind the results* a given customer wants—or says he wants. Different customers will want the same result for different reasons, and this means that each one's Concept of the result you can deliver is going to be different. Attitude Questions should always be used when you know that Jim wants the Model 1205, but aren't sure exactly why. If you sell him the Model 1205 without understanding *what that does for him personally,* you're still selling with inadequate information, and that may undermine your relationship with Jim, if not on this sale then on future ones. Better than any other kind of question, Attitude Questions help you focus, on every sales call and through all the stages of a long selling cycle, on the *person* behind the title on the door. So they are always appropriate when you need to know more about what makes that person tick.

The key words and use of Attitude Questions are summarized in the box on page 92.

Commitment Questions

We've said that salespeople frequently ignore Confirmation Questions and shy away from Attitude Questions. This is not the case with the fourth question type. The one type of question that no seller ever ignores or shies away from is the Commitment Question. In fact, a great deal of traditional "question skill" training is geared to developing new and more subtle ways of asking the ultimate closing question, "Are you ready to sign the contract today?"

KEY WORDS:

What, which, why, how, in conjunction with words that solicit a judgment such as: opinion, feelings, attitudes, reaction.

WHEN USED:

- When you want to get a handle on the customer's feelings or feelings of others as seen by this person.
- When you want to help identify Wins.
- When you want to understand what's behind the Results demand.

When we speak about "commitment" in Conceptual Selling, we do not mean simply the final step in the sale, the signing of the order. Getting the order is *part* of commitment, and "asking for the order," in all its guises, is part of getting commitment. But it's an error to think that it's the only part—or to believe that it's the most important part. In a good selling process, with each sales call, the seller should move the sale closer to an ultimate Win-Win commitment in a *series of graduated steps*. Getting the order is only the *last* step—and you cannot make that step happen unless, on previous sales calls with this customer, you have gone through the previous steps.

Early steps of commitment may include your customer's promise to present your product specs to one of his superiors, or an agreement to let you make a demonstration to a purchasing committee. On an initial call to a new customer, "commitment" may be something as "minor" as an agreement to set up the next appointment.

The level of commitment, therefore, will vary considerably from one sales call to the next. The *purpose* of a Commitment Question, as we define it, is to *tell you exactly what level you are at,* at a given point in the selling process, and at the same time to *make it possible for you to move toward the next higher level.* In other words, a good Commitment Question does more than simply move you toward the close. It also gives you information that tells you how far away you are from the close. And last, but *certainly* not least, it tells you what aspects of your customer's Concept are blocking your forward progress. Commitment Questions serve as a kind of compass to keep the salesperson aware of his current position, and of the rate and direction of his movement.

Because of their value as "place-testing" devices, Commitment Questions often function well at or toward the end of a sales call. In Gene's Chicago call, for example, after he had confirmed the manufacturer's problems and asked New Information and Attitude Questions to clarify his understanding of those problems, he posed this end-of-the-call question: "Are we in agreement that the next logical step is for you to set up a date when we can survey your food service patrons and analyze the current operation?" That question looked both backward and forward. It summed up the understanding of the meeting—that Gene's company was going to be a prime candidate for the replacement contract—and it defined exactly *what had to be done* next to move the selling process forward.

But beware of asking Commitment Questions *only* at the end of the sales call. A Commitment Question is appropriate whenever you need a check on your current position, and one advantage in asking these questions at every step of the way—that is, on every sales call—is to avoid the all too common situation where you come to the "final" call, the ink-on-the-paper call, only to discover that the rubber stamp is not a rubber stamp, or that Janice in Accounting hates your company, or that there's still a review committee that needs to be heard from before your proposal can be approved.

A summary, and further examples of Commitment Questions, are given in the box.

COMMITMENT QUESTIONS

Purpose:

• To move toward closure

• To determine where you are in the sale

Examples:

"Are you willing, with the information you have, to recommend this proposal to the committee?"

"Do I understand that you now plan to approve this with regard to specifications?"

Phrasing Commitment Questions. The key words that are most appropriate in phrasing Commitment Questions are those that relate to *future efforts*—either yours, or the customer's, or both: verbs like *determine, plan, mean to,* in constructions that focus on *what still needs to be done,* on this or future sales calls, in order to keep moving toward Win-Win.

Like Confirmation Questions, Commitment Questions can often be phrased effectively in the form of a statement-plus-question combination. Gene's Commitment Question, for example, might have been phrased: "It seems that the next logical step would be for us to survey your patrons and analyze your operation. Are we in agreement that you'll set a date for that now?"

There's a critical point to remember here, which is implicit in the sample questions we have mentioned. We say that Commitment Questions relate to the future efforts of both you and your clients. But the burden must be on the *client*. When we say that the Commitment Question focusses on what still needs to be done, we mean something that the prospective customer has to do, or be involved in doing, to move the sales process forward. "Do *you* plan to approve?" "Will *you* set a date?" and so on. We'll expand on this point in a moment.

When to use Commitment Questions. We've emphasized that Commitment Questions are commonly, and most effectively, used toward the end of a sales call, when you need to know how far you've come and where you still need to go. These questions may also be used, however, at *any* point during the sales call where the seller is *uncertain about the current level of commitment,* or *unsure what progress has already been made* in getting concurrence for his or her proposal. You should not follow our four-question-type format in a strict 1-2-3-4 pattern: that kind of rigidly sequential thinking is a legacy, and a fallacy, of track selling. Whenever you feel uncertain about your current position vis-a-vis a given customer, and whenever you are uncertain about what needs to be done to move a selling process forward—that is the time to ask your customer a Commitment Question. The timing and phrasing of these questions are summarized in the box on page 96.

Mutual Commitment. The bottom line here is *mutual* Commitment. That's why we stress the need to get the client to do something. Obviously, there's going to be plenty for you, the seller, to do too, but you already know that, and by virtue of the fact that you're working toward the sale, you've committed yourself to doing it. What you don't know is whether or not your customer is *also* com-

KEY WORDS:

Decide, plan, going to, intend, agree, direct, determine, mean to, propose, recommend, commit, secure.

WHEN USED:

- When the sales representative needs to determine what progress has been made in getting concurrence.
- To determine what remains to be done.

mitted to carrying the buy/sell process forward. Asking for his involvement in the next step is your way of testing that commitment, and to do this properly you have to be very concrete: what you want from your customer is a promise to *do something specific,* whether it's as major as pulling together a final approval committee or as minor as setting up a new meeting.

It's unrealistic to suppose, as do many traditionally trained salespeople, that you can always get the order on any call, if you only work yourself hard enough, or if you give your customer enough blatantly manipulative choices like, "Would you like to sign the contract today or Friday?" But it's also unrealistic to suppose that you can manage any selling process to a Win-Win conclusion unless you get *some* commitment to action on every call you make. If you've just spent twenty minutes with Mr. Hackford and he seems delighted with your general presentation, but all that he will say is "Give me a call sometime," then you might as well forget it. Commitment means a time and a date. It means Mr. Hackford is interested enough in what you've said to bracket out another twenty minutes next week, or next month, so he can hear more. If he's not willing to at least make that commitment of *his* time, we advise you not to waste *your* time "giving him another call." Because that's exactly what you'll be doing: *giving* him something for nothing.

We will be discussing this point in more detail in the chapter on Getting Commitment. For now just remember the basic point: A good Commitment Question elicits three things: an understanding of *where you are,* and understanding of *what remains to be done,* and a commitment from your customer to invest some of *his* time in doing something concrete.

Personal Workshop: Questioning

You're now going to have the opportunity to apply the principles in this chapter to your own upcoming sales calls. In the last chapter we presented you with a "laundry list" of common problem areas in sales—areas where salespeople typically lack information—and asked you to identify, with regard to your own sales situations, the areas where you were "information poor." You're now going to take that process of surfacing gaps one step further, by drafting a set of questions that you can use on your next sales call to get the information you're missing.

The following Personal Workshop includes four Steps, and should take you about fifteen minutes.

Step 1: Select your critical areas. First, taking a closer look at the information poor areas you identified on the laundry list, you should zero in on no more than *five or six* areas where you are a) most in need of information now, and b) most likely to get that information from the person you're next calling on. In other words, we'd like you to select a manageable handful of problem areas that are both *urgent* and *possible* areas to attack, given the sales call coming up.

By "urgent" we mean something you need to know *now*—something you need to know before you can move the call toward the next level of commitment. If you're about to make a second call on Mr. Chadwick, and you know that the typical selling process to a company like his takes six months, it's not urgent for you to know now all the details of the final contract review process. If you're two weeks from a close and you still don't know those details, that *is* an urgent area of missing information.

By "possible" we mean information that the specific Buying Influence you're calling on can actually get his hands on, and will be willing to give to you. There's no point in asking a vice president in charge of operations how many units rolled off Line 0321 last week, and no point in asking the plant manager for that line details about the corporate P & L profile for the coming year. You know who your Buying Influences are, and you know (or should know) their individual areas of expertise and responsibility. As you're focussing in on the five or six areas where you need information on the next sales call, be sure that the person you're calling on has responsibility in those areas—or at least can point you to someone who does.

Once you've selected the five or six most important areas, write them down in your notebook. You don't need to go into detail, and you don't need to phrase questions at this point, just make yourself some notes about the areas where you're lacking in information. The list might include things like "Need to know more about purchasing decisions in Louisville plant" or "Need information about competitor's new line." When you're finished, you'll have a brief and very focussed list of problem (and opportunity) areas that your next sales call might help to clear up and capitalize on.

Step 2: Construct your "Question Grid." Now that you've narrowed down the areas where you need information to the five or six most important, the next step is to construct a planning device that will help you organize those problem areas most effectively, so that you can ask the right questions in the sales call. We call that device the "Question Grid." The way you'll construct it is very simple.

First, down the left-hand edge of a page, write in the brief descriptions of the problem areas that we laid out in the previous chapter: these seven general category descriptions will divide the page into seven equal horizontal rows. Then divide the rest of the page vertically, into four vertical columns, and at the top of each column, write the name of the four question types: Confirmation, New Information, Attitude, and Commitment. When you're finished, you should have a grid that looks something like this:

	Confirmation	New Information	Attitude	Commitment
Buying Influences				
Buyer Needs				
Buying process				
New Players				
Competition				
"Resistance"				
Uncertainties				

Step 3: Categorize your problem areas. Now, go back to the laundry list from the last chapter, and put each of your five or six critical problem areas under the appropriate category in the left-hand vertical column. We've written in a couple of examples here to show you what we mean.

	Confirmation	New Information	Attitude	Commitment
Buying Influences				
Buyer Needs				
Buying process *Purchasing in Louisville plant				
New Players				
Competition *Their new line				
"Resistance"				
Uncertainties				

Step 4: Phrase appropriate questions. Now, using the key word constructions that we presented in this chapter, draft questions designed to get you the information you need in each of your five or six "information poor" areas. Write

them in at the appropriate places on the Question Grid, as in the examples given here.

	Confirmation	New Information	Attitude	Commitment
Buying Influences				
Buyer Needs				
Buying process *Purchasing in Louisville plant	"Is Charley still involved in this type of purchase?"	"What's his current role?"		"Are you able to recommend my proposal?"
New Players				
Competition *Their new line	"Am I correct that you now have a second supplier?"		"How do the quality control people feel about this line?"	
"Resistance"				
Uncertainties				

You're not playing "20 Questions" here. This is not an exercise in filling up space, or in coming up with more questions than the "average" salesperson. Don't try to fill in all the boxes. What you should be aiming for here is not quantity or "completeness" but quality. You may come up with questions in every question-type category and you may not; you may come up with no questions in a given category and several questions in another. That's fine. As long as each question you draft is phrased so that it will be most likely to elicit the information *you* need, then this exercise will have its maximum effect.

To provide a check on the effectiveness of your questions, we suggest you ask yourself the following:

- For every Confirmation Question: Is this question phrased to help me verify (validate or invalidate) the data I already have?

- For every New Information Question: Is this question designed to help me update my information, fill in the gaps, resolve discrepancies, and/or get information about my customer's results?

- For every Attitude Question: Is this question likely to give me information about this Buying Influence's personal values, attitudes, needs, and opinions regarding my current proposal?

- For every Commitment Question: Will this question tell me exactly where I am in the selling process, and what still needs to be done to move me and this person toward the close?

One other proviso. Although we don't advise you simply to "fill in the grid," we do suggest that you try to come up with at least one well-phrased question in each of the four question-type categories. Our experience shows that, without this proviso, many sales professionals will spend the majority of their time drafting nothing but New Information Questions. Those questions are essential, of course. But you cannot manage a sales call profitably by relying on them alone.

With the questions you've written in on the Question Grid, you should now be in a much better position to get the information you need to get on your upcoming sales call. We've said, though, that before you actually ask those questions, you need to do some thinking about sequence.

Guidelines on Sequence

Your goal in thinking about sequence before the sales call begins is to avoid the common error of submitting your customer to a barrage of disconnected queries—and to be able to direct the course of the interaction in a way that is profitable to you both. In ordering your questions into the most effective sequence, remember the following:

- It is almost always safe to begin a sales call interview with a Confirmation Question. These questions can also be used before presenting new product data and in building a foundation for a close.

- New Information Questions are an appropriate follow-up to Confirmation Questions, especially when the response to the Confirmation Question is unexpected. They are also appropriate when the seller needs missing information or wants to open up the interview.

- Attitude Questions are used when you want to identify the personal needs, interests, and concerns of your individual customers or prospects: that is, when you want to get more information about the feelings behind someone's answers.

- Commitment Questions are used when you need to know where you are in the sale, and to identify reasons why the sale is not moving forward as expected. It's usually appropriate to end a sales call with a Commitment Question.

An important proviso is in order here, however. We present the four question types in a given sequence because we have found that, as a *general guide,* this 1-2-3-4 sequence is an appropriate one. But this is not an "ideal" sequence, and it's certainly not meant to be viewed as a rigid, prearranged game plan. In an actual sales call, for example, you may have to ask several of one type of question before going on to another type. Or the answer to an Attitude Question may suggest that you have misunderstood something basic about the situation—and lead you to a Confirmation Question to clarify your understanding. And of course your prospect or customer will have his own agenda, and will be asking *you* questions. All of which will make it unlikely that you can follow *any* rigid plan with success.

We've ridiculed track selling for exactly this kind of rigidity, and we need to emphasize that sticking to any prepared list, and ticking off items as you go, is an almost ironclad guarantee that you will *not* get the information you need. Good sales call management, like good interviewing, is always a matter of being responsive to the individual situation—and to the constant changes in that situation.

Tom Brokaw tells a story on himself that illustrates this point very well. In an interview with Barry Goldwater in the mid-1970s, Brokaw asked the senator about Watergate. "I knew ten days before Nixon resigned," Goldwater said at one point, "that he was not going to stay." The appropriate response to that bombshell would have been, "*How* did you know?" But that's not what Brokaw said. Evidently his interview script only left a certain amount of time for Watergate, and so the reporter moved on, asking Goldwater about his recent trip to China. It was only after the interview ended, Brokaw later admitted, that he realized the magnitude of his blunder.

This is a perfect example of how even a veteran interviewer can foul up the communication process by a too close attention to the "numbers." That's why we say that the best gauge of when to ask a given question is to *remain attentive to what your customer is telling you.* The important skill to develop is to understand, at any given moment, which phase of the sales call you are in, so you can decide where you want to go next. You do that by communicating, both ways. The best sequence of questions in the world can still turn into a nonproductive monologue unless the questioner puts energy into *listening*.

We'll talk more about listening now.

▸ 5 ◂

CREATING POSITIVE INFORMATION FLOW

In the 1970s, educational researchers completed a series of studies on the effectiveness of different teaching styles. They found that one instructional style was invariably more effective than all others, especially in the presentation of complicated scientific information. It was a style that relied heavily on two-way communication between teacher and student, that aimed at creating a positive flow of information in both directions, and in which the pauses between questions and responses were typically much *longer* than in other teaching styles.

Since we have long believed that the Getting Information phase of the selling process and the teaching process are almost identical in terms of the flow of information, we decided to apply these findings to our own area of expertise. About six years ago, we started employing the teaching style that the researchers had recommended in our own selling situations, and we started incorporating it into the Conceptual Selling design.

The results have been extremely encouraging, and they have overwhelmingly supported our belief that good information gathering is a type of good teaching. By employing this unique selling "style," we have found, sellers are able to dramatically improve the information flow between themselves and their customers and prospects, and are able to bring about, in even the most difficult situations, what we call a Superb Communication Process. In the box below we've summarized what we mean by this process, and what it can mean to you. In this chapter we'll be describing the process more fully, and explaining how you can make it happen in every face-to-face situation with a customer.

SUPERB COMMUNICATION MEANS

- Maximum understanding between Buyer and Seller.

- Maximizing the **quality** and **quantity** of information flow between Buyer and Seller (two-way flow).

- Maximizing WIN–WIN—minimizing the chance that someone loses.

- Maximizing questioning/listening/responding activity on the part of seller; minimizing telling, describing, showing, demonstrating (at least in the opening stages of the interaction).

Question Shock

In the description of the ideal teaching style we just gave, we said that it involved *longer pauses between questions and answers* than other teaching styles. That's really the key point here. That seemingly simple feature—the extending of the length of time between questions and answers—is not just a teaching (or selling) "gimmick"; it is a tested and universally reliable technique for creating Superb Communication. But unfortunately this simple technique is still extremely rare in the selling world.

Many sales professionals, when they take the time to ask questions at all, seem less interested in hearing the buyer's responses than in running down a list of their own queries, and getting as quickly as possible to the end. You know the kind of rhetorical, rapid-fire questioning we mean. It's the style that the Music Man uses when he asks and then answers his own question: "Am I right? You know I am." It's the style that the old-time drummer uses when he supplies his audience's answers for them: "What can I sell you today? How about a nice bottle of Sam Slick's Superfine Snake Oil #31? Good for whatever ails you, step right up . . . " And it's the style that seems to be favored by journalists in political press conferences: "I have a followup question, Mr. President, and then a follow-up to the follow-up."

This type of questioning style—where you throw all your queries in the listener's lap at the same time—may be a necessary evil of the thirty-minute presidential press conference, where there are fifty other journalists trying to ask questions in front of you, and where you've got to impress the editor or station manager back home. But it very seldom leads to positive information flow, and it seldom creates a good communication process. In fact, what this "whack-whack-whack" interrogation style usually leads to is exactly the *opposite* of communication. It leads to the person being questioned clamming up or dodging the question or scratching his head in bewilderment. You see this all the time in press conferences, and it doesn't necessarily happen because the person being questioned wants to be evasive (although that's obviously sometimes a factor). Sometimes it happens because the guy is suffering an acute attack of the syndrome we call *Question Shock.*

Question Shock is what happens when a whiz kid like Perry Mason or Sam Donaldson strings together fourteen probing insights in one sentence and asks you to field them all at once. The whiz kid's got the questions written down, and he's rehearsed them, so there's little chance *he'll* be confused. But you don't have them written down, and you haven't rehearsed the fourteen replies he wants, so there's a better than even chance you *will* be confused. No matter how bright you are and how experienced you are at thinking on your feet, if somebody zaps you with more information than you can comfortably process on the spur of the moment, you are going to experience some level of cognitive confusion or uncertainty or hesitancy about responding. That's what we call Question Shock.

Everybody experiences it. Jack Kennedy was probably one of the most articulate fielders of questions that ever sat in the Oval Office, but even he was not immune to Question Shock. He'd get around it by smiling the JFK smile and joking, "What was that third question again, Chet?" But it was Question Shock all the same. And because they submitted him to this cognitive confusion, his questioners got less reliable and less complete information than they would have gotten if they had simply *slowed down.*

What we're saying here is even more relevant to the selling world than it is to the mouth dance that is politics. If you subject your prospective buyers to a barrage of questions without pausing, if you are continually ready to pounce with a follow-up probe, if you answer your own questions before the client has a chance to do so—you are going to put him, every time, into Question Shock. And you are going to throw a logjam into the information flow.

Our application of educational research to selling has revealed some startling statistics. We actually measured, with a stopwatch, the pauses in sales transactions. This is what we found to be typical:

- First, in many sales transactions, sellers who are questioning their customers can come out with *four, five, or more questions every minute.*

- Second, after asking a question, sellers often wait only about *one second* or less before either rephrasing the question, asking another question, answering the question themselves, or making some other comment.

- Third, after receiving a *reply* to a question, many salespeople tend to wait *less than one second* before commenting and moving on to the next point.

What does this data suggest? We think it suggests very clearly that, in probably the majority of selling situations, the salesperson is impeding the positive flow of information by moving things forward too fast. How much real thought can you expect a customer to give to your question, after all, if you only give him one second to answer it? How much thought can you be giving to his responses if you spend less than a second analyzing them before getting the ball rolling again?

The answer is damn little. As a result, the *last* thing the typical, rapid-fire questioning style leads to is Superb Communication.

It's not surprising that the figures we've given here are so low. Salespeople have traditionally been told that it's death for a sale if there's silence. Keep it moving, we're always told. Silence makes people uneasy. Don't give him too much time to think. And—probably most pointedly of all—if you're talking, you're in *control* of the sale; if the "conversation lags," you've lost control.

We say these slogans are nonsense. They arise from a common confusion about "controlling" vs. "dominating" the sale. In a sales call interview, the person who does the most talking is in fact dominating the call; but it is the person who is doing the listening who is actually in control. The key to really "controlling" the sales call, and the key to creating Superb Communication, is the same thing. It's to ask one question at a time and then keep quiet while you *actively listen.*

Golden Silence

What we're saying can be put to immediate and practical use with a technique we call Golden Silence. Golden

Silence is the only reliable "cure" that we have ever seen for the Question Shock syndrome. As you can see from the diagram presented here, it is a straightforward and elegantly simple cure:

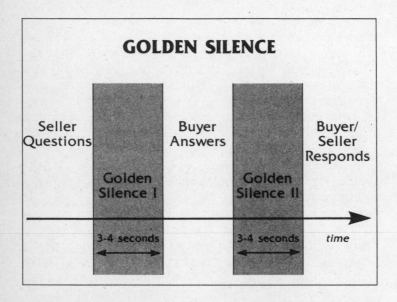

All that Golden Silence means, as the diagram indicates, is that you, the seller, need to *pause* for approximately *three or four seconds* at two different points in the questioning process: after you ask a question, and after your buyer responds. The first 3-4 second pause is what we call Golden Silence I; the second pause we call Golden Silence II. Introducing these two kinds of pauses into your sales call questioning will, we guarantee you, dramatically—and immediately—improve the quality and the quantity of the information you are getting.

The reason for this is simple. When you practice Golden Silence I by giving your customer a moment to think about what you've asked him, the information he gives you is much more likely to be solid information than if you had given him half as much time. When you practice Golden

Silence II by waiting after he speaks, you are giving yourself a better chance of understanding what he has told you than you would if you'd spent half the time. The result of using Golden Silence I and II together is a more leisurely, more thoughtful, and ultimately far more *productive* flow of information than you can possibly create any other way.

Now, we're not saying that you should carry a stopwatch into your selling encounters, that you should follow this technique slavishly to the exact second, or that you should use it in every question-answer exchange on every sales call. Obviously each selling encounter is going to continue to have its own rhythm and pace, and you need to adjust to that reality each time you sit down with an individual customer. Our point in teaching Golden Silence is not to give you a rigid game plan, much less a new gimmick. It's to give you a tested conceptual format for *understanding* the individual rhythms of your calls, and for turning down the volume and pace of conversations that are full of sound and fury, but no commission. As you practice the technique more and more in actual selling situations, you will know when to speed up and when to slow down. Hopefully, you will slow down far more frequently than you speed up. In any event, the basic point of the technique remains the same. It's to introduce into your selling situations those *essential periods of silence* without which positive information flow can never develop.

We're well aware that the Golden Silence technique can make you uncomfortable at first. Sellers are so used to jawing their way through any obstacle that keeping quiet seems unnatural. In the words of a colleague who initially resisted the idea, "When I first started using Golden Silence, I felt like the sphinx on parade. I was sure my customers were thinking, 'This guy is Dennis the Dense.'" Many of our program participants report similar cases of "silence nerves" when they first practice asking a question and waiting.

But this is a problem that diminishes very quickly with practice, and it points up again what we're saying about Golden Silence not being just another Motor Mouth gimmick. When we say "Ask the question and then keep quiet," we don't mean you should stare stonily ahead, as if you're challenging the person to open up. And we're not talking about the manipulative closing advice that says "He who blinks first, loses." Good selling is never a game where you try to overpower or psych out your customer. When you use Golden Silence, you still have access to all the body language and nonverbal cues that any good salesperson (or conversationalist) uses in a one-to-one exchange, and those techniques continue to be important. If you're uncomfortable just "sitting there," you can nod, lean forward, knit your brow, establish eye contact, and so on—just as you would do to generate fluidity if you weren't using Golden Silence.

Furthermore, when you're using the Golden Silence method, you have to be sensitive to those instances where the client simply doesn't understand you, and where "waiting him out" leads to nothing but a Leaden Silence. If you ask a question and after four or five seconds you have still gotten no response, the chances are good that he didn't comprehend the meaning of your question. At that point it's appropriate—indeed, it's essential— to rephrase the question or ask another one. One very effective technique of doing that is to say, "My intention in asking that question was to . . . " and then explain what you were trying to find out. This broadens the focus of the original question, and makes it clear that you are working at a dialogue, not a drill.

Our point is that the Golden Silence technique is meant to expand, not limit, the possibilities of Superb Communication. When it's used with discretion and flexibility, it does more for creating positive information flow than any other communicational skill we know. But it's not a magic wand and, yes, it can be used with too much rigidity—in which case it will lead to Leaden Silence. The way to avoid that misuse of the technique is to be sensitive to what your customer is saying—and that includes what he's saying nonverbally. The thing to remember is that silence is not golden in itself: it's "golden" because of what it brings you, the salesperson, in terms of the information that you need to proceed. If your silences are not bringing you that information, clearly it's time to adjust. Our experience has been, without exception, that when the technique is used with a close attention to *how the customer is reacting,* it vastly improves the seller's chances of making a Win-Win sale.

This is particularly the case when you're presenting something to a group or committee rather than to an individual. Many of our program participants have told us that, before learning the Golden Silence technique, they had been terrified of presenting to a group; the technique, they've said, enables them to set up a communication dynamic where the committee ends up doing most of the work. Our friend Gene, who used the technique effectively in his Chicago call, makes the point well: "You ask a committee one question and you give them five seconds to respond; I guarantee you it will be another five minutes before you have to ask them anything else."

Benefits of Golden Silence

We've said that Golden Silence is the cure for the common customer "disease" of Question Shock. That's a "negative" benefit of using the technique. There are numerous positive benefits as well. Here are several that we have found to be extremely common:

1. The *number* of customer reactions increases. When you use Golden Silence, you are much less likely to be stonewalled by people who feel pressured by fast-talking salespeople, or who are simply too "slow-thinking" themselves to be able to respond well to a rapid-fire style. Giving your prospective buyers the courtesy of a pause after your questions tends to increase their comfort level and make it easier for them to respond. This is especially useful with those who tend to process information slowly. Some people need more time to think than

others—which doesn't mean that they're stupid. Golden Silence gives them that time.

2. The *length* of responses increases. Since Golden Silence gives your customer time to think, it also gives him time to formulate more comprehensive answers. It offers him the opportunity to expand on his feelings about the sale, the results he needs, and his Concept of what you're trying to do for him.

3. The *reliability* of the information you get increases. Since the customer is being given more time to reflect on the situation, he or she is more likely to come up with considered responses, not just ad lib speculations. In a Golden Silence format, answers tend to be more objective as well as fuller.

4. The number of *relevant unsolicited responses* increases. The person who is given adequate reflection time is more apt to provide you with information you haven't specifically asked for, but that can still be critical to your understanding of the situation.

5. The number of *customer's questions* increases. Again, this is a logical outcome of being afforded more thinking time. Buyers who are given this time tend to ask you more questions regarding your product or service, and obviously this is to your benefit, since such questions help to move the sale toward closure.

6. The incidence of open-ended, *speculative thinking* increases. The customer tends to explore more alternatives, more possibilities of a fit between your product or service and his needs. This obviously sets up a golden opportunity for you to proceed toward a mutually satisfying sale.

7. Golden Silence tends to shift the *focus* of the discussion, during that critical pause period, onto the *customer's* real wants and needs, rather than on what the seller initially "wants" or "needs" to sell.

Again this increases the exploratory possibilities, and creates better chances for a Win-Win outcome to the sale.

8. Last, but certainly not least, Golden Silence gives the *seller* additional time to think about what information is still missing, to formulate additional questions, and to make those questions more pertinent to the specific situation and specific buyer. Invariably the Golden Silence technique improves the quality of the seller's questioning—and this in turn improves the *quality of the information received*.

"Techniques" to Avoid: Dangerous Verbal Signals

We said at the end of the previous chapter that there are right ways and wrong ways to phrase questions. We've just given you a technique, Golden Silence, that will enable you to present your questions in the most productive manner. But there are also several techniques you should avoid, if you are to make the best use of Golden Silence. In our experience, there are a variety of extremely dangerous verbal signals that interfere with Golden Silence, impede the positive flow of information, and drastically undermine communication. We caution you in particular against the following five signals. We've found them to be perfect techniques for the salesman to shoot himself in the foot.

1. "Think about it." There are two basic problems with this extremely popular "pre-closure" directive. The first problem is that it is vague. We've emphasized in the last chapter, in the section on Commitment Questions, that you always want to leave your customer, at the end of a sales call, with something specific to *do,* as a way of demonstrating his or her commitment to continue the selling process with you. The phrase "Think about it"—whether it's used in the middle of a call or as a parting gesture—

gives the buyer absolutely nothing specific to do. It's eyewash, pure and simple. Someone who has been asked to "think" about a proposal or a set of specs for your product has every right to do just that and nothing more; he has every right to say to you, when you return for a follow-up meeting, "I've been thinking about it, as you asked, but I just haven't made up my mind." That will get you, and him, exactly nowhere.

The second problem with "Think about it" is that it is a subtle put-down. When you direct somebody to do some (more) thinking about a topic, you're implying that he hasn't done any so far—or that the thinking he has already done has been so bush league and inconclusive that he'd better get himself in gear and do some *serious* thinking from now on. *We do not help people to think better by asking or telling them to do so.* The only way to get your customer to do the kind of thinking you want him to do before the next meeting is to give him *specific information* or materials around which to organize his thoughts. We'll be talking extensively about how to do this in the next chapter.

2. Mimicry. Somewhere along the line in sales training, the "experts" have gotten the idea that one good way to indicate to a person that you've heard and understood what he just said is to give it back to him verbatim. Mr. Hardwick ends a long explanation of his payroll situation with the observation "So as a result we have a constant cash flow problem," and the listener, ever sympathetic, responds, "You have a cash flow problem?" What is Mr. Hardwick going to make of this? If he's like any of the professionals we know, he's *not* going to nod sympathetically back and think "This guy really understands me." Instead, he's going to mentally check out the acoustics in his office, or start thinking, "I'm talking to a damn parrot."

Mimicry of the last crucial phrase spoken by the customer runs a very high risk of coming off as *condescending* behavior. You may not mean it that way. Who would? But it's risky business all the same. That's why we advise our clients never to "parrot back" a comment unless there's a pressing need to verify *factual* information or clarify very *complex* ideas. At other times, if you want to demonstrate to your customer that you've gotten the point of what he's just said, a nod will do quite well. An exploratory New Information Question is even better. In the example we gave above, for example, an appropriate and productive response to Mr. Hardwick would be "Can you *tell me some more* about the cash flow situation?"

3. "Yes . . . but" When a conversation includes a high level of "Yes . . . but" or other "give and take" statements, the probability is very good that that conversation is *stalled*. When a sales call is going nowhere, this phrase becomes a frequent refrain—on both the buyer's and the seller's part. Almost always it indicates the rejection of a just proposed idea or train of thought. For this reason, it tends to derail productive exploration, and to set up a broken-record syndrome, where the buyer's objections are countered by the seller's, and vice versa—and no real information gets exchanged.

Because we insist that good selling is a matter of information *flow,* because we believe that you find the proper "fit" in any sale largely through exploratory discussion, and because we have learned that the exploration of possibilities is always impeded by a "Yes . . . but" interjection, we advise you to avoid this phrase at all times. You cannot control your customer's "Yes . . . but" statements, but you can control your own. And limiting this distractive and confrontational verbal signal is essential to all good selling.

Instead of countering the customer's observations with "Yes . . . but" responses, we suggest you use an alternate phrasing that does *not* retract with the left hand what you've just offered with the right. Good alternate phrases include: "If that's the way it is, then how . . . ?" or "What kind of data do you have on that point?" Also, you can always move a potentially confrontational discussion in the direction of a Win-Win outcome by asking the exploratory New Information Questions we mentioned in the discussion of mimicry. Instead of "Yes . . . but," try "I don't understand fully yet what you mean. Could you expand on your production down-time problem?" Or: "I'm not sure I agree, Joe; could you tell me some more?"

4. Rhetorical questions/tags. A rhetorical question is one to which you don't expect an answer, or to which you think the answer is obvious. "Sure is hot, isn't it?" or "Isn't this new tax proposal outrageous?" Often such so-called questions (they're really not questions, but statements in question form) are preceded by, or followed by, traditional "tags." Three such tags are extremely common. They are the introductory "Don't you think that . . . " and the suffixes "Isn't it?" and "Right?"

The not-so-subtle purpose behind the use of such verbal persuaders is to get the listener to go along with what the questioner has already decided. The question "Don't you think you'd profit from a higher-density alloy here?" does *not* mean "Would you profit from a higher-density alloy?" It means "I have a higher-density alloy to sell you, and I don't care if you'd profit from it or not: sign here." The purpose is to *close off the customer's options* rather than opening them out. Since you know how we feel about closing off options, you can imagine how we feel about this tactic. It's at *best* a merely useless "filler" tactic. At worst it's an aggravating presumption that serves to alienate any potential customer who does not want his mind made up for him.

The "Right?" and "Isn't it?" tags are often used in telemarketing today, and we have a friend whose method of countering this technique is brutal but perfectly appropriate. "When a phone solicitor calls me to say that they've got something that will solve all my problems, I listen quietly up to the point where they make the first 'commitment break'. I let them say, 'Now that sounds like a pretty good deal, doesn't it?' Then I say, 'No, it doesn't' and hang up." We fell that that's exactly what a customer, *ought* to do when a salesperson asks him presumptive, rhetorical questions. And today, more and more people are doing just that. So we warn you away from these tags completely.   They do not lead to *finding* a fit, but only to some customers (like our friend) *throwing* a fit.

5. *"Why?"* We've already explained how this little word can put people on the defensive, and we've said that it should be kept to a minimum in the Questioning Process. This has a particular relevance to the development of positive information flow, for nothing can so immediately and disastrously impede the flow of information as a person who feels he's on the defensive.

If you are uncertain about why a client has said or done something, therefore, we advise you not to phrase your clarifying questions in the "Why" or "Why did you" form. Instead, use the equivalent, but not nearly so challenging, word "How." This may seem like a small and insignificant change. It's not. There is a considerable amount of communications research which indicates that a questioner can nearly *double* the amount of useful information received from a question if he or she prefaces it with the set-up word "How" rather than the potentially offensive "Why." "*Why* did you decide to change the monthly schedule?" comes off as a demand for *justification.* "*How* did you decide to change the monthly schedule?"   only asks the person to *describe his or her actions.* Because this phrasing is perceived as less threatening, it can actually *get* you the information, while asking somebody to explain "why" a given decision was made may get you nothing but evasion, rationalization, and defensiveness. The difference between the two question tags, it would seem, is perceived by the person being questioned as the difference between *conversation* and *interrogation.*

Of course a conversation, as opposed to an interrogation, always has two parties involved. Up to now we've been focussing on what we call Phase One of the sales call—the essential and often beginning phase where you, the seller, elicit the information you need. We're going to move now to Phase Two—to that equally essential part of the sales call where the other party to the conversation, your customer, gets the information *he or she* needs.

‣ 6 ‣

PHASE TWO: GIVING INFORMATION

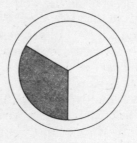

Giving information is supposed to be what the professional salesperson does best. Just as selling is often considered the art of persuasion—of telling the customer why he should want what you have—the most "important" part of the sales call is often seen as the display of your extensive product information. The heart of any pitch worth its salt, it's sometimes assumed, is the intensive, one-two-three rundown of the product's features and benefits.

But there's a problem with this whole approach. Of course a good salesperson has to know his product well, and of course letting the customer in on the product's impressive catalogue of capabilities is a necessary part of many sales calls. The difficulty is that the information you have about your product, the information that you consider important, may or may not be the information that your potential customer needs to hear in order to make a sensible buying decision. That's why, in the Giving Information phase, the Conceptual seller needs to perform a careful selection process before the sales call, so you can be sure that the information you give out will best serve your own, and your customer's, needs.

In order to be most effective, the information you give your customer has to do two related things:

- First, it has to help you make the Product Sale by relating your product or service to his or her Concept. The Giving Information phase of the sales call is what enables you to link your two selling tasks: the Concept Sale and the Product Sale.

- Second, it has to make it clear that your solution to his or her problem is in some significant way *different* from the solutions being offered by the competition. This means that the information you give out must do more than show him you're a candidate for his business; it must show him you're the *best,* indeed the *unique,* solution.

This second, critical point about Giving Information is what puts the Conceptual Selling approach years ahead of the old-fashioned "features and benefits" game. We're saying that, when you get down to showing off your product or service, it's never enough to establish that you can do the job; you have to give the client information that *differentiates* you from everybody else. That means you have to be expert in a very special, and specialized, kind of "telling."

Differentiating: Why It's Important

Buying, as we said earlier in the book, is always an exercise in *decision-making.* Some buying decisions are made impulsively and almost unconsciously; others are made after long and careful consideration of all the variables. But *all* decisions to buy are ultimately the end result of a mental process by which the buyer comes to a decision.

That process, we have found over and over, is an internal selection process which allows the buyer to distinguish between the various options open to him. He can perform that selection process in one of two ways. He can make the selection at *random*—by throwing dice, drawing straws, or just guessing. Or he can make the selection by *differentiating*—by acting on a perceived distinction between one option and all the others.

Of these two ways of deciding, differentiating is by far the preferable one, and for good reason: being able to select rationally among options is one of the things that makes us human. Nobody makes a decision—especially a potentially costly buying decision—by random choice unless he can see no difference in the options. *Whenever possible, people decide by differentiating.*

Think back to the last major purchase you made yourself—your automobile, an insurance policy, your VCR. Think about how you came to buy *that* particular automobile or policy or VCR, from *that* particular seller at *that* particular time. Chances are you didn't throw darts at the Yellow Pages. If you're like most informed buyers, you did some comparison shopping first. You checked out a few car dealers, you asked for brochures from several VCR stores, you asked friends and business associates about their experiences with different insurance companies—all of this as a way of seeking out a distinctive feature or capability, so you could make a wise decision. That's typical of intelligent buying. And it's precisely the kind of decision-making process that you want to help your customers to perform; the fundamental purpose of the Giving Information phase should always be to *help them to differentiate, but in your favor.*

The reason it's critical to provide this kind of help to your customer is that, if you *don't* help him to see a distinction that works in your favor, he will *create one of his own*—one that may *not* work in your favor. This point bears some clarification.

Let's suppose you're in the carpeting business, and you've been given an option to bid on a subcontract for a new office building. You're one of three top carpet vendors being considered for the job—not the biggest or most prestigious of the three, but still one of the chief contenders. Let's suppose further that, because you've already done the necessary groundwork in defining the prospect's Concept, you know that your company can do the job: the carpet your company can deliver to the office building will meet the design specifications. It's time now to link the potential customer's Concept to your particular product line, by giving him product and service information that he needs to have to make a decision. There are three basic ways you could go about this.

First, you could lay out your product specs and service capabilities exclusively on their own merits, and assume that the excellence of your wares will automatically incline him in your favor. In other words, you could simply ignore the competition, tell your story as fully as possible, and let the buyer decide. This is what we call "letting the buyer do the sorting," or "buyer differentiation." It's a common, and deadly, approach.

Second, you could size up the capabilities of the competition and try to convince the potential customer that you can do everything they can do—that your carpet is *as good as* anyone else's in the business. This is what we call the "me too" or "I'm just as good as Xerox" approach. Just like the approach that ignores the competition, it asks the buyer to do his own sorting. Faced with three "identical" vendors in this kind of scenario, guess which one the buyer is going to choose? The cheapest or the known brand, most of the time. And that may or may not be you.

Third, you could *help the buyer with the sorting,* by emphasizing what is different about you. Not what's "good" or "just as good" as somebody else, but what is in fact *unique* to your company and its capabilities. Maybe it's a quarterly cleaning program that nobody else can match, or a recently developed stain resistant formula, or the widest available color selection. Whatever it is, the thing that's significantly different about you is what we call a *Unique Strength.* In giving your customers information, *it's only by stressing your Unique Strengths that you make differentiation work in your favor.*

We realize that, strictly speaking, "unique" means "one of a kind." But we use the word in a slightly more flexible manner than Webster does. In sales reality there can be, and often is, such a thing as "relative uniqueness," where a company is able to offer something that is *different to a significant degree* from what everybody else is offering. In Conceptual Selling we say it's reasonable to speak of such a degree of difference as a Unique Strength too.

To sum up what we've said so far: Buying is an exercise in decision-making, and people make decisions, whenever possible, by a process of differentiating. In order to differentiate intelligently, people need to perceive a *distinction;* if they don't, they will create one of their own. Your fundamental task in the Giving Information phase of the sales call, therefore, is to highlight those areas where you are different from everybody else giving your accounts information: in other words, it's to focus on your own Unique Strengths.

Unique Strengths

You can see by what we've been saying that our concept of Unique Strengths is quite different from the traditional, product-related notion of "features and benefits." The basic difference between the two approachs to giving product information is that the "features and benefit" idea always *starts with the product,* while Unique Strengths starts with the *customer's Concept,* and then enables you to *relate* the product to that Concept.

This is a subtle but critical distinction. The limitation of feature and benefit selling may be summed up very simply: it *assumes that every product feature has a benefit,* and thus that if you only describe the feature glowingly enough, the benefit will be obvious to the prospect. That only works when the prospect has *already* recognized and accepted the value of the "benefit" you're offering him. The feature "tenderness" in a T-bone steak has absolutely no benefit to a vegetarian. That's why pushing any product's "inherent" benefits is a self-defeating proposition—

unless the seller first determines that those benefits link up to the prospective buyer's Concept. The value of the Unique Strengths approach is that it begins by asking "What does this customer really need?" and then proceeds logically to the next step: "How can I, *uniquely,* deliver it?"

In short, features and benefits selling begins (and often ends) with the product. Unique Strengths lets you look for a *fit.*

There's one other reason that Unique Strengths is a more reliable method of Giving Information about your product than even the best features and benefits pitch. It's that many features and benefits are *common* to a number of competitors, and so they do not enable you to differentiate yourself from other potential suppliers or vendors. Your stain-resistant carpet material may be an attractive feature to your customer; but if everybody in the carpet business uses this material, it's hardly a Unique Strength. The lesson is that *product strengths alone are never enough.* You've got to be able to give information about those product strengths that makes you stand out from all the others.

This is particularly important in an era when there are so many competing firms for every piece of business, and when the products that they are able to offer the customer so often seem indistinguishable. In a highly competitive environment, unless you move beyond product specs, you're going to be right back to the "me too" scenario, where the customer is forced to do his own sorting—and where he'll do it, nine times out of ten, on the basis of price or availability alone.

One of the greatest advantages of emphasizing the Unique Strengths you have to offer, in fact, is that it *diminishes the importance of price competition,* and allows you to do "value added" selling.

Look at IBM, for example. Why have they kept on top of one of the most competitive markets in the world for going on fifty years? Is it because they sell the most powerful computers in the business? Not at all. The IBM computer line is excellent, of course—but so are several dozen other computer companies' lines, and computer people themselves will tell you that, if you judge them on the basis of pure engineering alone (that is, on their inherent features), the computers put out by Big Blue are no more innovative than those put out by Hewlett-Packard, Digital, and the other front runners in the field. IBM has maintained its lead in this highly competitive field for many reasons, but one of the most important is that, since the days of founder Thomas Watson, the company has put an almost obsessive premium on *instant service response.* You can own an IBM mainframe in the middle of the Amazon jungle. If it malfunctions on a Tuesday, by Thursday morning a service representative will be on your doorstep, ready to get it running again. One of IBM's most important Unique Strengths has been its fanatical commitment to responsive service. And because they value that strength—because they know it can help them out in distress—customers have always been willing to pay a premium price for IBM products.

We mention this example as representative, but it's not necessarily going to be typical of your company. A world-famous service capability is something that is unique to IBM, and of course to many other value-added companies. It may not be your Unique Strength, however. You can have (and develop) Unique Strengths in any number of different areas. We've highlighted some of the most important areas in the box on page 127.

Obviously some of these areas will be very relevant to your type of business, and some will be less so. In addition, a Unique Strength in one area may appeal to a given customer, and be of no particular interest to a different one—even a different one for the same product. If you're selling color televisions, for example, your state-of-the-art technology may be seen as a Unique Strength to an electronics whiz; but that same technology may seem irrelevant to someone who just wants a cheap second TV so he can watch the Celtics in his workshop. One customer may be happy to wait two weeks for delivery, because he's going to be on vacation until then anyway; another may want delivery tomorrow. To the second person, your 24-hour

AREAS OF POSSIBLE UNIQUE STRENGTHS

- people
- product
- process
- knowledge
- service
- implementation
- delivery
- experience

- organization
- customer base
- technology
- reputation
- application
- training
- logistics

delivery promise will be seen as a Unique Strength; to the first one, it won't.

It all comes back to customer Concept. In the Giving Information phase of the sales call, no less than in the Getting Information phase, you always need to begin with what the *customer* is thinking about what you can do for him and his company. In selecting which of your various possible Unique Strengths to emphasize in any given sales call, you should always be asking yourself the question: "How does this strength meet *his* need? How does it hook up to the solution image *he* has in mind?"

Now, to put this all into an immediate, practical focus, we'll give you the chance to do a Personal Workshop on the concepts of differentiation and Unique Strengths.

Personal Workshop:
Unique Strengths

First, at the top of a sheet of notebook paper, write the heading "Unique Strengths." Then, underneath that title, write down the following information:

- The name of the client or potential customer that you're going to be calling on in an upcoming sales call.
- Your single sales objective with regard to that person and his company: that is, *what* you want to sell him, *how much* of it you want to sell, and by *when*.
- The particular product or service solution that *you* can offer for his or her current problem.
- The solution that is being offered, or can be offered, by your *chief competitors* for this business.

Obviously, this last point may involve some speculation on your part. You're never going to know as much about your competitors' solutions as you know about your own. But if you're totally in the dark about them, then you're selling from a position of profound weakness. If you can't say anything about what your competition has to offer, you need to *highlight this as an area of missing information*, to be tackled by New Information Questions on your next sales call.

Keep in mind also that one of your chief "competitors" in any sales situation is the customer's own status quo. Whenever you try to sell someone something, you're telling him in effect, "I can help you do something better than the way you're doing it now." To get that something better, he has to accept the *change* that is represented by your solution—and many people, are highly resistant to change. So always consider your accounts' current state of affairs as something you have to compete with.

Once you're written this basic identifying information in your notebook, take fifteen minutes to focus on your Unique Strengths.

Step 1: Draw your Unique Strengths chart. Underneath the heading and the list of four items you've just identified, divide the page into four vertical columns. At the top of each column, place a heading, as we've done in the example below. Also as in the example, list in the left-hand column the fifteen areas of possible differentiation that we mentioned earlier in the chapter. And add to that list, at the bottom, the catch-all "Other" category, to cover things that may be relevant to your business but that we haven't mentioned. When you're done, you'll have a worksheet that looks like this:

Unique Strengths

Area	Unique Strengths	"So What?"	"Prove It"
People Product Process Knowledge Service Implementation Delivery Experience Organization Customer Base Technology Reputation Application Training Logistics Other			

Step 2: Identify your Unique Strengths. Now, using the left-hand column as a guide, write down in the second column any Unique Strengths that you possess, for *this* particular sales objective to *this* customer. You're not going to find an entry to write in for each category—if you did, you'd probably already have made the sale. Try to come up with several areas where the solution you're offering this customer can be clearly differentiated, in your own and the customer's mind, from the solution your competition is offering.

Two provisos for this Step. One, you should avoid listing "strengths" that are no different from those of your competition. We've emphasized the hazards of "me too" selling and marketing; don't fall into the "as good as Xerox" trap here. Avoid listing "strengths" like "Our great service capability" and "Our rock-bottom cost" unless you have an IBM-style service record and your prices really are below everyone else's.

Two, keep in mind our concept of "relative uniqueness." You don't have to confine yourself to those areas of possible differentiation in which you're *absolutely* distinct from everyone else. Being truly, gramatically "unique" is only an ideal. In listing your own Unique Strengths for this sale, focus on capabilities that *approach the ideal,* and that therefore put as much distance as possible between you and the "me too" vendors. Concentrate on those areas where you are "unique" to a *greater degree* than anyone else offering solutions.

Step 3: "So what?" Now, for every Unique Strength you've listed, put yourself in your customer's place and ask yourself the question "So what?" This exercise, which often produces some startling gaps in information when our program participants perform it, is designed as a first-level test of the *validity* of your information.

You're testing validity here by focussing on your *customer's Concept.* You can bring out the most impressive list of Unique Strengths in the world, but if they don't relate to the solution image a client wants, they're going to be useless—and even worse than useless, because they'll distract him and you from finding an appropriate fit.

As an exercise in relating each of your Unique Strengths to his or her Concept, therefore, write down in the third column of the chart the answer that you would give *this* person if he or she asked you "So what?" Put down clearly and concisely how you would demonstrate that the Unique Strengths you're highlighting do actually tie in with his or her needs.

For example, let's say you're trying to sell a production line maintenance program to a large industrial manufacturer. Among the Unique Strengths you've listed are "Dramatic reduction of machine down time" and "Our unique training program for line operators." The plant manager you're dealing with in this sale has been consistently plagued by machine breakdowns, but he is also a fanatic about his company training its own people. Putting yourself in his place, you ask yourself "So what?" about the two items we've mentioned. What are you going to find out? You'll find out that the first Unique Strength—reduction of down time—will tie in perfectly to his needs. You'll also find out that the second Unique Strength—your ability to train his people—isn't a strength at all, as far as he's concerned. And if it isn't a strength to him, then by definition it's not the kind of information you want to be giving *this* customer. So you can scratch it from your list and save yourself some grief.

Filling in this third, testing column will probably leave you with fewer Unique Strengths than you had (or rather thought you had) before. But the remaining ones will be real. They will focus much more directly—and therefore, for you, more productively—on relating your product or service to this individual customer's Concept.

Step 4: "Prove it!" Finally, a second and even more demanding test, to further focus your Unique Strengths listing. In the fourth column of the chart, write a brief sentence for each Unique Strength entry *proving its value for this sale.* In our corporate programs we ask participants to do this by completing two sentences, and we'll ask you to do the same. For each Unique Strength you've listed, write an ending to these two sentences:

- We are the *only* ones who_____.
- We are *different* because_____.

There are no right or wrong answers here, and your "proofs" don't have to be elaborate. In fact, they shouldn't be. You ought to be able to say very briefly why you're the "only ones" for this sale, and why you're different from the competition. If you can't, then you need to do some more thinking about what your Unique Strengths really are.

In proving the validity of your solution to your actual clients, of course, you're not necessarily going to produce a written statement like the ones we're suggesting in this exercise. You can prove your validity by giving references from satisfied customers, by giving a written guarantee, by bringing in an expert witness to vouch for your capabilities, and/or by actually demonstrating them with presentations, examples, or previous successes. If any of these "proofs" are what you would normally offer a customer, fine: write that very fact down in the fourth column of the Unique Strengths chart. For example, you might say "We're the only ones who will give you a six-month written guarantee" or "We're different because of past success; we can provide testimony to our effectiveness from ten satisfied customers."

Once you've made sure that each of your potential Unique Strengths is in fact related to your client's Concept, and once you've further tested the value of each Unique Strength by "proving it" to yourself, you'll have gotten your list of differentiating qualities down, probably, to three or four. That may seem like a small amount of information to be providing on the next sales call, but it's not. When you've clearly identified the Unique Strengths you want to highlight, you're already miles ahead of the salesperson who goes in with a head full of "dynamite" data but no plan for "relating" it to the customer. Giving your customer just three or four pieces of concrete information *that effectively link your product or service to his Concept* is a far more efficient use both your time than winging it on a satchel full of bells and whistles. And it always gets you better results.

Of course, once you meet the person, you will also be asking further questions, and these questions will no doubt surface further gaps in your information, which will necessitate a reexamination of your Unique Strengths. To stress once again a point that is central to the use of our system, the three "phases" of the ideal sales call are not to be seen as sequential Parts One, Two, and Three. They are to be seen, collectively, as a framework within which you can move most freely and effectively from asking, to listening, to telling, and back again. The Giving Information phase of the sales call, just like the Getting Information phase, has one central underlying purpose: to maintain that positive information flow, both ways, that leads to Superb Communication.

So that this kind of communication moves consistently forward from one sales call to the next—that is, so that you know where you are and where you still have to go on every call—you need to be able to move, just as freely and effectively, in and out of the third phase of the sales call, the phase we call Getting Commitment. We move to that third phase now.

▸ 7 ◂

PHASE THREE: GETTING COMMITMENT

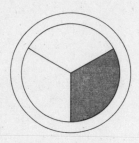

It's been recently estimated that the typical face-to-face sales call today may cost the selling organization as much as $500. The price, which includes such obvious price-hikers as accommodation and transportation expenses, has escalated tremendously in the past decade or so, and that's one of the reasons that so many large organizations are moving more and more of their precious selling resources into less expensive avenues like 800 lines and telemarketing.

Of course there is still no substitute for face-to-face interaction, providing the expected sales revenues justify it, and for that reason the field salesperson, the person who actually sits down with the customer, is still the mainstay of the selling profession. The question, therefore, isn't whether or not there is still a place for the one-to-one personal sales call: there will always be a place for that. The question is how you, as a professional seller, can utilize your time and resources to get the best possible return from every individual sales call you manage. At half a grand a crack, it's obvious that costwise companies are going to be more and more concerned with how the salesperson spends his valuable selling time—and their money. A successful sales call today means, above all, ensuring that every time you go out, you come back with something to show for your time and money.

As we said in the chapter on questioning, that something doesn't always have to be the order. Because of the nature of their business, some salespeople do write first-call orders. But many do not. What you do have to get, on every call, is a degree of *Commitment* that indicates your time has not been wasted.

Getting Commitment: Key Ideas

Every time you go out on a sales call, by definition you have committed your own time and resources to a possible buy/sell relationship. The main idea with regard to Getting Commitment is that you should not be the *only* person in that relationship who has extended himself in this way. For a sale to end up Win-Win, the seller must accept two responsibilities: one to himself and one to the other party. But the *buyer* must accept those two responsibilities also. Until your customer commits, you do not have a Win-Win relationship.

On the first call to a new customer or prospect, you have no choice but to commit yourself. If you're going to write any business at all, you have to spend that initial $500: that's a kind of seed money to get the ball rolling, and you have to be willing to risk it with no guarantee of customer Commitment. But that's the first and *last* time that you should sell from this position of unilateral risk. You cannot leave that first call, or any subsequent call, without involving the prospective buyer in Commitment. Practically, this means every sales call must end with the customer understanding *what he or she is going to do* in order to move the process forward.

The customer must know, in other words, that if he's considering doing business with you, *there is no free lunch.* Both of you Win, or nobody Wins. The way your customer indicates to you that he's interested in having *you* Win is by committing himself to do something before the next time you meet.

His Commitment has to be concrete and focussed to a particular time frame. Vague promises to "think about the proposal" or "get back to you sometime next month" are worthless as signs of Commitment. What you want, before the end of every sales call, is a *promise* to perform some *action* by a specified *date.* For example: "I'll give your proposal to the Planning Board this Friday." Or, "After I've had a chance to review these figures, I'd like to meet with you again before the end of the month." Specific actions, specific dates. Not an evasive "sometime" or "soon."

In addition to being specific and related to a time frame, your customer's promise of action also has to demonstrate to you that he is willing to spend some of *his* time and resources, just as you have. If he's not willing to put himself out—if he's not willing to share some of the risk of Commitment with you—then he's asking you to carry the freight by yourself. Translation: he doesn't care if you Lose. He wants the free lunch—and you pay. The only way to ensure that you don't end up in this kind of losing situation is to expect, and receive, Commitment on *every* call.

Incremental Commitment

But that's only the beginning. The second key point to remember about Getting Commitment is that, as your time and energy increase throughout the selling process, your customer's *degree* of Commitment *has to increase as well.* Your customer's Commitment to Win-Win, no less than yours, has to be *incremental* throughout a multi-call selling process. Otherwise you're just spinning your wheels.

At the initial stages of a selling process, the degree of customer Commitment can, and probably will, be modest. If it's the first sales call you've ever made on Mr. Stein, you might be satisfied with the input you got about his organization's needs, and his Commitment to set up a second meeting with other Buying Influences. There's nothing wrong with that kind of low-level Commitment as long as you're still getting started. But when you go back to Mr. Stein the next time, and you deal with the concerns he has about your literature, and you spend another hour of your time trying to zero in on his Concept, then the Commitment at the end of that second call had better be something more substantial. By the end of that second call, you've put in a thousand dollars of your company's time. That should be worth something more to Mr. Stein than one more brochure-ruffling session.

You might ask him to introduce you to the person who gives final approval, or to show your proposal to a relevant committee with his recommendation, or to give you the Finance Department's reaction to the preliminary specs that you've outlined. But whatever action he agrees to perform, it should indicate an increase in *his* Commitment that will justify *your* spending another $500.

If you've been in selling for more than a few months, you've probably been involved in "limbo" sales—sales where you're never quite sure, from one sales call to the next, how close you are to getting the business—or whether the guy is "giving you the business." You've met a certain customer three or four times, and you seem to be getting along well. He's seen your material, he's "thinking about" what you've told him, you've taken him to lunch a couple of times, your conversations are always pleasant—but the whole thing doesn't seem to be *moving* anywhere. Every salesperson we know has found himself in these situations, and very often the response is to let things slide— to put the pleasant but noncommittal prospect on the back burner for a while, and "get back to him" periodically, in the hope that, eventually, something will break and you'll get the sale.

Forget it—it never happens. Invariably when a sale goes into "limbo" like this, it's because the salesperson has neglected to get Committment on the sales calls he's already made. And letting a piece of business like this slide is a surefire way of ensuring that it will never get off the back burner. The only way to ensure that you don't fall into these limbo situations in the first place is to strive for *incremental Commitment* every time you go out.

Remember this especially if a potential customer asks for a proposal. We often see salespeople commit to submitting a proposal without asking for any specific action in return. Yet you know how long drafting a proposal can take. You can't knock it off in half an hour while you're unwinding at the 19th hole. So if a prospect, toward the end of a sales call, says, "That sounds good; why don't you send me a proposal?" you have every right to respond, "I'll be happy to do that; *what will the next step be* when you receive it?" In other words, "What will you *do* with it?" Not asking for this kind of Commitment means you are setting yourself up for a Lose.

The fundamental issue here is time. Every salesperson's single most valuable resource is that precious commodity, selling time. We don't mean time in general, but the time you actually spend, face to face, with your prospects and clients. Nobody ever has enough of it. So it's essential that what you expend not be wasted. When you agree to commit your time to a customer without getting something in return, you're saying, "My time is not as valuable as yours. I'll do all the work on this sale if you'll only, please, please, give me an order." With that kind of relationship as a basis, even if you *do* get the order, eventually with this person you're going to Lose.

When You Can't Get Commitment

What about those times when you just can't get Commitment? The times when, no matter how brilliant your presentation and no matter how good the rapport, he still won't agree to do anything more substantial than "think about it and get back to you"?

Everybody runs into situations where the sale just seems to be stalled, and nothing you can do or say seems to be able to move it forward. Sales reps have a million reasons for explaining why this happens. We've heard them all. "The timing isn't right now, I guess." "Our price must be too high." "They're too strong for our competition." "The guy is stubborn; he just won't see reason." And our personal favorite, "It's politics." These excuses usually go along with the sound of madly spinning wheels and the image of a guy scratching his head. Sometimes they're fairly close to reality, and many times they're light years away. *Never,* in our years of experience, do they describe the *real* reason any sale slows down.

No matter what the excuse, and no matter what the particular situation, we have found that there is always only *one reason* that a person won't give Commitment.

> *Whenever a customer refuses Commitment,*
> *it's because he feels he's going to Lose with*
> *your solution.*

That's the bottom line, every time. You can have the best product in the world, it can be perfectly suited to a given person's real needs, and you can spend half the national budget taking the guy to lunch. If he doesn't perceive that the sale you're trying to make is going to be a *personal Win for him,* there is little chance that sale will move forward. Each of us has been personally involved in hundreds of sales calls. In every single case where the selling process was stalled by a "stubborn" or "difficult" or "price-sensitive" buyer, his or her reluctance could be translated into the same two words: "I'm Losing."

Because a customer's perception that he's Losing can spell death for the most "surefire" sale, it stands to reason that being able to pick up on a customer's "I'm Losing" signals is a valuable part of sales call management. The sooner you as a seller are able to spot and deal with a potential buyer's "Lose" feelings, the sooner you'll be able to move the selling process forward. Until you get to that point, you'll just be taking the excuses for the reality. That's why the first practical step in Getting Commitment is digging for *why* the person feels that he's Losing.

In Conceptual Selling, we define that digging process in a very particular terminology. We say that, whenever a customer feels that he's Losing, there is a *Basic Issue* involved. Your primary task in Getting Commitment is to *uncover* and then *resolve* Basic Issues.

Basic Issues Defined

A Basic Issue is any *personal* feeling an individual may have that results in his or her believing "I'm Losing." Note our emphasis on "personal." Basic Issues are not concrete, quantifiable, "objective" realities, waiting to be tinkered with and fixed up by the savvy, product-wise salesperson. Basic Issues arise from deep within the customer's individual experiences and value system. So they cannot be "overcome" or talked around like a reluctant buyer's objection.

A Basic Issue and an objection, although they may both impede the selling process, are two very different things. An objection is merely the manifestation of an underlying Basic Issue; or, to put it in more scientific terms, the Basic Issue is the *cause* of the customer's reluctance, while the objection is the *effect*. When someone raises an objection, he's always giving you a signal that something underneath is troubling him. That "something" is a Basic Issue.

Another difference between an objection and a Basic Issue is that an objection is usually tangible and product or implementation related. A Basic Issue is not. Basic Issues are related to the individual's mental picture, or Concept, about the sale; and like any mental picture, they're generally intangible and personal.

"Overcoming an objection," therefore, is very different from dealing with a Basic Issue. It's no less than the difference between cause and effect, and sellers who consistently achieve Win-Win outcomes in their sales are never content simply to deal with effects. They know that dealing with causes is fundamental not only to Getting Commitment, but also to any long-term business relationship.

In the box below we've listed some possible Basic Issues that you may encounter in your selling situations. These are, of course, only examples, since there are really an unlimited number of Basic Issues. But they should be enough to give you the idea of what we mean.

As the list clearly indicates, Basic Issues are *specific* to

POSSIBLE BASIC ISSUES

(How the Person You're Calling on Feels He or She Will Lose)

- loss of power
- loss of control
- get less leisure time
- lack of skill development
- decrease of personal productivity
- lack of being an instrument of change
- not seen as a problem solver
- lack of recognition
- lack of contribution to organization
- decrease in growth potential
- lose social/professional status
- less time with family
- less self-esteem
- loss of flexibility
- lose security
- being seen as a malcontent
- not invented here
- seen as poor performer
- loss of leadership
- loss of credibility
- seen as me-too
- incur indebtedness
- decrease responsibility/ authority
- stuck in a rut
- lose freedom of choice
- pigeonholed
- put in a double-bind (catch 22)
- not fun anymore; no laughs

individual buyers—that is, they are highly *personal.* That's the fundamental point to remember about them, and it's why they're often difficult to get at. Two related points bear some emphasis:

1. You cannot *judge* a Basic Issue. It's like what a somewhat cynical philosopher once said about the state of the world. "The world isn't good or bad; it simply *is.*" That's true of every Basic Issue, too. A Basic Issue is what someone is *feeling,* deep down, about what working with you will mean to him. There are ways to analyze and discuss and work with those feelings, but the one thing you should not do, ever, is to deny their validity. One of the surest ways we know to kill a selling process on the spot is to say to someone with a Basic Issue, "You shouldn't be feeling that way."

2. You cannot assume that you know what the *particular* Basic Issue is. Since the "I'm Losing" perception and non-Commitment are always linked, it's safe to assume, when you cannot get Commitment, that there's *some* Basic Issue involved. But it's hazardous to assume that you know what that Basic Issue is. Dealing with Mr. Franklin's fear that he's going to lose power, when in fact he's not worried about power at all but about a perceived lack of recognition, will do nothing but waste time. As this example suggests, it's easy for a salesperson to confuse one possible Basic Issue for another. That's why we reiterate the principle of "No assumptions," and why we say that identifying specific Basic Issues is so critical to Getting Commitment.

Basic Issue Symptoms

Before you can identify a specific Basic Issue, however, you need to be able to recognize the underlying fact *that* a Basic Issue exists—in other words, to recognize when your customer feels he's Losing. You do that by attending to what we call Basic Issue Symptoms, outlined in the box on page 143.

BASIC ISSUE SYMPTOMS

- Hesitation
- Questioning Attitude
- Grunt and Groan
- Argument
- Hostility or Passive Resistance

(Severity increases down the list)

The symptoms we've listed here are fairly self-explanatory, and we're sure you can understand why we say a hesitant or argumentative customer is very likely concealing a Basic Issue. One thing about this list is not self-evident, however. You'll notice a vertical arrow pointing downward to the left of the symptoms. This is to indicate that the severity of the symptoms *increases* as you go down the list. At the same time, the probability of a good sale *decreases*. If you're dealing with a merely hesitant client, therefore, you generally still have time to identify and resolve his Basic Issues before the situation deteriorates. If your prospect has become outright hostile, it's unlikely that you can save the sale.

In many sales situations, moreover, the severity of the customer's Basic Issue symptoms *increases over time,* unless the seller intervenes. A sales call that begins with the customer just asking questions can turn into a buyer/seller argument later on unless the Basic Issue is met and resolved.

This means that the seller has a certain level of *control* over where the sales call is going, but also that this level decreases the longer he ignores the Basic Issue.

Since every sales call is unique, there is no absolute "symptom level" at which a salesperson loses control of the sale. Generally, though, once responses have gotten beyond the "Grunt and Groan" stage, it's very hard to turn things around. At that point the typical buyer's perception seems to be that "all is lost." Therefore, we say that responsible selling means intervening *no later* than the Grunt and Groan stage. If you don't intervene by this point, the situation is almost certain to deteriorate further, and quickly.

But when we say "intervening," we mean something very specific. We mean asking a *Basic Issue Question* to search out and surface the hidden reason he feels he's going to Lose.

Basic Issue Questions

As we use the term in Conceptual Selling, a Basic Issue Question is a specialized type of Commitment Question. In our description of Commitment Questions in Chapter 4, we said that their purpose was to show you *where* you were in the sale, and what still needed to be *done* to move the selling process forward. A Basic Issue Question does exactly that, in the context of a customer's reluctance.

Basic Issue Questions have a dual purpose. On the down side, they help you to understand your customer's reasons for feeling that the situation is a Lose. On the positive side, they help you to uncover what still needs to be done to turn the situation into a Win. This dual purpose, with a few examples of how Basic Issue Questions are phrased, is given in the box on page 145.

You'll notice in these examples that a common thread is the sense of *uncertainty* or *concern* that leads to non-Commitment in the first place. This is reflected in the key words that we recommend you use in phrasing these ques-

BASIC ISSUE QUESTIONS

Purpose
- To uncover Basic Issues
- To reveal unmet Wins

Examples:
- "Is there anything about which you're uncertain?"
- "Are there any other concerns that need to be resolved?"
- "What might upset or worry other people?"

tions. Since you're trying to elicit information about a grey and potentially shaky area in the buy/sell encounter, it's appropriate to use key words like *doubtful, puzzled,* and *unclear.* See the box on page 146 for more examples.

When should you ask a Basic Issue Question? There's a general and a specific answer to that question.

The general answer is that you should ask this type of question *whenever* you sense in the sales call that your customer is in an "I'm Losing" mode. In other words, whenever you spot a Basic Issue Symptom, no matter how "trivial" it may seem, it's time to head off future trouble by seeking, *at that moment,* for the cause of the problem.

The specific answer is to ask this type of question as a final test of your customer's Commitment—that is, at the *end* of every sales call. We've already explained that our questioning process sequence is to be taken as a general

KEY WORDS:
Uncertain, doubtful, hesitant, questioning, dubious, in a quandary, puzzled, uncomfortable, unclear, concern.

WHEN TO USE:
Essential to use as final test to make sure of Customer commitment.

guide, not a rigid format; that goes for Basic Issue Questions too. Still, there is one point in the sales call where it is almost always appropriate to surface your customer's concerns, and that is just before you leave. Every sales call should end, you'll recall, with an understanding of *what the customer should do,* before the next call, to make his or her Commitment level clear. Asking a Basic Issue Question toward the end of a sales call is one good way of determining just what the current level is. In the box you'll see that we've identified this last-minute usage as the one *essential* usage of Basic Issue Questions. It's a solid way for you to make sure, before you walk out the door, that the client understands not only what you're going to do for him, but what he's expected to do for you.

The "Unstuck" Sale, or "Buyer's Remorse"

Now, you could just slip quietly out the door and hope that, since you're still talking, everything will probably be all right. This is a not uncommon way of going about things with sellers who feel that no news is good news. But it's a self-defeating tactic in the end, because it leaves you knowing less than you need to know to keep all the variables of the sale under control. Failing to ask enough Basic Issue Questions on a sales call is just asking for misinformation; and when you're burdened with misinformation, you're in an even worse position than the seller with no information at all. What you tend to do, when you're burdened with (comforting) misinformation, is to build yourself a mental Fools' Paradise, where what you don't know can't hurt you. You end up assuming your way out of the sale.

Or something even worse can happen. You can go along with the numbers game philosophy that instant volume is all that matters. You can forget about resolving Basic Issues, ignore your customer's puzzled or uneasy looks, and make the sale *in spite of* his resistance. It happens all the time. And it sets up what we call Buyer's Remorse.

In the typical pattern of Buyer's Remorse, a customer goes along with a persuasive salesperson in spite of his feelings of uneasiness, and lives to regret "being sold." Not all customers, after all, have a clear, conscious handle on their Basic Issues. Often a customer will have only a vague sense of uncertainty or dissatisfaction, and be unable to articulate what's causing it. A salesperson who is concerned only with getting the order and getting the hell out can "help" a prospect to ignore these feelings. But the long-term outcome of such sales is not good. Typically, two weeks or two months down the line, the customer finds out that the product didn't solve his problem, or that he's lost credibility because of the deal, or that the sale has made his job more rather than less difficult—in short, that for any one of dozens of reasons, the sale has become a personal Lose. The result is Buyer's Remorse: that gnawing and humiliating feeling that he's been taken for a ride.

When a customer experiences Buyer's Remorse, the implication for the seller is always bad because one way or another, down the line, this sale and future sales will become "unstuck." Which is just what you should expect when you stick it to the buyer. Even if the person doesn't send your product back to the factory or make your service manager's life a nightmare, the very least he's going to do is to back away from doing future business with you. At worst—as we'll explain in the following chapter—Buyer's Remorse will lead to Buyer's Revenge. You'll have taken the order and run, all right, but just like the old-time snake-oil drummers, you'll soon find that you can't *stop* running.

This can happen even if you're not *trying* to Win at your customer's expense. It's very tempting, even for the most ethically minded salespersons, to ignore their customers' Basic Issue concerns unless they actually surface as objections. Many salespeople still seem to have the idea that only the *stated* objection really matters: if the person is willing to sign, it must mean he's satisfied with the sale. As countless "unstuck" sales illustrate, that attitude can be deadly to long-term business.

Because of their hidden power to undo your good work, you have to make a conscious and very *active* effort to seek out and deal with Basic Issues. We emphasize "active" as another way of highlighting the critical distinction between a Basic Issue and an objection. Sales reps are taught to *react* to or *ignore* objections. It's never enough to react to a Basic Issue, and it's often deadly to ignore it. It's like the difference between a visible and a hidden weapon. Basic Issues are the hidden weapons threatening every sales relationship. You've got to go after them *before* they surface.

You're going to do that now, in a Personal Workshop.

Personal Workshop: Basic Issues

We've said that not all Basic Issues are clear to the potential buyer; they can be either conscious, or hidden and poorly understood. Even when they're conscious to him, though, they can still be hidden from you. So we break this Personal Workshop into two parts. In Part A, you'll clarify your understanding of those Basic Issues you've already identified. In Part B you'll work at identifying those that are still unknown to you.

At the top of a notebook page, write the heading "Basic Issues." Then, with a specific client and a specific working proposal (that is, a specific sale-in-progress) in mind, complete the following exercise.

Part A: Known Basic Issues

Step 1: Describe the customer's Basic Issues. Using the Possible Basic Issues list that we presented earlier in this chapter as a guide, start by listing all the areas of concern that this person has *already* expressed to you regarding the proposal you're offering him or his company. You can focus on the appropriate areas by asking yourself the general question, "How is this individual Losing right now—or how does he think that he's Losing?" You may come up with one or two or ten areas of concern here: every one, if left unattended, can eventually undermine your sale, so don't be shy about listing even areas of "marginal" concern. A marginal concern can become a major one unless you bring it to the surface and resolve it.

Step 2: Confirm these Basic Issues. Since you will be meeting this person in the near future, and since the selling process can be stalled if you go in there with false assumptions, it's important to think out in advance how you will *verify* your current understanding of his or her concerns. You'll remember from Chapter 4, on questioning, that verification is accomplished with Confirmation Questions. So, for each of the Basic Issues you've just listed, write down one Confirmation Question that you can ask on your *next* sales call with *this* individual to validate or invalidate your understanding.

Example. If Ms. Beddoes in quality control has expressed concern about the security of her position, you might begin the next call on her with this Confirmation Question: "You had shown a little uncertainty about the effect of my proposal on job security. Do you still feel that's a possible problem here?" The goal is to have a specific and properly phrased Confirmation Question to address *each* of your customer's *known* Basic Issues the next time you get together.

Step 3: Can you help? Just because you know what's bothering your customer doesn't necessarily mean you can solve his or her problem.   In this Step, for each known Basic Issue you've listed, ask yourself the following qualifying question: "Am I in a realistic position to help this customer reduce or eliminate his Lose perception?"   If the package you're offering Ms. Beddoes will bring her instant recognition and thus enhance her job security, then the answer is obviously Yes.   If her feeling of uneasiness is related to something that's outside of your control, then the answer is No.   Being as realistic as you can about your own capabilities, identify which Basic Issues are within your power to affect, and which are beyond your control.

One way to check your understanding in this Step is to refer back to the Unique Strengths workshop you did in the previous chapter.   There you highlighted areas where your proposal and your company could have a positive impact at this time on your customer's problem or problems.   In addressing a customer's Basic Issues, it's always best to work from a position of strength; reviewing your own Unique Strengths is a way of ensuring that you're doing that.

Don't be surprised if you find Basic Issues here that you aren't capable of resolving—areas where you *can't* eliminate the Lose.   But don't be disappointed either.   Finding out that there are aspects of a sale that you are not able to handle at this time can be just as valuable a discovery as finding out that you've got an answer for everything.   In fact, it can be far more valuable. Let's face it, nobody has an answer for everything every time, and the sellers who say that they do are the "refrigerators to Eskimos" kind of people who rarely sell the same customer twice. Later we'll talk about those sales where the wisest course of action is to recognize that you can't help—and walk away. Surfacing your customer's currently unresolvable Basic Issues is a step toward that sadder but wiser understanding.

Step 4: Identify appropriate actions. Now that you've sorted out the Basic Issues that you can address from those that you cannot, you should identify, for each resolvable Basic Issue, a specific, concrete action that you can take on the next sales call with this individual to reduce or eliminate the Lose. "Action" here is really another word for "Giving Information." What you're trying to do here is to identify the information that you can give on the next sales call that will best address his or her Basic Issues. Again, your Unique Strengths listing from the last chapter should be of benefit.

When you've identified appropriate actions/information for each Basic Issue, write them down in your notebook. For example: "Tell Jane Beddoes how this package got her opposite number at Wilson a promotion." We don't pretend that writing yourself messages like this is going to instantly solve your problem, or your customer's. What it will do is to make *visible* to you those areas of remaining difficulty, so that you can pay attention to them next time out. This action list is not a blueprint; but it can be a valuable pre-call "rehearsal" tool. So hang on to it. By checking it over before you go in to meet Beddoes again, you'll be better equipped to give her information that can turn her Lose into a mutual Win.

Part B: Unknown Basic Issues

As we've said, there are usually known and unknown Basic Issues in most buyer/seller relationships. If there's been a Commitment problem with your sales calls to a given individual, but you can't pin down why, we encourage you to do the following exercise to prepare for your next sales call on that person.

Step 5: Is there a Basic Issue? First, determine whether or not the problem you've been having with this customer is a Basic Issue problem. Ask yourself whether or not the selling situation as it stands now fits the typical pattern of sales being blocked by Basic Issues. In that pattern, we've found, three elements are present:

- First, there is a real match—or at least a "good potential" match—between the seller's product or service and the customer's solution image. In seeking out unknown Basic Issues, be sure first of all that there *really is a fit* between what you have and what the customer needs.

- Second, there is a feeling of uneasiness for the *seller* as well as the buyer. If every time you come out of a meeting with this person, you feel aggravated and/or confused, there's a pretty good chance that you're picking up on *his* signals of uncertainty.

- Finally, there's no movement toward Commitment. In spite of the good potential match, you cannot get him or her to agree to do anything but schedule one more meeting. So you're doing all of the work.

When one or more of these three elements is present, you can be confident there's a Basic Issue involved.

Step 6: Phrase Basic Issue Questions. The next step is to phrase good Basic Issue Questions that will help you identify *which* Basic Issue is involved. Since you don't really know what you're looking for, and since you don't want to put words in your customer's mouth, it's important not to ask closed or "leading" questions, but to help him to surface his own concerns. Refer to the Basic Issue key words we suggested earlier in the chapter, and try to come up with two or three well-phrased questions that you can ask next time out to find out why this individual thinks that he's Losing.

It's hard to give specific phrasing guidelines here, because each buyer/seller relationship is different. We know one exuberant young sales rep who, when he senses a customer is Losing, throws his cards brashly on the table: "Jan," he'll say, "there's something that's bugging you here, and I can't figure out what. I know you're not happy. What's wrong?" He can get away with that (most of the time) because of his particular warmth and charm, although for many of us such a direct method would be a disaster. You have to set your own style of questioning, depending on your individual relationships. But we can give you three hints.

First, we've found that the key word *concern* generally tends to get better results—that is, more reliable information—than almost any other key word. It seems less threatening to most people than the potentially condescending "puzzled" and "upset." "What are your concerns with this proposal?" is one of the best of all Basic Issue Questions.

Second, you can sometimes get a reluctant buyer to talk more freely if you ask the Basic Issue Question in a *positive* rather than negative manner. If he's hesitant to tell you why he's concerned, you might ask: "If I could give you a proposal that would make you entirely comfortable, what would it look like?"

Third, asking a customer to identify what's making him *uncertain* can sometimes help reduce or eliminate the uncertainty. We've said that people don't always understand consciously what their Basic Issues are. Asking "Is there something you're uncertain about here?" can often help both you and the customer to bring his Basic Issue to the surface.

Fourth, always use your *own* feelings as a guide. You project your own uncertainties and concerns out onto your clients no less than they do onto you. Therefore, if you're uncomfortable with the way you've phrased a question— if you feel uneasy about asking it—*rephrase it* so you are comfortable.

Step 7: Do you need coaching? Finally, we'd like you to consider the possibility that, for this individual at the present time, you need to seek coaching from someone *else* in order to get reliable information. There are essentially three ways to get Basic Issue information. One is to guess, which is worthless. Another is to ask the relevant customer directly, and that's what you've been practicing in this Personal Workshop. A third and often very valuable way is to ask about your customer's possible Basic Issues from someone who knows him or her well, and who is in a position to give you reliable data. This is an especially useful method in those cases where the person himself *doesn't know*—or doesn't want *you* to know—why he feels that he's Losing.

Of course you can't ask just anybody. When you're trying to verify information regarding a customer's Basic Issues, we advise you to look for potential "coaches" who a) trust you and your company personally; b) are trusted by the customer's organization; and c) want you, for whatever reason, to make *this* sale. If you test your potential information sources against these three criteria, you can dramatically increase the probability that the data they give you about the person is going to be accurate and useful.

Once you've found out from your customer and/or from other sources what his Basic Issues are, the "unknown" obviously becomes the "known." And when each Basic Issue becomes known, you can then go back to the beginning of this Personal Workshop, and run it through Steps 1 to 4, as a way of further clarifying your information.

Commitment Signals

One final point. We've said that if the seller ignores or tries to avoid a Basic Issue, he is in effect ignoring the customer's Lose perception—and thus setting himself up to Lose too. Oddly enough, sellers often also ignore their customers' Win perceptions. The results of that are no better. In order to escape this trap, you need to be attentive to what we call Commitment Signals.

A Commitment Signal, as we define it, is a message from the buyer to the seller indicating the *action he is ready to take* to move the buy/sell process forward.

Since we've emphasized that Getting Commitment means getting the client to *do* something, you might think that salespeople would be continually alert and ready to pounce when they heard a Commitment Signal. Not so. We've found that, although *the buyer will invariably tell you when he is ready to buy,* many sellers never hear the message and as a result they lose major business. There's the VCR salesperson who's so busy showing off bells and whistles that he doesn't hear the prospect say "I'll take it." Or the software sales rep who ignores his customer's query, "When can we get the training started?" and goes rattling on about the features and benefits of the product.

This kind of all too common behavior is what we call "snatching defeat from the jaws of victory." It happens generally because salespeople mistake a Commitment Signal for "just another question" or because they have not thought out clearly in advance what kind of Commitment they want on a sales call—and so they miss it when it is offered.

In order to actually *get* the Commitment you want when it's offered, you have to attend to the buyer's signals. Luckily, they're not difficult to identify. Commitment Signals are almost always phrased in the form of a question or statement about *implementation.*

Implementation can refer to a huge range of issues, although generally speaking they all relate directly to the "end business" of getting an order. Some major implementation areas are itemized in the box on page 156.

The questions that are typically asked with regard to these implementation areas have to do not with *whether* the seller can deliver what the buyer wants, but *when* and *under what conditions.* Sample implementation questions from the customer:

- "How long will it take for delivery?"
- "When can my operators be retrained?"
- "How much lead time will we need to schedule a pilot run?"
- "Will you be able to give us a loaner until ours arrives from the factory?"
- "I'd like to check out three references."

Notice that behind all these sample questions and statements there is the same basic implication. It's that the client is ready to give Commitment, and that he just wants

IMPLEMENTATION AREAS

- cost
- timing
- references
- installation
- training
- administration
- conversion
- servicing
- credit
- terms

- financing
- payments
- demonstration
- trial run
- pilot program
- tests
- validation
- spec measurements
- logistics

to be told *how*. It should be clear why we call such questions and statements Commitment Signals—and why you have to respond to them when they happen.

It all comes back to *hearing your customer*—to listening to what he or she has to say, whatever phase of the sales call you are in, and whether what he or she has to say is favorable, or unfavorable, or indifferent. The entire information-exchange process—call it a teaching process or a selling process—begins with what's in your customer's mind, with his Concept of what he's trying to accomplish.

As our discussion of the three phases has made clear, the only truly effective way of tracking and working with your customer's Concept is to ask much more than you tell, and to listen—really listen—to the answers. That's the way positive information flow develops. It's the way you ultimately get Commitment. And it's the way, over the long run, you nurture the Win-Win relationships we all need.

In the next section of the book, we'll be talking in more detail about those relationships, and explaining how Joint Venture selling can make Win-Win a reality.

GETTING TO
WIN-WIN

▸ 8 ◂

YOUR ULTIMATE GOAL: WIN-WIN

Underlying every program we teach at Miller-Heiman is a commitment to what we call Win-Win selling. In Win-Win selling, both the buyer and the seller come out of the sale understanding that their respective best interests have been served—in other words, that they've both Won. It is our firm conviction, based on thousands of selling situations, that over the long run the only sellers who remain truly successful are committed to this Win-Win philosophy.

The reason isn't just "philosophical." In this era of intense competition and sophisticated customers, the successful sales professional cannot rely, *practically* speaking, on "taking the order and running like hell." We doubt if it was ever enough simply to "win" the order and leave; certainly it's not enough today. Today, to ensure that your success will *last* from client to client and from sales call to sales call, you need the following:

- Satisfied customers
- Long-term business relationships
- Solid repeat business with your "regular" customers
- Enthusiastic referrals to new prospects

If you don't consistently and predictably get these four things out of your sales calls, sooner or later your business will be nothing but a series of one-night stands. You may be writing orders at a record pace, but in today's markets that pace *cannot* last if you're in business for the volume alone. That's a major paradox of modern selling. The salesperson who takes the money and runs eventually finds himself running in place; the salesperson who knows that getting the order is only the *beginning* finds not only that he's writing *more* orders than the competition, but also that those orders are *solid:* they are linking him up to an ever expanding network of future business.

The reason for this is to be found in the nature of selling itself. In selling, two parties—a buyer and a seller—have to come to an agreement before any deal can be made. This means that any sales transaction involves *mutual dependence.* Our philosophy of Win-Win selling recognizes that mutual dependence and gives you a reliable method for building on it, long term.

The Win-Win Matrix

It's one thing to say that both the buyer and the seller should Win in each sales transaction. It's quite another to bring that about in the real world. We'll be the first to admit that what looks simple and basic on paper isn't always easy to carry off in an actual selling situation. Especially when the competition is breathing down your neck, the sales manager is demanding that you meet quota or else—and you're not even sure that your prospect *wants* to play Win-Win with you anyway. We recognize the problem, and we have some news for you: it'll happen again. All sales professionals confront situations where they try to get to Win-Win, but just can't make it come out.

The first step in getting the Win-Win philosophy to work for you is to recognize that a Win-Win outcome is only one of *four* possible outcomes that can happen as a result of any sale. We're not talking here about those selling situations that turned out to be near misses, or where you got aced out by the competition. We're talking about sales where you've already ostensibly "won" because *you got the order* and the commission. Since there are always at least two parties involved in these sales—you and your customer—there are a total of four scenarios or outcomes that can exist after you have the money in your pocket:

- *Win-Win:* This is where *both* you and the buyer feel satisfied with the deal after it's done, and you both feel satisfied with your business relationship.

- *Win-Lose:* This is where *you* feel good about the sale but the buyer feels that, for whatever reason, he or she has gotten the short end of the deal.

- *Lose-Win:* In this scenario, your buyer is satisfied but in some way you've had to "buy the business"—so you feel *you've* gotten the short end.

- *Lose-Lose:* Here, in spite of the fact that the sale has been made, you both wish you'd never done business together—and you are probably determined never to do it again.

We represent these four possible scenarios in a diagram we call the Win-Win Matrix, pictured on page 162.

You'll see in this diagram that we've shaded the upper left hand, or Win-Win, quadrant. The reason should be obvious. This quadrant is where everybody—at least everybody in his or her right mind—wants to hang out all the time. It's the goal of all intelligent sales call management to put you and each of your clients in this quadrant, and keep you there.

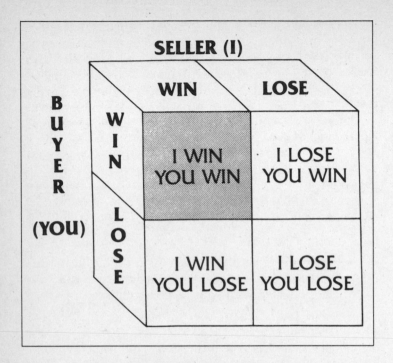

Win-Win: Why It's Attractive

Why? Why do people find the Win-Win quadrant so attractive? There are three basic reasons:

- First, the Win-Win quadrant is more *profitable* than any other scenario. As we've already pointed out, a Win-Win outcome generates not just "the order," but an expanding network of future business. Which means that Win-Win salespeople make more money.

- Second, the Win-Win quadrant is more *stable* over time than the other quadrants. In the dynamic world of selling, of course, change is always part of the picture. But a sale which is solidly understood as having benefited both parties is much less likely to deteriorate later than one where one party feels he's Lost.

- Third, being in the Win-Win quadrant is more *comfortable* than being in the other quadrants. When you manage a sale with a client so that both of you feel well served, then you don't feel guilt at having cheated him or resentment at his having cheated you. He doesn't feel guilt or resentment either. And as any freshman psychology major will tell you, you've gone a long way toward a sense of well-being when you've gotten rid of resentment and guilt.

The Win-Win outcome, in short, is the only outcome to a sale, or to a sales call, that is likely to lead to *enduring* success. No wonder sales professionals who know where their bread is buttered would like to end up there all the time.

Win-Lose: The "Backlash" Quadrant

That doesn't always happen, though. Frequently when it doesn't happen it's because the salesperson has not made a dedicated enough effort to *make sure* it happens. Most commonly, he has assumed that *his* Win is all that really matters—or at least that it's more important than the customer's. Or he hasn't thought about it at all. And he ends up with Win-Lose.

Sellers play Win-Lose for a variety of reasons, but probably the most common one is greed. Here's an everyday example.

You make a reservation at a fancy restaurant for a special occasion, and you fully expect the establishment to live up to its reputation: you're going to be shelling out good money for the meal, and you expect it to be a Win. But the evening turns out to be a disaster. The restaurant has severely overbooked for that evening, and you're kept waiting an hour for your reserved table. The food is late and overdone, the orders are scrambled, and you end up paying a premium price for service you could have gotten at Sloppy Joe's. The restaurant, with its eye on short-term profits, comes out of the evening with a Win; but you, and all the other buyers that evening, come out of it feeling abused. That's a classic "seller Wins-buyer Loses" scenario.

Now, in this scenario it's probably safe to assume that the restaurant management didn't actively *set out* to Win at the customers' expense, and that brings up an important point about Win-Lose. *Win-Lose selling can be either conscious or unconscious.* You don't have to *want* to burn your clients in order to give them that impression. In many cases, customers will feel they've Lost even when you believe they've Won. When such a situation occurs, the "facts" of the case don't really matter. What matters is what the client *believes* to have happened. If he or she sincerely believes that you've been playing a Win-Lose game, then *that* is the reality you have to confront.

You may not have to confront it immediately. Whether the Win-Lose scenario is conscious or unconscious, sometimes it takes a while before the client's Lose perception sets in. It may take weeks or months, for example, in cases where an industrial parts salesperson sells a factory obsolete machinery, or where she exaggerates her company's service capabilities. But whether the buyer finds out immediately or later, the eventual result is the same: "backlash." Backlash is an *inevitable* consequence of allowing a sale to end on Win-Lose. It usually comes in two stages.

Stage One: Buyer's Remorse. In this stage, the client you've burned recognizes what has happened and takes the guilt and resentment on himself. He realizes that the software you've sold him is obsolete, or that she's paid too much for the car, or that the service policy is not what he thought it was—and he starts kicking himself for being a jerk. "How could I have been so stupid?" he asks himself.

Stage Two: Buyer's Revenge. In this stage, he gets the answer to his question. He feels he's been sold a bill of goods by a sharpie who didn't give a damn if he Lost or Won. Once he feels that he's been "sold," the burned customer's resentment miraculously shifts away from himself and out onto the seller. He's got somebody other than himself to blame. If that somebody is you, look out. Because somebody who feels you have tricked him into buying (whether it is true or not) will inevitably be looking for revenge.

Buyer's Revenge can take many forms, and none of them is good for the seller. The very least that a beaten buyer will do is to decline future business with the offending salesperson; that is, he'll simply *get out*. That's bad enough. But a more dangerous, and more common, scenario is for the wronged party to *get even*. If you make a Win-Lose sale with a client, bet on having made an enemy for a long time. Bet on him making sure that, if he can foul up your business *anywhere*, not just in his own company, he will do it. With a satisfied smile.

A study conducted for the White House Office of Consumer Affairs in 1985 makes our point well. The study uncovered the following sobering statistics:

- 96 percent of unhappy customers never complain *directly* to the seller about their dissatisfaction.
- But 91 percent of those dissatisfied customers *will not buy again* from that seller.
- In addition, the average unhappy customer will talk to at least *nine* people about how he or she got burned by the seller.
- 13 percent of those customers will tell over *twenty* other people what happened.

The lesson for the professional seller is brutally clear. Trying for Win-Lose with a customer—or even allowing a Win-Lose to happen—not only ensures that your professional reputation will be damaged; because of that "non-complaining" 96 percent, Win-Lose almost guarantees that your "beaten" customer will be getting even *without you knowing that it's happening*. That is the insidious nature of Buyer's Revenge.

The revenge might not come immediately. It might take weeks, months, or even years. And sometimes, of course, it might not come at all, because the person you've burned moves to another state, or dies, or just doesn't have the leverage to do you substantial harm. But even in that kind of "good" situation, you're still going to have to be wary— of things he or she *might* say or *might* do. The salesperson who has "successfully" played Win-Lose is like the young punk who has just outdrawn the old gunfighter. He's got the notch on his gun, all right, but he's going to spend the rest of his life looking over his shoulder. He's Won a round. But eventually he is going to get it in the back.

This points to the basic problem with Win-Lose. We've said that Win-Win is a *stable* quadrant, relatively speaking. That cannot be said of Win-Lose. Eventually this kind of selling works against you as well as against the buyer. Win-Lose is highly unstable: it almost always deteriorates into Lose-Lose.

Lose-Win: Giving Away the Store

This is even more dramatically the case in the scenario known as Lose-Win, where you make a conscious sacrifice for your customer as a way of getting the business.

In an "I Lose-You Win" scenario, you get the order by *giving something away*—by allowing yourself and your company to Lose in the hope that you'll make it back in future sales. Maybe you offer the customer a ridiculously low introductory price, or a special volume discount, or service conditions that are out of this world. Whatever it is—time, terms, price, training, financing—you're essentially saying to the client, "I'm letting you Win at my expense, because I value your business."

Now, there's nothing fundamentally wrong with a "loss leader" or "investment" strategy; retail stores use it all the time, and with very good results. The problem for most sellers comes about because such a Lose-Win proposition is by its very nature a *temporary* expedient. It cannot possibly be offered, to any customer, every time—and yet that's exactly the way many people read it. You offer a customer an extraordinary payment schedule on an initial contract, as a way of attracting his business. You know it's only a one-time, special arrangement, but he doesn't get that message. He thinks the extraordinary schedule is your *typical* schedule. When contract renewal time comes up, and you tell him, "Harry, we'll have to return to our normal payment schedule for this contract," he acts like you've just stolen his car. "What do you mean normal? I thought we had a deal!"

You did have a deal, but Harry has failed to appreciate its particular, temporary nature. Because he believes that the current arrangement is normal, he has false expectations; so, without even meaning to, you've set him up. So he takes your sacrifice as a ploy, and soon you're both in danger of Losing.

Setting the customer up with false expectations is a danger in every Lose-Win scenario. Here's a recent example from the news.

You probably remember that in 1985 the American car manufacturers, following the lead of General Motors, embarked on various "incentive-rate" financing programs as a way of edging out the Japanese. These were classic "loss leader" or Lose-Win programs, where the customer would be drawn into the showroom with the promise of 6.5 percent financing (or, alternately, a whopping cash rebate). The hope was that, once the consumer's loyalty was regained, the industry could return to a more "normal" level of time payments.

The idea backfired in two ways. First, large numbers of consumers decided that, even at 6.5 financing, they weren't ready for what they saw as shoddy merchandise, compared to the Japanese models—they were willing to pay Toyota's 12 percent rates in order to get a car that they believed wouldn't fall apart in three years or break their budgets on fuel costs. So they rejected the Lose-Win offer because they saw it, underneath, as Lose-Lose. Second, customers who were still shopping for American models started to see basement-rate financing as *normal*—and forced the manufacturers into a percentage points war that made the Lose-Win scenario even more unreal. In the words of

Newsweek, "GM didn't anticipate the extent to which introduction of incentive-rate financing would steal sales from the future. The other companies had to follow GM into the subsidized-financing business and now wish it would go away."

The GM case points up the two things that most often happen when you employ a Lose-Win strategy. Customers either suspect there's a trick involved somewhere (since we all know you don't get something for nothing) and back out of the room with their hands on their wallets. Or they buy in to the Lose-Win option, and expect it to go on forever. Either way, you eventually Lose.

We've said that when the customer feels you've taken advantage of him, the situation eventually deteriorates into Lose-Lose. The same thing happens in Lose-Win, when you let the buyer, in effect, take advantage of you. But you get to Lose-Lose in this case by an indirect route. We've pictured that route in the diagram on page 169. You can see that it's a kind of dogleg.

In the first part of the "leg," you see what happens when you tell the "favored" client that things are now about to return to normal. He doesn't see it that way; he thinks you're trying to do him in, and his perception becomes that he's Losing. Thus you end up, without trying to, being the villain of a Win-Lose scenario. In the second part of the "leg," the inevitable happens: the buyer who thinks that he's Losing gets out, gets even, or does both. And you both end up in the doghouse, at Lose-Lose.

Now, in a case like this one, it's not always the seller alone who sets up the false expectations. Many times, customers will *ask* for Lose-Win, because they believe (mistakenly) that it's to their long-term advantage. A client will demand a better credit structure or a more favorable price than he, or anyone else, has ever gotten in the past—because he knows you want his business so badly that you're willing to hock the store to get it. The interesting thing here is that such a customer, far from stealing a march on the "sucker" salesperson is usually just setting up his *own* false expectations, and therefore *setting himself*

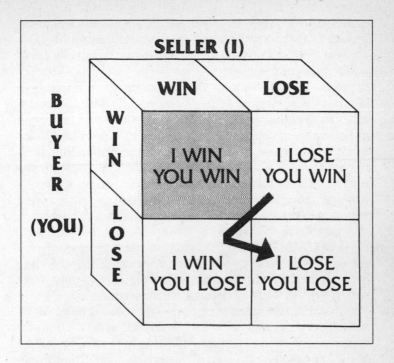

up to Lose. The bottom-line lesson is the same. No matter who initiates the idea of Lose-Win, it's almost always, in the long run, a double-fault game.

When It's Worth the Gamble

We say "almost always," and that suggests there may be situations where the calculated risk is worth taking. You may want to consider Lose-Win in situations where the potential return is *so* good, and where the prospects for long-term business are *so* promising that you'd feel like a fool just walking away because the special deal they're asking for is "impossible." Obviously there are no rules we can give you for determining which accounts these are, because nobody knows your business like you do. But we can give you a story that makes the point.

A friend of ours recently started a plant-care service in Manhattan: she supplies and supervises the care of decorative plants for corporations and large retail outlets. Several months ago, she was offered the opportunity to supply the plant decor for one of the largest banks in the city—a company with dozens of locations which could have doubled her income overnight. Because she was so eager to get in the door, she agreed to supply and service plants for a midtown location for six months at approximately half her usual rate. At that kind of introductory discount, she made nothing at all on the deal. In fact, she lost money. But she considered it worth the gamble because of the expected return. Our friend explains how she presented that gamble to the bank:

"What I do, I do extremely well—but there was no way the bank would have ever found that out if I'd had gone head to head with the competition. They would have priced me out of the business with no trouble. So I told the bank I did something unique—that they'd be getting a value-added service with me—and that I was willing to prove that to them by taking a bath on the trial period. I spelled it out very clearly. I was giving away the store up front, and I told them so, *in writing.* And I made it perfectly clear that, if they wanted my service to continue, it would be at my usual rates. I've now got a ten-site contract for two years, and I never had even a hint that they thought I was 'upping' my prices."

That illustrates perfectly not only the single exception we're pointing out—that is, not only *when* it's all right to operate in a Lose-Win fashion—but also *how* to do so. Our friend "spelled it out very clearly," and she did it *in writing,* up front. The reason that Lose-Win so often degenerates into Win-Lose, and then into Lose-Lose, is that the salesperson *fails to point out to the client that he or she is getting a special deal.*

The lesson here follows directly from what we've been saying throughout this book about *communicating* with the people you sell to. If you find yourself in a situation where Lose-Win seems a reasonable gamble, fine: go for it. But be up front with your clients. Tell them what you're doing. Admit this is difficult for you and your company. Tell them why you think their business is worth it. And—most important of all—tell them exactly when, and under what "new" conditions, reality is going to be reintroduced into your relationship. That's the only way you're going to be able to manage a Lose-Win scenario—or, for that matter, any scenario—into a long-term Win-Win outcome.

Lose-Lose: The "Magnet" Quadrant

We say "manage," because experience has taught us that Win-Win selling is never the result of accident or luck or good intentions. It's always the result of a *conscious decision on the part of the seller to work actively toward mutual satisfaction*. We believe that as a salesperson today, you have two basic responsibilities:

1. You have a responsibility to help your *buyer* Win.
2. You have a responsibility to help *yourself* Win.

Both responsibilities are equally important, and indeed in Win-Win selling, they are inextricable from each other.

When you fail to perform *either* of these two responsibilities, there is one inevitable result. The selling process always degenerates, sooner or later, into Lose-Lose. In Conceptual Selling, the sales professional not only makes a conscious *choice* to work toward Win-Win outcomes; he or she also does whatever is necessary, from one sales call to another, to keep the selling process moving in that direction. This is essential because, *if left unattended,* every sales scenario you've ever seen will eventually degenerate into Lose-Lose.

The Lose-Lose quadrant, in fact, seems to exert a kind of "magnetic" influence on sales. Whether it's because of inertia, or laziness, or neglect, or a combination of factors, all potentially good buy/sell interactions have a natural tendency to move toward disarray. The only way to prevent that from happening is to consciously and actively *manage* every one of your sales calls in the direction of Win-Win.

We don't say this is easy. What's easy, in most cases, is to consciously or unconsciously manipulate the customer into buying (Win-Lose) or to give away the store to get the business (Lose-Win). Staying Win-Win can be hard work. We're not minimizing the difficulty—only saying that it's worth the effort, because it's the only thing that can keep you both from Losing.

Problems in Staying Win-Win

Let's talk about some specific difficulties. When we tell our clients "Always try to remain Win-Win," we frequently encounter objections, and in this section we'll discuss the four problems that our clients most commonly bring up. We don't have solid, surefire answers to these problems, and those who say they do haven't been in the selling world very long. But we can give you some guidelines.

Problem One: "There's no fit." What if the product or service you're selling doesn't have a clear "fit" to the customer's current business or personal needs? Is it possible to have customers Win when you sell them something that does not clearly, and uniquely, provide answers to their "solution images"?

The simple answer is No. So you should walk away from that business. The more complicated answer is Maybe—*if* you can bring them and/or their companies something that nobody else can provide. If the piece of machinery you're selling the XYZ Corporation is only 95 percent as efficient as the machinery your competitor is prepared to offer, you might still make the sale come out Win-Win if you have a solid-gold support system, if your service policy rivals IBM's, or if you're willing to run out the payments for twenty months longer than the competition's. Nobody today *simply* sells product. So you might be able to construct a "fit" from follow-up or other intangibles. Just be sure, if you're selling in this kind of situation, that you make it very clear to the client, up front, exactly what you're offering, and where the critical difference lies. There's no point in giving anyone a great deal on service and then trying to make him or her believe that you've sold state-of-the-art technology. Or vice versa. The point is to *level with your customers.* If you do that, you can sometimes make a fit that isn't obvious. If you don't do it, no matter what kind of a "fit" you make happen, sooner or later it will blow up in your face.

Problem Two: "I've got to meet quota." It's a fact of modern corporate selling that the people you would most expect to be on your side in developing Win-Win scenarios often feel like your worst enemies. We're talking about sales and marketing management. Not *all* sales and marketing management. Just those far-seeing, numbers-crunching whiz kids who tell you three months before you've ever gone into the field exactly what you're going to bring back when you go there. The guys who check out the Dow-Jones and the market share and their astrological signs, and then pronounce, with no hint of humor, "Your quota this quarter is 6 billion units."

We have nothing against marketing projections per se. But to anybody in sales it's very obvious that the figures you're given each quarter—whether they come from the branch manager or the Central Office—only bear a marginal relationship to what's happening, day to day, in the field. That's why you, as the person who's closest to the sale, have a responsibility to *educate* your management: to explain, just as we've explained it here, that you will all reap bigger benefits in the long run by working *with* your customers rather than against them. Sometimes this will mean pointing out that meeting quota in a given quarter actually goes *against* your long-term best interests.

It's very common for sales representatives to get mixed signals from sales management. On the one hand it's the old bromide "We're out to meet the needs of our customers." On the other hand it's "Make him need what we have. Make quota, however you do it." We hope what we've been saying in this chapter is ample evidence that such mixed signals are counterproductive.

Problem Three: "My competition is undercutting me." Problems One and Two here are problems of having to stay Win-Lose, whether you want to or not. Problem Three we've already hinted at: it's the dilemma of trying to decide whether or not you should stay Lose-Win, when your competition, on the surface, is offering the potential customer a better deal. In this kind of situation, when matching the competition's offer would clearly be a Lose for you, you have a choice of three options. You can a) choose to stay Lose-Win for now, in the expectation of future returns—and we've already pointed out the hazards of that approach. You can b) sell your product or service on a "value added" based by showing the client that, in spite of your competition's better price (or delivery schedule, or whatever), you can offer better *value* for his money. Or, if neither of these options works, you can c) choose to let this particular piece of business go. Sometimes this last option, although it looks unattractive, is the best option, long term, because it acknowledges one simple fact: If you're committed to Win-Win selling, you *cannot sell everybody,* every time.

Many salespeople, holding on to the "volume first" philosophy, would probably prefer the first option—going Lose-Win as an "investment." We don't say that's wrong. We only remind you that, if you decide to do this in order to nail down future business, make sure that the temporary sacrifice is likely to be worth it—and make sure your customer understands, on paper, that you're playing Lose-Win *for this time only.*

Problem Four: "My customer won't stay Win-Win." Face it. No matter how hard you try to work it out with each individual client, there's always going to be someone who *likes to see you Lose.* Not you particularly, but everybody. There are always going to be those charming characters who get their jollies from seeing other people squirm. You can give them everything they want, and they're still going to be hanging around, hovering like vultures until they see an opening, and they can feast on your Lose.

Luckily these characters are rare (maybe the bulk of them have been done in by ulcers). But you're bound to meet one now and then. When you do, our advice is very simple. After you've sized up the situation at length and determined that the person does not care if you Lose, get up, explain, "Sorry, we can't make that come out"—and back quietly out the door.

Not exactly your basic Selling 101 advice, we realize, but it's good advice nonetheless. You cannot stay Win-Win with everybody, and you sure can't stay there alone. Therefore, if you're truly committed to Win-Win, you have to be able to size up those situations that are inherently no-Win. And you have to be willing to walk. To reiterate a point we made just above, *either* you try for Win-Win, *or* you try to sell everybody, every time. You cannot have it both ways.

Win-Win: Basic Objectives

We'll end this chapter with a summary of the basic objectives you should keep in mind every time you go out on a sales call.

- *Don't oversell on expectations.* Don't overpromise so that you're forced to underdeliver. Be straight with your customer from the start. This is in your own best interest as well as the client's, because if you oversell at the beginning, both of you will be undersold by the end.

- *Don't get suckered into a giveaway.* Don't be so eager to get a particular piece of business that you forget what you're in business for: to satisfy your customers *and yourself.* One without the other won't do.

- *Hear the buyer out.* Don't assume you know what he or she is thinking about you and what you're trying to do for his or her company. Let your customer talk.   That's the only way you can be sure of getting the information you need to manage the sale into Win-Win.

- *When in doubt find out.* Ask the questions you need to ask to discover what your customer actually thinks about the situation, and especially about how he or she can Win.   Test your understanding of this critical information at every step of the way in the selling process, that is, on every sales call. The key to every good sale is solid, up-front *communication.*

- *Be willing to walk.* Be willing to let a piece of business go if it's clear you can only get it with somebody Losing.   If you're not willing to walk *sometime,* then face it: you're only playing lip service to Win-Win, and you'll always end up at either Win-Lose or Lose-Win.

Personal Workshop: Win-Win

With these objectives in mind, you can now make the concept of Win-Win real to you by applying it to your own situations.   In your notebook write down the heading "Win-Win," and set aside about fifteen minutes.

Step 1: Define your past sales. Think back over the sales you've made—that is, over the orders you've actually gotten—in the past couple of months.   Below the heading "Win-Win," list six or seven of these sales at the far left edge of the page.   You can identify them simply: "The 3100 deal with Macro," "service renewal with the Comram Group."   Just be sure you understand, for each individual sale that you list, exactly what *account* you are talking about, exactly *what* you sold them, and *when.*

Now, for each sale that you've listed, write down a brief description of how *you* and the *customer* both felt at the end of the sale, We emphasize the end of the sale—and by that we really mean how you both felt a month or two *after* the customer had the opportunity to understand what the sale meant to him or her. We realize this is going to be speculative in terms of how your customer felt; just do the best you can in assessing, in a brief description, how you and the person you sold to probably felt two or three months down the line.

Look over the comments you've made, and *compare* how you felt about these representative sales with the way your customers probably felt. If your sales have a high percentage of "I felt great-customer felt lousy" comments, then the chances are pretty good that you've been playing Win-Lose. If you have a preponderance of comments that sound like "He got a great deal, I got burned," then the chances are equally good that you've been playing Lose-Win.

There are no right answers here. Our point in asking you to review the history of your own recent sales is to make you aware of the Win-Win possibilities—and of the various ways in which those possibilities are often thwarted. We suspect that what you will find from this Step is that the sales where you have actively and vigorously served your customer's interests as well as your own have been the sales where you came out feeling good; and the sales where you have actively (or inadvertently) thwarted that interest have been those where you have also, albeit unwittingly, thwarted your own.

Step 2: Assess your current Win-Win position. Now apply the Win-Win way of thinking to your current accounts. Pick two or three of the upcoming sales calls that you're using as models in this book. For each of those upcoming calls with specific individuals, ask yourself the following questions:

- Am I firmly committed to finding a fit between my product or service and what this customer actually needs? In other words, do I want him or her to Win?

- Does this person fully understand that I want him or her to Win? What evidence do I have that he or she believes this?

- Is this person clearly committed to having me Win, or is he or she aiming for a good deal at my expense?
- Have I made it clear to the customer that he or she must share the responsibility for making the sale come out Win-Win?

Obviously, there are no right answers to these questions either. We urge you to ask them so that you can get a preliminary "fix" on your current position with regard to each of your clients or prospects. If it helps you to write down brief notes about each customer, do so; anything that makes your position more visible to you works to your long-term advantage in maintaining a Win-Win relationship.

Step 3: List actions to get you to Win-Win. We've stressed that Win-Win is not something that simply "happens" to lucky salespeople. Getting to Win-Win is a conscious and active choice, and on any individual sales call you can make a decision as to what "quadrant" you want to be in. That decision won't guarantee that you'll end up where you want to go; but failing to make the decision will almost certainly propel you toward the "magnet" quadrant of Lose-Lose.

In this Step, therefore, we'd like you to think about specific actions you can take on the next sales call with your client to manage the selling process toward Win-Win. We suggest you ask yourself one question, but that you ask it in three different forms:

- What *can* I do to assure Win-Win?
- What can *I* do to assure Win-Win?
- What can I *do* to assure Win-Win?

You'll notice that the first form of the question stresses *reality:* in listing actions you can take, you have to start with the immediately possible. Say you're meeting Harrison at the end of next week, and she has been playing an obvious Lose-Win game with you, by demanding that you cut your price to an impossible level. Your company simply won't allow that kind of discount, so there's no point in listing an action like "Agree to the rock-bottom suggestion." You can list a more realistic compromise like "Counter offer at ten percent above their figure" or "Explain to Harrison how her suggestion will set us both up to Lose."

In the second form of the question, you focus on your *personal* responsibility. If credit terms in your company are governed by an unchanging formula over which you personally have no control, don't bother listing "Try to rearrange the credit terms." What you can do personally with Harrison might be to "explain our credit options more fully" or "arrange a meeting with our credit manager."

Finally, in the third form of the question, you focus on what is *actionable* and *concrete*. You need to identify actions that relate directly to what the client thinks he needs from the sale *and* that still allow you to Win. The actions you list should be specific, and should be designed not just to "keep the ball rolling," but to move the selling process forward. And they should be actions that you can perform, face to face, with the customer on the upcoming sales call.

The term "action" here might be misleading. We don't mean only physical actions like "Take him to lunch at Sardi's" or "Deliver the new spec sheet by Friday." Those kind of actions may be fine, but remember that *questioning* is also a type of action; and it's a type you can definitely perform in that upcoming sales call. If you're not in the Win-Win quadrant with a client, or if you're not sure where you are, the "actions" of choice should always include drafting questions that are designed to improve your understanding. And, since Winning is so intimately connected to people's personal feelings, we urge you to pay special attention to drafting good Attitude Questions. Asking Harrison how she *feels* about the credit arrangements can be one of the best actions you can take to move her in the direction of Win-Win.

This exercise won't give you all the answers. We know that. But it should give you a handle on which of the four quadrants your sale is in at the present time. With that preliminary fix in mind, we're now going to show you a method for moving from wherever you are now toward a Win-Win conclusion. We call that method Joint Venture selling.

▶ 9 ◀

YOUR PATH TO WIN-WIN: JOINT VENTURE SELLING

Every time you begin a sales call, you make a conscious or unconscious choice between two basic methods of selling. In the more common and popular method, you assume that your prospect has a need for whatever you're selling, and you try to manage the sales call so that he or she acknowledges that need. In the less common method, you don't assume this need, but instead search for a fit between what the buyer *may* need and the solution your company can offer. This second, less well-recognized approach to selling is what we call Joint Venture selling. In this chapter we'll be explaining why in most cases it's the better method to get you to Win-Win conclusions.

The fundamental reason that Joint Venture selling is effective relates to what we said at the beginning of this book about your buyers' *decision-making process*. To reiterate the points we made there:

1. Buying is a special case of decision-making.
2. Whenever someone makes a buying decision, he or she does so in a series of predictable and logical steps.
3. These steps take place in an equally predictable and logical sequence that you, the seller, can track.
4. It's only by following this sequence that you can ensure quality sales.

In short, there is a *natural order* to every decision-making or buying process. And because buyers tend to feel more comfortable when they follow this natural order, there should also be a natural order to *selling*. Joint Venture selling works because it follows this natural order.

Three Types of Thinking

When we say "natural order," we're not talking about physics or cosmology. The natural order of selling has to do with the way the human brain functions, and specifically with the *three types of thinking* that we as a species engage in every time we grapple with a decision.

These three types of thinking were identified and explained several years ago by UCLA psychologist J.P. Guilford in his book *The Nature of Human Intelligence.* Guilford found through clinical research that human decision-making involves three distinct but interrelated thinking processes, which serve the decision-maker much like computer "subprograms," each with its own function and applicability. Furthermore, these three subprograms do not function haphazardly; in any decision-making process, even though the subprograms are different from and independent of each other, they almost always appear in the same order or sequence. It's possible to subvert or ignore this sequence, as we'll show you in a moment. But for any soundly reasoned and coherent decision-making process, this is the natural order of the three types of thinking:

1. The first type of thinking is what Guilford called *Cognition* thinking; it allows the decision-maker to *understand* the situation he or she is facing.
2. The second type is called *Divergent* thinking; it helps the person to *generate* options and solutions.
3. The third type is called *Convergent* thinking; it lets the person *select* the best solution.

The three types of thinking are represented in the diagram below. Let's see now how they work.

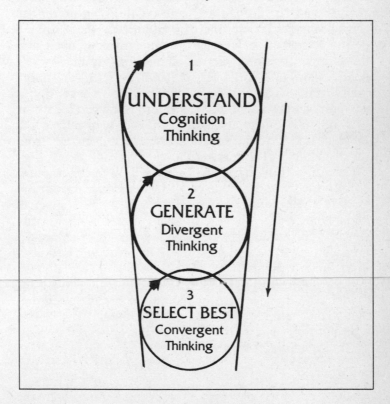

Cognition Thinking

Whenever anyone is faced with a situation in which he or she has to take some action, the first thing that has to occur is for the person to acquire a clear understanding of the situation. When a decision for action is required, all your senses come into play inputting raw information into your brain. Cognition is the process by which that raw information is given *sense* and *structure;* it's what provides you with a mental picture of the situation that has shape, dimension, size, and other relevant parameters. If you could record this internal process, Cognition would sound like this: "What . . . ? How much . . . ? Where . . . ? When . . . ? Why?"

Until you go through a Cognition thinking process to clarify your understanding of a situation, you are like a person locked in a darkened room, fumbling and stumbling into furniture. Cognition thinking is turning the light on: it won't solve any problem by itself, any more than turning on an electric light will unlock a door. But it will perform the essential first step of letting you see where you are. Without good Cognition, it is only by pure, blind accident that anyone ever reaches a sound decision. And the probability of that is very low.

Cognition thinking is critical in selling because unless both the seller and the buyer fully *understand* the parameters of their mutual situation, there's no way short of blind chance that they're going to reach a satisfactory conclusion: the buyer won't know what he or she really needs, and neither will the seller. The result will be a poor fit and a poor solution.

We see the results of bad Cognition all the time in selling. Frequently, the sales rep who has an incomplete Cognition of a client's situation will end up frustrated after pitching a product that has no relevance to the customer's needs. Or the salesperson may get an order for twenty units of Product A and walk away from an order for 100 units of Product B because the buyer's Cognition of the seller's product line was incomplete. In good selling, both the potential buyer and the seller have good, complete Cognition, and they are able to build on that Cognition to generate real matches and real solutions.

We said earlier that sound selling always begins with

what's in the customer's mind—that is, with his or her Concept of what your product or service can do. And we said that good questioning is the principal way of understanding the client's Concept. This ties in precisely with Cognition thinking. Asking good questions to clarify the customer's Concept is an integral part of Cognition thinking: it's the way that both buyer and seller can make sense of the basic situation.

We emphasize *both*. It's just as essential for the prospect to understand what you're about as it is for you to understand his or her needs and problems. Good questioning serves both these purposes. We've mentioned that people don't always understand their own problems and needs as well as a seller might like them to. Questioning helps you over that hurdle. It invites the client or prospect to find out *with* you what are the parameters of his or her Concept. In other words, it makes it possible for you to engage in *mutual* Cognition thinking. That's where every good sales call should begin.

Divergent Thinking

The second stage of the decision-making process is called Divergent thinking. It is *necessarily* the second stage, because you cannot do good Divergent thinking until you first have a clear Cognition of the situation. In Divergent thinking, the decision-maker considers a variety of solutions that might answer to his or her particular needs. Divergent thinking sounds like this: "How about . . . ? We could . . . What if . . . Let's consider . . . " It's a creative and often freewheeling process designed to generate *alternatives*. In everyday language, it's what is often called "brainstorming"—except that, since it follows Cognition, it's a focussed and precise form of brainstorming.

As anyone who has ever conducted a brainstorming session knows, Divergent thinking works best when there are no constraints put on the person who is looking for solutions. Say you're the moderator of a study group that's trying to solve an inventory control problem. If you open the first meeting of that group by demanding nothing but "solid, well thought out" suggestions, you're going to get damn few suggestions. If you want any Divergent thinking/brainstorming exercise to be truly productive, you've got to be willing to consider *all* suggestions, no matter how "offbeat" or unconventional. You'll get a lot of junk ideas, sure, but you'll also get far more good ideas than you would ever be able to get if you limited the discussion to so-called good ideas.

The point of Divergent thinking is to *explore* possibilities, not to *exclude* them. This is as important in an interaction with a potential customer as it is in any group brainstorming session. Once your buyer understands the basic situation through Cognition thinking, he then has to be able to spend a reasonable amount of time in sifting through *all* the possibilities. Not just the "obvious" solutions, or the "most reasonable" solutions. And not just the solutions *you* can offer him. For the three-step thinking process to work properly, you have to let your prospect's Divergent thinking subprogram run its natural course. If you don't do that, you're inevitably going to generate confusion, resentment and, very likely, a no-Win outcome to the sale.

Convergent Thinking

Once the decision-maker has had the opportunity to consider all available options, the final step is to *select the best one* for his particular situation. He does this in the mental process called Convergent thinking. It's called Convergent thinking because when we converge on a solution, we are narrowing and focussing our viewpoint; we are zeroing in on "the answer." Thus, Convergent thinking might sound like this: "We should . . . The logical choice . . . It's obvious."

There's an interesting paradox associated with Convergent thinking. You might think that coming up with "the answer" would be the hardest and most tedious aspect of a decision-making process: after all, you don't want to choose wrong, so it might be expected that you would spend inordinate amounts of time in determining that your final selection is the right one. Actually, in a good decision-making process, this isn't what happens at all. The only time you have to agonize over the selection phase of the process is *when you have not spent enough time* in the previous two subprograms. If you spend sufficient time developing a sound Cognition of the problem and considering the available options with Divergent thinking, then finding the answer with Convergent thinking often becomes an almost automatic operation.

Time and Direction

You can see what we're saying here illustrated in the diagram we presented on page 183. To understand why good decision-making often makes the answer almost obvious, note three things about the diagram.

First, note that the circles indicating the three thinking subprograms are not all drawn the same size. This is not accidental. The size of the three circles corresponds to the amount of time a decision-maker ideally should spend on each of the three thinking steps. This follows the way our minds work. We have found over and over again, in a variety of selling situations, that the more time you give potential customers to do Cognition thinking, the easier it becomes for them to do the Divergent thinking that must follow. And the more time you allow them to generate possible solutions with Divergent thinking, the less time will ultimately be required to zero in on the best solution.

Second, note that the three circles in the diagrams are not isolated from each other: they overlap. We draw them that way to indicate that the three thinking processes are interrelated, just as the subprograms of a computer program are interrelated. The interrelationship is important because if any of the subprograms is faulty or incomplete—that is, if you don't allow the decision-maker to "run the program out" at his or her own pace—then it becomes difficult, if not impossible, to proceed logically to the next step in the decision process.

Finally, note that there is a specified *direction* to the three-part decision-making process. That direction is indicated by the arrow to the right of the diagram. In every sound decision-making process, Cognition comes first, Divergent thinking comes next, and Convergent thinking comes last. Since buying is a form of decision-making, this means that selling *ought* to follow the same sequence. The seller ought to perform Cognition thinking with the prospect first, to fully understand the Concept; help him or her to perform Divergent thinking next, as a survey of all possible Concept solutions; and encourage the prospect to perform Convergent thinking only *after* the first two steps have been adequately performed.

But that's seldom what happens.

Upside Down Selling

Instead, what salespeople typically do—because it's what they've historically been trained to do—is to *turn the customer's decision-making process on its head,* as indicated in the diagram pictured on page 189.

Sellers have typically been told that their job is to *make the customer need* whatever they have to sell. They've been told that the whole point of selling is to get him to see *you* as the answer—in other words, to make the final, Convergent thinking selection in your favor in spite of the fact that he hasn't been through the two earlier subprograms of the decision-making process. Much sales training, in fact, tries to obliterate those earlier subprograms entirely, because they "get in the way" of pushing the product and getting the order.

As the diagram indicates, this means that the typical salesperson is actually moving *against* the natural order of the customer's thinking by asking the person to

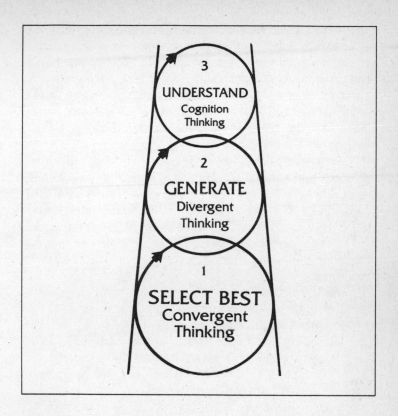

select first, think about alternative options later, and come to an understanding of why he's bought last—if at all. What this says to the potential customer is: "I've got the best possible product out of the few (or no) others that you've looked at, for a situation neither you nor I understand."

Crazy, isn't it? And yet it's being done all the time—by salespeople who come away without an order, wondering why the stubborn jerk wouldn't buy after they gave such a super presentation.

Why would any seller approach a customer in this bass-ackwards way?

The answer is that it looks easier and safer. It looks more straightforward and efficient than working your customer through all that Cognition and Divergent and Convergent, thinking. It's commonly assumed, by some gung-ho sellers, that the quicker you get the order, the better. And the quickest way to get the order is to keep control by putting on a great floor show, slip the pen in his hand while he's smiling, and dance out the door to the next town, talking all the while. It's Product Pitch again, with a vengeance.

This type of upside down selling, while it may work on some customers some of the time, is increasingly becoming a liability. "Slam-dunking" the client into Convergent thinking before he fully understands what he's getting into is a classic case of playing Win-Lose, and in today's markets, where customers are more savvy than ever, that's bound to backfire—usually sooner rather than later.

In addition, and again contrary to popular opinion, asking your customer to perform Convergent thinking first is not nearly as "quick and easy" as it looks. In fact, this kind of selling is actually much *slower* and *less efficient* than following the customer's natural thinking process. Why? Because if you force a customer into a decision before he is mentally ready for it, one of two things is likely to happen. Either a) he'll balk, throwing up roadblocks and objections until you're entirely on the defensive, and Losing; or b) he'll cave in, sign the order and then, after thinking about it, have a severe attack of Buyer's Remorse. Whereas if you prepare the way by enabling him to understand what you're doing, there's a far greater chance you will create that positive information flow that is at the heart of all Win-Win selling.

The principal lesson here is one that we outlined in the first chapter. *People love to buy, but they hate to feel they've been "sold."* When you perform what we've been calling "upside down selling," you're very often going to be seen as the typical pushy hustler, trying to "sell" somebody something. As a result, very often, you'll be left out in the cold, doing your great floor show for yourself.

"Unilateral" vs. "Joint Venture"

Because the "upside down" method of pushing product often leaves you talking to yourself, we also call it Unilateral selling. Unilateral means "one-sided," and that's exactly the situation you put yourself in when you adopt a Unilateral method. All the pressure for "making" the sale rests on you; you get no help from the buyer, because you don't ask for it. So you're left alone, trying to cram round pegs into square holes, and seeing the potential customer as the opposition. Whenever you ignore the client's Cognition process (and your own) and try to force the sale, you set yourself up to be isolated in this way.

But at the same time, in Unilateral selling, you often give up to the buyer the one thing you should be in charge of: drawing the necessary connection between your product or service and his or her Concept. When you sell unilaterally, you confine yourself to product pitching—and you rely on the Buying Influence himself to connect your product with his experience. That dramatically limits the percentage of potential clients who can become real buyers, because it's just not logical to assume that all people *have* a real need for your product or that, even if someone does have a need, that he will necessarily be able to understand it. The double mistake in Unilateral selling is the same double mistake we outlined in talking about Product Pitch: it assumes first that *all* potential buyers can use your product, and second that if you only "show and tell" them about it—get out the dancing dogs again—they'll appreciate the obvious benefits and rush to buy from you.

We're not saying that you should *never* engage in Unilateral selling. We've already acknowledged the importance of Giving Information, and of maintaining positive information flow with your customers—so we're obviously not opposed to the seller talking. At certain points in every sales call, it will probably be entirely appropriate for you to show and tell about your product. The potential problem we're identifying here is in letting that go on too long, so that you end up locked into the 80 Percent Syndrome, with the seller in a virtual monologue.

To make sure you don't end up in a monologue, you should be thinking, on every sales call, about how to get your customer *involved,* so that both of you can be participants in a truly two-way conversation. We don't mean a rigid plan of I talk, then you talk, then I talk again. We mean an active, fluid *exchange* of ideas. The method we recommend for accomplishing that kind of exchange we call Joint Venture selling.

As the name implies, in Joint Venture selling, the burden of "making" the sale rests on both buyer *and* seller. As we pointed out in the section on Commitment, it's up to both the buyer and the seller to move the buy/sell process forward, by mutually encouraging positive information flow. There's no assumption that the buyer already has a need for the seller's product. On the contrary, the entire questioning process, and the entire Cognition phase of the sales call, is geared to determining, up front, whether or not there really is a need. Thus Joint Venture selling follows the natural order of decision-making, by beginning with Cognition, moving next to Divergent thinking, and ending with Convergent thinking.

As we've mentioned before, such a "customer-driven" selling process is threatening to many traditionally trained sales professionals, because they confuse "domination" of the call with "control" of the agenda, and they fear that letting the client become a partner in the call will cause them, the sellers, to lose control. But as we've also pointed out, this is exactly the opposite of what usually happens. In good Joint Venture selling, the seller's insistence on asking questions to discover the customer's real needs ends up giving him or her *more* control than is possible in a "show and tell" presentation. In Joint Venture selling, you control the agenda because the basis of that agenda is mutual understanding and information flow. You direct the potential customer through the natural three stages of decision-making, because you know that only those sales where he or she has been able to go through this process are going to end up at Win-Win.

Making It Easy on Yourself

Directing your clients through the decision-making process makes it much easier on them to come to sound buying decisions than they could if you'd forced your product down their throats. But it's easier on *you,* too. That's one of the principal advantages of using a Joint Venture approach. Because it's a natural, fluid method, salespersons who use it typically report that their sales calls become far less stressful, and far more predictable, than they had ever been before. There's a real psychic boost that comes with the realization, as our friend Gene recalled about his Chicago meeting, that he "didn't have to *sell* these guys." All he had to do was to make it logical and easy for them to buy.

Gene's case is not isolated. It's typical. What he found is what all Joint Venture sellers soon find: that searching for a match—as exacting and challenging as that can be—is still infinitely less of a burden than the old game of cramming product. It's a more flexible, freer way of selling. As many of our program participants tell us, Joint Venture mentally *liberates* them.

We're not being touchy-feely or philosophical here. When we say Joint Venture is liberating, we mean that it frees you, in very practical terms, from the burdens of selling conventions—and especially from the oldest convention of all: the idea that your job is to *make someone need* your product, no matter how impossible that may seem. With the dead weight of that convention lifted, you're free to get down to the real business of selling, which is to provide your prospects and customers with solutions.

We're not saying that providing solutions is easy, or that if you practice Joint Venture selling the orders will fall in your lap. Joint Venture salespeople work as hard as anyone else. But they work with far greater *efficiency.* The energy they put into sales calls isn't misdirected, butt-your-head-against-the-wall energy.   It's energy that leads, logically and naturally, to results.   In the words of another colleague, "For most people, making a tough sale is like driving a hundred miles with the emergency brake on. Joint Venture takes the brake off."

Joint Venture and the Thinking Process

It may already have occurred to you that the three stages of decision-making can be directly related to the three phases of the sales call that we described in Part II of this book.   When you practice Joint Venture selling, the following usually happens:

- Cognition thinking, both for your customer and for you, is fostered by the questioning process that is involved in Getting Information.
- Divergent thinking is encouraged in the Giving Information phase of the sales call, where you point out the Unique Strengths of your product or service.
- Getting Commitment through the resolution of Basic Issues enables your customer to "zero in" through the process of Convergent thinking.

Obviously, the correlation between the three thinking sub-programs and the three phases of the sales call is not absolute.   There's no reason it should be.   Just as you will move from one phase of the sales call to another without being confined to a rigid "schedule," so too you will find yourself encouraging Divergent thinking toward the end of certain sales call interviews, and focussing on "best choice" selection toward the beginning of others.   But the basic point remains valid.   No matter where you and your customer are in a given sales call situation, he or she will always prefer to make his or her buying decision *after* having gone through the three subprograms of decision-making, not before.

This fact can be turned to your advantage, because knowing that your clients want to work through the three thinking processes sequentially gives you a unique method for spotting and resolving trouble. Take a typical scenario. You're trying to get through a brilliantly conceived program about why your company's solution to an engineering problem will save the Winger Company millions of dollars a year. Winger's head honcho of engineering, though, is continually shooting you down—finding off-the-wall, irrelevant reasons that your solution just won't work.

A traditionally trained salesperson in this kind of scenario would just bull his way through, overcoming each individual objection as if he were kicking pebbles from his path. If you're attentive to the client's decision-making process, however, you'll take a more sophisticated approach. You'll be able to realize that the Winger engineer may have been inadvertently rushed through some previous stage of the thinking process, and is resistant to your solution at this point because there are gaps in his (or your) information regarding Cognition, or Divergent thinking, or both. Knowing that, you'll be able to move back: to restate a previously agreed upon understanding, to clarify your idea of the Concept, to do whatever is necessary to work, step by step, though the process again. By doing that, you'll have a much better chance of eventually ending up at Win-Win than you would have if you forced his decision.

We summarize what we've been saying about Joint Venture and Unilateral selling in the comparative "Methods" chart on page 196.

Input, "Ownership," and Commitment

Although, as we've acknowledged, there are places in a sales call where you may be doing most of the talking, there are *very few* selling situations where it is appropriate for

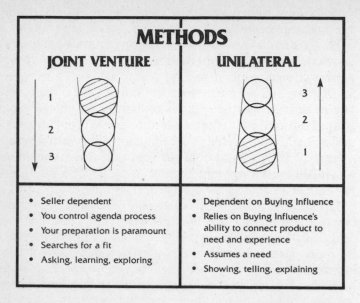

METHODS

JOINT VENTURE	UNILATERAL
• Seller dependent	• Dependent on Buying Influence
• You control agenda process	• Relies on Buying Influence's ability to connect product to need and experience
• Your preparation is paramount	
• Searches for a fit	• Assumes a need
• Asking, learning, exploring	• Showing, telling, explaining

you to *limit the input* your customer has in the call, or in the solution. One of the main reasons we caution you about Unilateral selling is that it has a tendency to do just that: to cut down on the client's involvement.

This is hazardous because it leaves you open to making sales that can easily become "derailed" later on. We've quoted the company executive who says that people "don't resist their own ideas." The opposite of that dictum is also true. People do, actively and vociferously, resist ideas that they do not "own"—even when they've ostensibly accepted them by purchasing a product or service. So when you make a sale without developing customer ownership, you set yourself up to Lose down the line, when the person discovers he or she has been "sold." On the other hand, when you actively engage the buyer's input in the decision-making process, you allow him or her to buy into a mutual solution. When a customer owns a solution in this way, he or she will fight to keep it in place.

And not just for the present. When you work with a customer through all the necessary stages of a Joint Venture selling process, you lay the groundwork for a long-term commitment that is going to be far more profitable to you over the years than any one-time commission could ever be. We've seen this happen countless times. Here's just one example.

A friend of ours had some carpentry work done several years ago. It was complicated trimwork, and the carpenter that he hired was at the time the new kid on the block. Our friend wasn't really sure that he was going to be up to the job, but he came through beautifully. It wasn't just that he knew how to handle a hammer and saw. The young carpenter actively *involved* our friend in the design and construction of the work. He went over blueprints with him, had long conferences with him and his wife, made absolutely sure at every step of the decision-making process that the trimwork was a perfect fit to what our friend had in mind. "When he put on the finishing touches," our friend told us, "it was exactly what had been in our mind's eye. He had done the cutting and the planing, but the finished product was *ours*."

That was ownership. But it was only half of the story. About two years later, after the carpenter had become pretty well established, our friend hired him again. This time the work wasn't so great. The carpenter had taken on three helpers by this time, and one of them was not up to scratch. Halfway through the second project, our friend started to spot obvious defects in the workmanship. But—and here is the point we're making—because he had established such a sound Win-Win relationship with the carpenter on the previous job, his reaction was very different from what it might have been if he had been dealing with someone to whom he had no commitment. "If anybody else had put that kind of work in my house," he confided to us, "I would have cancelled the contract on the spot. With Jim, I had such a good feeling—such a good history of working together—that I bent over backwards trying to keep him on board. I went to him directly, pointed out my concerns, and gave his firm a month longer than I would have given anybody else to get the work back up to par. We worked it out together, so that a project that once looked like terminal trouble has turned into another mutual Win."

The lesson is clear. By making your clients *part of their own solutions,* you make an investment in the future that no amount of quick fixes could ever bring you. In all good Conceptual Selling, the input of the client leads to owner-ship—and ownership leads to long-term commitment.

Personal Workshop: Joint Venture

In this Personal Workshop you'll relate the concept of Joint Venture to your own selling by running through the three subprograms of the thinking process from your prospective customer's point of view. Pick one of the model calls you've been working with, and be sure that for this call you have a clear sales objective in mind. Remember that by "sales objective" we mean whatever you want to have happen in the account that isn't happening right now; remember, too, that the objective must be tangible, mea-surable, and tied to a realistic time line. When you've chosen the objective and the specific sales call, write the heading "Joint Venture" at the top of a notebook page, and give yourself about twenty minutes.

Step 1: Cognition. Put yourself in your prospective cus-tomer's place, and write down a brief description of *his or her* Cognition of the situation. You're trying here to think with your client's mindset, and we know that isn't easy. In our programs, the participants often find that they can come to a clearer understanding of this mindset if they complete the following sentences *as they think the client would complete them:*

- The situation today is . . .
- The budget is . . .
- I need to get approval from . . .
- My key supporters/detractors are . . .
- What's in it for me is . . .
- I'll Win in this situation when . . .

Write down the completed sentences in your notebook. Keep in mind that, although you're trying to think with the client's mindset, the answers you put down must also relate to your specific sales objective: in fact, when we say "situation" here, we mean the very fact that you are trying to get the client to decide in favor of your sales objective.

Step 2: Divergent thinking. Now, still thinking with your prospective customer's mindset, generate the alternative solutions that he or she is likely to be considering with regard to the current situation. To help you do that, complete the following sentences.

- I've thought about . . .
- We've agreed to . . .
- So far we've already looked at . . .
- The options we've considered are . . .

Fill in one or more of these sentences the way you believe the client would fill them in, and write down the completed sentences in your notebook.

One subtle point. Remember that, when potential buyers consider alternative options, they are going to be looking not just at a range of possible purchases and possible vendors, but also at changes in implementation, at modification of existing procedures—and at the very real possibility that the best course of action may be to stay with the status quo. For this reason the status quo is always a kind of "competitor," and you should therefore consider the possibility that, as your client is weighing different actions, one action will be to take no action at all.

Step 3: Convergent thinking. Finally—still with your client's thinking cap on—consider the selection process he or she will probably be going through in converging on a "best choice" solution. You can do this by completing the following sentences:

- This is important because . . .
- I want to/must accomplish . . .
- The final solution here will have to . . .

Again, write down your client's probable answers in your notebook. Be especially attentive in this Step to how well, or how poorly, these answers relate to your stated sales objective. If a client's Convergent thinking does not relate in some way to the objective you're trying to accomplish, then the chances are good that you and/or the client has missed something earlier in the thinking process. It may be useful for you to review the Cognition stage of that process again, to see if you have clearly understood what you're in this selling situation for, and whether or not it hooks up clearly to the client's Concept.

We don't expect that this Personal Workshop will give you detailed, clear insights into *what* your client is thinking. What it should give you is two important things:

- A sense of *how* each of your potential clients arrives at a buying decision
- An understanding of the *gaps in your information* with regard to decision-making for this sale

In other words, the exercise should help you discover where you still need to find answers; it should help you find out what uncertainties you need to address in the Getting Information phase of your next sales call on this prospect or client.

In order to manage that sales call efficiently, you need to *plan* for it in advance. In the next chapter we're going to introduce a practical tool that will enable you to do that most effectively: a tactical Planning Matrix.

‣ 10 ‣

LINKING TASKS AND METHODS: THE PLANNING MATRIX

Every time you go into a sales call, you have two essential *tasks* to perform: first, you have to make the Concept Sale, and then, when appropriate, you have to make the Product Sale to relate your product or service to the client's needs. To perform these two tasks, you have access to two basic approaches, or selling *methods,* which we have just described as the Unilateral method and the Joint Venture method. You're always going to get the best results in sales calls when you spend some time in advance thinking out which combination of tasks and methods you want to be using in the call. It's for that reason that we present the planning tool we call the Planning Matrix. It's a unique organizational device that will help you link tasks and methods most effectively.

The Planning Matrix is depicted below. You'll notice immediately from the diagram that there is a surface similarity between this Matrix and the Win-Win Matrix we introduced in Chapter 8: both matrices plot the possible selling situations into four boxes, or "quadrants." But the two matrices are not the same.

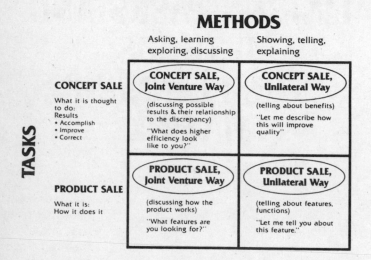

METHODS

	Asking, learning exploring, discussing	Showing, telling, explaining
CONCEPT SALE What it is thought to do: Results • Accomplish • Improve • Correct	**CONCEPT SALE, Joint Venture Way** (discussing possible results & their relationship to the discrepancy) "What does higher efficiency look like to you?"	**CONCEPT SALE, Unilateral Way** (telling about benefits) "Let me describe how this will improve quality"
PRODUCT SALE What it is: How it does it	**PRODUCT SALE, Joint Venture Way** (discussing how the product works) "What features are you looking for?"	**PRODUCT SALE, Unilateral Way** (telling about features, functions) "Let me tell you about this feature."

(TASKS — vertical label at left)

When we spoke about the Win-Win Matrix, we said that it's always desirable, if not always possible, to position yourself in the upper left-hand, or Win-Win quadrant; no matter where you may be at a given point in a selling process, the goal is to get to Win-Win. The same thing isn't always true of the tactical Planning Matrix. Although we have been emphasizing the importance of making the Concept Sale, and of making it in a Joint Venture fashion, it doesn't necessarily follow that you can be in the upper left-hand quadrant of the Planning Matrix at *all* times.

In fact, depending on where you are in a selling process, and depending on what specific information you need to cover in a given sales call, you may want to position yourself in any one of the four Planning Matrix quadrants. Indeed, within the time frame of a single sales call, it will almost always be appropriate to move into more than one quadrant, as the information requirements of the situation change. We'll explain this more fully now, by examining each of the quadrants in turn.

Quadrant 1: Concept/Joint Venture

When you and your customer choose to operate in the Concept/Joint Venture quadrant in a particular part of a sales call, the major emphasis is placed on what we have called Cognition thinking. In this quadrant, you spend much of your time asking questions—and probably your prospect does too—for you both to get a complete under-standing of his or her current problems. You also work with the person in an exploratory, mutual fashion to find out what results he or she needs, and to determine how you can help to provide them. The focus is on the customer's Concept, not on your product or service, and your questioning should be designed to elicit information about that Concept. Typical Concept/Joint Venture questions address the broad picture, not details: "If you could wave a magic wand here, Sarah, what would this organization look like?" Or: "Could you fill me in on your current quality control difficulties?"

Because it's essential to make the Concept Sale first, and because Joint Venture conversation with a customer is more likely to get you information about Concept than any amount of Unilateral "telling," this first quadrant is usually an appropriate one to aim for at the beginning of a call, if for no other reason than to confirm your understanding of his or her Concept. This is crucial when you don't know the customer well—for example, on an initial prospecting call—or when you're unsure of his or her interests and concerns. It's also appropriate to work toward the Concept/Joint Venture format when-ever an information gap surfaces in the context of a sales call interview. Since everything in Conceptual Selling begins and ends with the client's Concept, and since you can only understand that Concept by Joint Venture explo-ration, it's advisable to spend some time in the Concept/

Joint Venture quadrant on every sales call to every customer.

But you don't *always* want to be there.

Quadrant 2: Product/Joint Venture

When you're making a Product Sale in a Joint Venture way, you definitely shift the focus toward what *you* have to sell, but you do so in a way that still invites maximum participation from the prospective buyer. By both Getting Information regarding the client's specific product needs, and Giving Information designed to highlight your Unique Strengths, you are able to tell exactly what your product does in relationship to what he or she is trying to accomplish.

Questioning in the Product/Joint Venture quadrant would focus on the product itself, but seek to determine how the product ties in with the customer's stated needs. "If you could get only one feature with this type of unit, Mark, which one would you prefer it to be?" Or: "Do you feel comfortable with our spectrum scanning capability as a way of addressing your QC problem?" In making the Product Sale in a Joint Venture way, you definitely move in the direction of nuts and bolts, but you are constantly checking—discussing, exploring, learning—to be sure that every nut and bolt you're describing can provide a match to what the client really needs.

Notice that, when you're in this quadrant, it's assumed that you have *already made headway on the Concept Sale.* To reiterate one of the fundamental lessons of Conceptual Selling, *the Concept Sale always comes first.* Even if you're toward the end of a drawn-out selling cycle, it's not appropriate to begin a sales call by pitching the product. The ideal pattern is to cover the Concept/Joint Venture quadrant up front, and then move to the Product/Joint Venture quadrant so you can discuss in more detail how your particular Unique Strengths can address the customer's particular problem.

Quadrant 3: Concept/Unilateral

In the third quadrant, the salesperson makes the Concept Sale, but in a Unilateral way. That is, the focus of attention is on what the customer thinks the product or service will be able to do, but the bulk of the talking is done by the seller.

We realize this may sound self-contradictory, since we have continually emphasized the importance of listening and minimized the value of simply telling. But, as we pointed out in Chapter 9, that doesn't mean it's *never* appropriate for a seller to be doing the talking. As long as you don't *monopolize* a sales call interview, and as long as you remain alert to your customer's responses, there are situations where it is highly appropriate for you to be telling him or her about Concept.

Now, since the Concept is by definition something that's in the prospective buyer's mind, not yours, we don't mean you should be telling about *his or her* Concept. You never use Unilateral selling to tell a customer what to think. But you can use this method effectively to describe how *other* buyers, with similar Concepts, have benefited from your company's solutions. Say the issue concerning a given prospect is assembly line quality control. If you've addressed such a problem successfully in the past with another company's assembly line, then it's entirely appropriate to tell the prospect that directly. "One of our Bay City clients had a similar problem two months ago; this is what he wanted to accomplish." Or: "Let me describe the results we achieved for the other manufacturers we've worked with."

There's a possibility of fuzziness here on both your part *and* the customer's. On the one hand you're telling the client about what you've already been able to accomplish; in a sense that's a type of Product Sale, because you're focussing on your own company's solutions. On the other hand, you're relating those solutions to what you believe to be his or her real needs; in that sense you're definitely making a Concept Sale. The terminology is less important here than remembering what it is you're trying to do. In the Concept/Unilateral quadrant, you're doing the talking, but you are constantly checking, with questions, that what you're saying relates to his Concept. If you've already clearly identified the Concept, there really isn't anything wrong with running through a "show and tell" session. At some point in many sales calls, that may be exactly what the customer wants or needs to hear.

The danger is in slipping prematurely from this tricky third quadrant into the seemingly less tricky fourth quadrant, the one we call Product/Unilateral.

Quadrant 4: Product/Unilateral

When you make a Product Sale in a Unilateral fashion, you're falling back on the supposedly time-tested seller's basic tactic, which is to tell everything he knows about the product or service, so he dazzles the prospect into buying. When you make a Product/Unilateral pitch, you drag out everything you've ever learned about the levers and buttons, capacity and horsepower, safety checks and warranties and service specs. Whether you're selling airplane parts or banking services or answering machines, the bottom line message is the same: "Let me plug this baby in and show you how great it runs."

We've already described at length how limiting and dangerous it can be to rely on this kind of Product Pitch philosophy, and in fact the entire thrust of Conceptual Selling works against this "dog and pony show" approach. To highlight the basic point we made about this method in Chapter 2, the product-oriented approach is only effective *when a match has already been determined* between the product and the customer's real needs. Many salespeople never make that prior determination, and so they end up pitching their great product to people who don't have even a remote chance of wanting or needing it.

This is not to say that it's *never* appropriate to find yourself in the Product/Unilateral quadrant. Making the

Product Sale unilaterally may be helpful to the client in generating Divergent thinking, or in selecting a best choice through Convergent thinking. Certainly it can help you as a seller to place emphasis on your Unique Strengths. And of course if a prospect has asked for a demonstration or fuller description—if he in effect says "Show me the bells and whistles now"—you may want to consider doing so. Every salesperson loves to talk about his product, and when a customer asks you, "Push this button for me," the natural tendency is to push them all. Sometimes that's what's required.

But there's a danger in relying on a Product/Unilateral approach, even when the client has asked for it. We can explain why by telling a story on ourselves.

The Fourth Quadrant Trap

Years ago, when we had just started our business, we were asked to give a presentation to a large pharmaceutical company. There was good potential money involved, so we were there bright and early, raring to go. When we walked into the presentation room, we found a group of ten executives, only three of whom we had met, waiting for us to begin. The vice-president for sales, who had invited us in to make the presentation, introduced us to the group and then said, "OK, why don't you tell us what you do?"

With that invitation to "hit it," we launched into the greatest product spiel of our careers. For twenty-five minutes they sat enraptured as we described all our programs in infinite detail, explained how every one of them was perfect for their type of business, and gave them a slide show that made Hollywood look like Podunk. The Music Man himself would have been proud: we were the Bobbsey Twins on Broadway, to the hilt.

Well, not only did we not make the sale, but we weren't even invited back for a second chance. Our great floor show bombed completely—and that got us thinking about what we had done wrong. We know now that we had made at least two major blunders.

First, we didn't find out where we were. The *first* thing we should have said after being introduced was, "We've only met Don and Jane and Arnie. Could we find out who you all are, so we can get an idea of what might interest you in our programs?" Then we should have sat back and practiced a lot of Golden Silence while we found out why the ten of them were there—and, therefore, why *we* were there. By jumping head first into the presentation before we knew anything about the audience, we had simply set ourselves up. Instead of being able to tailor a presentation to the individual interests of *this* group, we *forced* ourselves into a Unilateral dog and pony show that may have had little or nothing to do with the individual interests of our listeners. So we were shooting in the dark—and wound up shooting ourselves in the foot.

Second, we ignored the Concept Sale entirely, and concentrated on pitching our product. We figured at the time that this was an acceptable tactical approach because, after all, it was what the client had asked for. But going along with that seemingly reasonable request proved to be a major blunder. It forced us into the Product/Unilateral quadrant and kept us trapped there throughout the whole sales call. The outcome was entirely one-sided. The pharmaceutical managers learned more than they ever wanted to know about our operation, but we learned nothing about them—nothing about their current needs, their problems, their reasons for calling us—that we hadn't known before we got there. When you go through an entire presentation without finding out anything new about the client, what you get is exactly what we got, and what we deserved to get: nothing.

We learned some valuable lessons from that experience, which we have since incorporated into all our programs:

1. You should *never, absolutely* NEVER, give a dog and pony presentation to a group whose members you don't know. If there's a surprise guest in your

audience, find out before you start who he or she
is—and why he or she wants to listen to you.

2. Even if you're only speaking to one individual,
   don't *start* with a product pitch. Find out early in
   each sales call interview what the *current* situation
   is regarding his Concept, and move to the Product
   Sale only when the client is ready to hear it.

3. Even when you're convinced that he or she is ready
   for the Product Sale, keep on *testing* that assess-
   ment by asking questions: "Is this what we should
   be discussing?" or "Am I addressing your concerns?"

4. When you find yourself trapped in the Product/Un-
   ilateral quadrant, *stop* and ask for *feedback* from
   the client. Even when you're asked to make a
   product pitch, involve the customer in the discussion by moving it from a Unilateral to a Joint
   Venture presentation method, and by keeping the
   presentation tied to the client's Concept.

We don't say that any of this is necessarily going to be easy.
The traditions of selling are tenacious, and there are plenty
of face-to-face situations where the customer seems to
want you to keep talking, seems to want you to push the
bells and whistles, even though the match between product
and Concept has not yet been identified. You've got to be
attentive to those situations, and strive constantly to redirect the discussion so that it puts both you and the client
where you mutually need to be at any given moment.

There's no way of saying exactly where you should be at
a given moment in a call, or of saying when you're in
danger of being caught in the fourth-quadrant trap. But
as a general guideline, we'd say that *four or five minutes* is
the maximum amount of time you should allow yourself
to pitch product without moving from Unilateral to Joint
Venture: that is, without asking for the customer's input.
If you've been talking for six or seven minutes without
getting any feedback, you're already trapped, and may not
know it.

The feedback may be a precisely worded question that asks you to expand on a certain area, or it may be simply a nod of understanding. Whatever it is, what you want is some indication that the client is *involved* in the call—that he considers it *his* call too—and that he's not expecting you to carry the ball by yourself. Remember, Win-Win says you and the client *share* responsibility for how the buy/sell process moves forward. This means that you don't simply "follow orders" when someone says "Give me a thirty-minute demo next Friday." Instead, you strive throughout the presentation to make it truly a *joint* venture.

You make the choices over how you want a sales call to evolve by thinking through in advance which quadrant of the Planning Matrix you should be in and how, if it becomes necessary during the call, you can move comfortably from one quadrant to another. We'll give you the opportunity to see this in practical terms now.

Personal Workshop: The Planning Matrix

You should work here with an account that is somewhere in the middle of the selling process: that is, one where you have already made at least one call on the client, and where you'll be making another one soon. Write the heading "Planning Matrix" at the top of a notebook page, and give yourself about ten or fifteen minutes.

Step 1: Identify the last quadrant. Think of the last call you made on this customer. Where were you positioned at the end of that call? Or, alternatively, which of the four Planning Matrix quadrants did you spend *most* of your time in on that call? (Ask yourself too, where you *should* have been.) To determine your most recent Matrix position, you might want to use these guidelines:

  • If you spent most of your time asking questions and together discussing options to determine the customer's Concept, you were probably in the Concept/Joint Venture quadrant.

- If you spent most of your time showing how your product or service would be likely to relieve his or her problem, you were in the Product/Joint Venture quadrant.

- If you spent most of your time discussing ways in which your other clients have solved problems similar to his or hers, you were in the Concept/Unilateral quadrant.

- If you spent most of your time telling how your product or service works, you were in the Product/Unilateral quadrant.

Under the heading, write down "Last Call," and next to it the name of the quadrant (or quadrants) where you spent most of your time. You're defining your current or latest position, so you can more realistically plan where you want to go next.

Step 2: Where is the client now? Now think about where the client was at the end of that same sales call, by asking yourself:

- What is this person's current solution image regarding the problem or urgency he or she is facing?

- What is his or her current understanding of my product or service as it relates to that solution image?

- What kind of information does he or she now have regarding the relation of my product or service to the problem?

- What kind of information does he or she still need in order to make a decision in my favor?

We realize we're asking you to speculate here on what's in your customer's mind. There are no right answers here. Our purpose in asking you to think about where your customer now stands is to help you focus on those areas where your information about the client's thinking is still deficient. If you don't know the answers to these questions, write *that* down in your notebook.

Step 3: Plan the next call. Once you've thought about where both you and your prospective buyer were at the end of the previous meeting, sketch out a game plan for the upcoming meeting. Remember that you can make a conscious *choice* about which quadrant of the Matrix you are in. So decide which quadrant or quadrants you should be in with this client the next time you meet so that, at the end of that call, both of you will be closer to a Win-Win conclusion than you are at the present time. Refer to the guidelines we gave in Step 1 of this Workshop, and write down the quadrant(s) you need to cover with this customer, in order to keep the information flow positive, and to heighten the likelihood of a quality sale.

Step 4: How will you manage the call? Finally, you should give some thought to *how,* specifically, you will cover the necessary quadrants. The way we suggest that you plan this is to take each of the necessary quadrants in turn and write down two or three good questions that you need to ask the client when you are selling in that quadrant.

For example, suppose you've been running down product specs for this customer at such a rapid pace that you're not entirely sure at this point that he understands the relevance of those specs to his organization. You want to move in the next sales call from a Product/Unilateral approach to a Product/Joint Venture approach. In this situation you might write down the question: "If we could provide these features, what impact would that have on your down-time problem?" Whatever questions you write down, be sure it is clear in your mind how each one will keep you where you want to be or move you from one of the four Matrix quadrants to the quadrant where you want to go.

Be sure, too, that whatever questions you devise will help you manage the call in a productive, Win-Win fashion. This is really the whole point of using the Matrix. We say you should *manage* your sales calls, not command or dominate or push them. Good sales call management, like good management of any kind, means being constantly attentive to the needs of all parties involved, so that "joint ownership" is sustained and so that you and each of your customers can come to the end of the selling cycle with a complete understanding of the route you have taken to get there, and why.

Again it comes back to the Concept. Whatever time you intend to spend in a given quadrant on a sales call, and no matter what questions you draft to get you from one quadrant to another, the fundamental thing to remember is that, on any Win-Win selling venture, the customer is encouraged to buy for reasons that make sense to *him or her.* By asking you to use the Planning Matrix as a way of "rehearsing" your next sales call, we're really saying not only that you should figure out where *you* want to be, but also that you should manage the call so your prospective buyer is positioned *with you* in the quadrant(s) where he or she can go through the decision-making process most efficiently. The ultimate reason that you want to prepare any sales call in advance is so that, at the end of that upcoming call, no matter where you are in the Planning Matrix, you and your customer will both be moving toward a long-term Win-Win outcome.

GETTING STARTED: THREE PREREQUISITES FOR THE SALES CALL

▲

▸ 11 ◂
CREDIBILITY

Up to this point we've been discussing tactical skills you can use when you're actually face to face with a client. But what about those situations where getting face to face is itself a major tactical problem? What about the guy who simply won't give you an appointment? Or the "hot tip" prospect who's a complete blank to you, so that you wouldn't know where to begin even if you could get to meet him. Does Conceptual Selling have anything to say about the salesman's ancient dilemma: not being able to get that first foot in the door?

Absolutely. We realize that the best tactical skills in the world will still be useless useless you can first open the door. So in this Part of the book, "Getting Started," we're going to focus on tactical planning that you can do in advance of your sales calls, to make certain that you do get in, and that you're properly positioned once you get there.

This pre-call tactical planning hinges on what we call the

three prerequisites for every sales call—elements that you have to have covered before you can even think about Getting Started. The first of these three prerequisites is Credibility.

The Importance of Credibility

Remember the old Richard Nixon poster with the caption "Would you buy a used car from this man?" It appeared some months before his resignation, and it made the beleagured president look like the protypically devious used car dealer. The implication was that "Tricky Dick" was no more to be trusted than Slippery Sam.

Whether or not this characterization of President Nixon was fair, the photograph did make a good point about selling. If you can't convince your potential buyers that you can be *trusted,* you're no better off than the lemon peddler whose income is based on deceit. In all sound selling—in all selling where long-term success is important—the credibility of the salesperson is a basic.

Generally speaking, we've found that there are five basic reasons that a potential buyer will refuse to agree to a sale.

1. There's *no need* for the purchase—no clear fit between the product or service and the buyer's wants.

2. There's *no money*—or not enough money in the budget, or no way to get it allocated—to make the particular purchase desirable.

3. There's *no desire* on the potential buyer's part to make the change that the sale would represent.

4. There's *no urgency* to make that change at this particular time.

5. There's *no trust*—no basis for the buyer to believe that the seller is concerned with both their interests.

Any combination of these elements can prove to be the undoing of a potential sale. But one of them stands out.

In our experience with thousands of selling situations, we've found that the last item, lack of trust, kills more sales than the other four reasons combined. The implication for the professional seller is dramatic. No matter what else you do well, if you don't have credibility with your customers, the rest of it will not be worth a damn. Almost nobody buys from a person he doesn't believe can be trusted.

There are occasional exceptions. If you are the *only* available supplier for a given product or service and the buyer is desperate to have it—in other words, if he thinks there's no alternative—then you can make a no-credibility or low-credibility sale. You can also trick some inattentive or impulsive buyers into trusting you temporarily when common sense says they should not. But such situations are extremely rare. And *you cannot build a business* on this basis. If you want to succeed in Win-Win selling— that is, if you want to develop satisfied customers, great referrals, repeat business, and enduring relationships— then you've *got* to have credibility.

Elements of Credibility

Different people will trust you for different reasons. Therefore, it's useful to understand the elements of Credibility. There may be dozens of these elements operating in any given selling situation, but we can break them down into four basic areas. These areas relate to your *experience,* your *knowledge,* the way you *present* yourself, and your *associations.*

1. Your experience. One of the first things a potential customer wants to know about you as a seller is your experience in your current business or a related one. Twenty-year veterans automatically have more credibility than the sales reps who pulled in their first commissions last month. And the more closely related your past work has been to the potential *client's* type of business, the more reliable you will look to him or her.

But it's quality, not quantity, that really counts. What your potential customers are looking for is not just twenty years of steady employment, but a *track record* that says you can deliver. Even if you're the new kid on the block, you can earn credibility with customers if you've accomplished something solid for them, or for someone with problems similar to theirs. Remember that credibility means you're *believable*. If you've come through for Mr. Harris with exactly the performance-improvement figures you promised, he knows you can do what you say. That's the kind of experience that counts. If you've been having that kind of experience—delivering what you've promised—for twenty years, so much the better.

2. Your knowledge. Even if you haven't yet delivered solid results to Mr. Harris, you may still earn his trust through your knowledge. Your educational background, your technical expertise, your demonstrated ability to understand his areas of expertise and responsibility—all these can be elements of credibility. Establishing trust through what you *know* is not quite as reliable as establishing it through what you've *done,* but it can be a pretty good second, *if* what you know eventually helps your client to accomplish something that he or she wants done.

That can be a big if, of course. There's nothing wrong with showing off your knowledge. But be wary of *simply* flashing the Stanford degree or quoting from the technical journals. Your knowledge by itself can set up a preliminary credibility. If you want to make it permanent, you've got to prove it—that is, to demonstrate the value of your particular expertise to the client's interests and needs.

3. Presentation. By "presentation" here, we mean the manner in which you present *yourself,* not your product or service, to the customer or prospect. Among the "softer" but still very important elements of credibility can be your personal appearance, your language and patterns of speech, your personality and demeanor, and your general level of professional courtesy. The way you look and sound to the customer, in other words, can go a long way toward getting him to trust you.

But appearance can be both misleading and overdone, and we don't mean to give the impression that credibility can be earned just by looking good. You can devour every "dress for success" and "business etiquette" manual on the market and still strike out with certain clients because they don't believe you're *more* than your clothes. Other things being equal, the person who presents himself in a clean, articulate, professional manner is going to earn greater credibility than the guy in the green suit who speaks in grunts. But your appearance, like your knowledge, just gets you started: it says to your customers that you are savvy enough to play in their league. Once you're in, you've got to show you can perform.

There is one aspect of the way you present yourself, however, that can be an extremely important element on its own. We've mentioned "professionalism" as an aspect of appearance. It's also an aspect of the selling *method* that we've defined as Joint Venture selling. The salesperson who shows up on time for the appointment, who is organized in presentation, and who listens attentively to what the prospective customer has to say is demonstrating more than mere "etiquette." He or she is showing that concern for the other person that defines good selling *and* good manners. When this method becomes an integral part of the way you deal with individual clients, and is not merely a slick, polite facade, it can be invaluable in developing a customer's trust.

4. Your associations. Finally, your personal and business associations. Mr. Harris may not know you from Adam. But if he knows your company, if he knows about you from one of your other customers, or if he knows about you from friends he trusts, you have a better chance than Adam would of getting him to trust you up front.

Associations of this order will seldom get you past that initial trust level, and we are certainly not suggesting that you can rely on "connections" to build credibility. We believe firmly that the days of relationship selling—of "Who you know" and the old boy network and the old school tie—are numbered; that kind of selling, by itself, is just not conducive to Win-Win outcomes. But, like your knowledge and like your presentation "manners," your relevant business and personal connections can have a good introductory effect: they can set up a temporary trust in situations where you otherwise wouldn't have it.

The emphasis here is on "temporary." As hard as it can be sometimes to gain credibility with your customers, it's extremely easy to lose it, unless you keep earning it, every time. For this reason, credibility has to be *checked* constantly, to be sure it is not being eroded.

We mean checked on *every* sales call, and as frequently on each call as it's appropriate. *The sales call where you assume you have credibility is the sales call on which you will lose it.* So we urge you to perform an ongoing checking procedure, with every account and every individual you deal with, that begins at the very first sales call and continues throughout the selling cycle.

The initial step in this ongoing checking procedure is to be able to determine when you do, and when you don't, have credibility with an individual client.

How to Tell if You Have Credibility

You're sitting across a desk from an important Buying Influence, and you've determined that you can probably solve his problem. But you've never done business with this person before, so there's no history of mutual trust. Or it's been six months, or six weeks, since you last met with him, and you're not certain he *still* trusts you. What you need are face-to-face clues to your *current* credibility with this person.

We call such clues the "symptoms" of having, or not having, credibility. They're outlined in the boxes below. As these symptoms suggest, there is a direct and clear relationship between credibility and customer "ownership." When a prospective buyer *believes* in you—when he's convinced you can be trusted—he naturally becomes more actively involved in the sales call interview than if

HOW TO TELL WHEN **DON'T** HAVE CREDIBILITY

- Negative body language:
  - (a) folds arms in front
  - (b) fidgets
  - (c) arms behind head, leaning back
  - (d) yawning
- Allows interruptions
- Your gut is churning
- Issues during conversation center around power/control

HOW TO TELL WHEN **DO** HAVE CREDIBILITY

- Positive body language:
  - (a) nods in agreement
  - (b) gives examples
  - (c) smiles and/or throws in humor
- Does not allow interruptions (e.g., "Hold my calls.")
- Asks questions that are on the mark, not about your credentials/ credibility
- Discussion centers on what the customer is trying to accomplish

he sees you as a threat or an unknown quantity. When you have credibility, your client is a "partner" in the interview: she asks pertinent questions regarding what you're trying to do, volunteers information that will help you to move the sale forward, and gives you her undivided attention because she feels involved in something that she "owns."

When you lack credibility, just the opposite happens. When the buyer is not convinced you can be trusted, he clams up or becomes antagonistic. He bombards you with questions *about* your credibility rather than about your possible solution to his problems. Rather than becoming a partner with you in the buy/sell process, he becomes an anti-sponsor instead, expending all of his energy trying to find reasons that your proposals won't work.

Because credibility has such a decisive effect on the way a prospective buyer is likely to interact with you face to face, it's essential to be attentive to the above signals from the first moments of a sales call. The quicker you spot the signals, the quicker you can shift tactical gears where necessary, and begin asking questions and managing the call so that you get the credibility you need.

But how do you do that? How do you "get" credibility if you don't already have it?

"Getting" Credibility

There's a three-part answer to that question, but we have to point out at the beginning that in a sense this is a trick question. Nobody ever really "gets" credibility once and for all. The trust that you need from your customers is something that you develop over time, and something that has to be reestablished every time you meet face to face. That's why it's more accurate to say that the Conceptual salesperson *gains* credibility in an ongoing process, rather than nailing it down for all time. Credibility is as fragile as it is valuable. Unless you pay constant attention to gaining and regaining it on every call, you can easily find yourself *assuming* a client's trust when it's long since flown the coop.

There are three basic ways to gain credibility. It can be *earned* by you personally, it can be *transferred* to you by somebody else, or it can be established by *reputation*. These three ways are highlighted in the box.

THREE WAYS TO GET CREDIBILITY

1. IT'S BEEN EARNED BY YOU

The Buying Influence has won with you as a joint venture partner In the past

2. IT'S BEEN TRANSFERRED

Credibility was transferred by a third party reference.
It's never as high as when earned

3. IT'S BEEN ESTABLISHED BY REPUTATION

If you represent a product or company that's highly regarded, you have more credibility than an unknown

---

1. Credibility earned. By far the *best* way to get credibility is to earn it yourself, with each Buying Influence. As we mentioned above in our discussion of the elements of Credibility, "results delivered" is a chief component of this selling prerequisite. If you've already had a successful Joint Venture sale with Mr. Williams in the past, he knows you care about his self-interest as well as your own—and a buyer who knows that is going to be willing to do business with you again. When you've delivered once to a customer, you're like the carpenter we mentioned in the chapter on Joint Venture selling: your performance is "money in the bank" to the client, and he's going to be much more eager to draw on that "money" in the future than to run to a rival seller from whom he may, or may not, get the same satisfaction.

2. Credibility transferred. Sometimes it's useful to think of credibility as an equivalent to credit at the bank. The best of all possible scenarios, as we've just described, is for you to earn the credit rating yourself, with the "reserve" of your own past performance. But, just as you can sometimes get bank credit by having someone else co-sign a loan, so too you can gain temporary credibility on the strength of someone else's recommendation—whether it's in the form of an introduction, a letter, or a simple phone call. If you have such an entree to the buyer from a respected colleague, a business associate, a past satisfied customer, or a friend whom the buyer trusts, then that person's earned credibility can be transferred to you. It will never be as high or as solid as credibility that you earn on your own merits, but it will still be "credit" you can draw on—a case of "credibility by association."

3. Credibility by reputation. Gaining trust because of reputation is another type of credibility by association. It's possible to gain temporary credibility if your company, or the product you represent, has its own good track record with your prospective client. Up to a point, the Hewlett-Packard or BMW or Kimberly-Clark salesperson has a built-in credibility with new accounts—a "credit rating" that a new kid on the block can't even begin to approach. But this works only up to a point—and, again, the credibility of an unknown representative for a major name firm is still never going to be as good as that of a salesperson for a smaller supplier who has already proved his or her value to the Buying Influence.

But no matter which of the three ways you use to get it in the first place, in the end *all credibility has to be earned.* Gaining credibility by association, like getting a bank loan on somebody else's recommendation, is at best a temporary expedient—what the new player usually has to do when he or she has not established a personal credibility history. Buyers, like banks, will take a chance on you if you come backed by the best. But they will not take a chance a second time, *no matter how glowing your references,* unless you prove your personal reliability with results.

Some of this "proving" can only come well after the sale has been made. But some of it can come along the way—in the face-to-face selling situations that together make up the selling process. You can, and indeed must, earn credibility as you go, in each and every face-to-face encounter. Here are some guidelines for doing this.

Earning Credibility: Guidelines

1. Ask precise questions. The more focussed and specific your questioning, the more it will be clear to the client that you have thought enough about your meeting with him or her to have done your homework. Vague, wondering discussions around the topic hinder the salesperson's credibility. Since the client's time is just as valuable as yours is, save both of you some aggravation by drafting precise questions in advance of your meeting. Doing this not only impresses the client with your preparation; it also makes it much easier for you to get the specific information you need to move a Joint Venture selling process forward.

This guideline may seem to be in contradiction to our advice in Chapter 4 that you should ask your customer open, exploratory questions. It's not really a contradiction. Yes, you should give your clients plenty of opportunity to expand on a cloudy point whenever the need arises. But make sure they understand precisely what it is you're asking for. "Tell me more about your operation here" is too diffuse to be of specific benefit. If you want to develop credibility, ask instead, "Can you fill me in on the details of the cost-control operation now in place?"

2. Listen intently. Demonstrate to the client that you're actively listening, with the appropriate body language and supportive responses. The purpose here is twofold. One, intent listening helps you to understand the Concept better—which is the bedrock of everything you do in Conceptual Selling. Two, it shows that you're concerned with *his or her* needs—with what he or she thinks and feels about the situation. Showing a real interest in what prospective customers are saying is one of the simplest of all methods for getting them to listen to *you.* And when the two of you are listening to each other, you've got fluid information exchange and mutual trust.

3. Be yourself. Maybe it sounds like a cliche, but it's good advice nonetheless. In Conceptual Selling, and especially in establishing credibility, the last thing you should do is play a role. Any role. In our combined fifty years of selling we have found it to be invariably true that salespeople who put on phony fronts—all the gleaming teeth and hand-pumping and soulful looks of mock concern—soon come off looking like fools. To today's customers, such game playing is increasingly transparent. Besides, if you've got a good product or service and you're honestly looking for a match to the client's needs, you don't need this buck-dancing to make the point. In earning a potential customer's trust, demonstrate straight out that you trust *yourself.*

4. Don't be a know-it-all. Don't give your prospect pat answers, and don't under *any* circumstances display the arrogance that says you know more than he or she does. Maybe you do know more. But that's irrelevant. In fact it's worse than irrelevant, because customers who get the message that you're condescending to them are never going to give you an order unless they have absolutely no other option. Millions of sales are lost every year by selling whizzes who try to establish their credibility by showing off how brilliant they are. That is one of the surest ways we know to *lose* your credibility on the spot.

We don't mean you should be Humble Harry. If your product knowledge is solid and extensive, and if you really do have superior insights about how a customer's problem might be solved, of course you should let him know that. It's the *way* you let him know it that's crucial. Credibility is never established by "wowing the customer." It's established by giving clear, comprehensive answers, and by giving them at the *client's* pace and level of understanding—not your own.

5. Stay Win-Win. Demonstrate to the prospective buyer that, even though you're not ignoring yourself, you also really care about *him or her* coming out ahead in this sale. This is particularly important when the prospect is negative or defensive. When a buyer is finding excuses to shoot you down, the natural tendencies are either to fight back—to play Win-Lose in response—or to play Lose-Win by being overly accommodating. If you want to earn credibility with a client, resist both those tendencies. Real credibility is only achieved in Win-Win scenarios. And there's nothing wrong with being blatantly clear about this with the buyer. If he's being "difficult" or "resistant," search for his Basic Issues; find out *why* he doesn't trust you; tell him, straight out, "Jim, I want us both to Win here, and I have a feeling that that's not clear to you. How could we make this situation become a Win for you?"

When you're faced with an antagonistic prospect, we also suggest the following:

- Ask for *specifics:* that is, defuse the general antagonism by focussing on the what, where, when, and how much of the situation;

- Make it clear, by means of precise questioning, that you're not aiming simply to overcome objections, but rather to gain a fuller *understanding* of what's happening;

- Hear the client out: don't interrupt or counterattack, but allow the customer to vent his or her feelings, until the anger runs out.

Sometimes, of course, the anger won't run out, and in these cases—as we discussed in Chapter 8—you just *can't* get to Win-Win. But those situations are rare. Most times, waiting out the antagonism is a necessary part of gaining trust. And you don't have to be a patsy to pull this off. If you can show by statement and example that you want both yourself *and* your client to Win, your chances for gaining credibility are high.

6. *Remember that you have to produce.* You will only get credibility for sure after you have *earned* it. You get long-term trust from a customer only by delivering the results he or she needs—by producing the mutual Wins that underlie all real credibility.

7. *Practice Joint Venture selling.* This means beginning with the Cognition phase of the thinking process, so you can understand and address the real reasons behind a customer's resistance, and then moving logically to Divergent, and then Convergent, thinking.

We summarize these guidelines in the box.

HOW TO EARN CREDIBILITY

- Ask precise questions

- Listen intently

- Be yourself

- Don't come across as a know-it-all, no pat answers, no arrogance

- Demonstrate that you really care; stay WIN-WIN, especially in light of Win-Lose behavior on Buyer's part

- Remember: Will get it **for sure** only when you've produced

- Practice joint venture selling

Personal Workshop: Credibility

To see how credibility has been a factor in your own selling situations, we'd like you to write the heading "Credibility" at the top of a notebook page, and then select *two* sales calls from the recent past: one in which you *did* have credibility (that is, were clearly trusted) by the client, and one in which you did *not* have credibility. Then take fifteen minutes to review specific elements of these two calls.

Step 1: List symptoms of credibility. Working first with the call where you did have credibility, write down the name of the account and the name of the Buying Influences you met with. Then list the symptoms that you noticed on the call that indicated to you that this Buying Influence trusted you. You can refer to the list of symptoms that we gave on page 223 of this chapter, and briefly jot down your recollections. "Jeffries had all his calls held while I was there," for example. Or: "She asked specific questions about our solution." The point here is for you to make visible what we often take for granted: the clearly definable signals that a customer believes you can be trusted.

Step 2: How did you earn credibility? Now, for the same sales call, identify *how* you came to be trusted by this particular Buying Influence. Remember that credibility is either *earned, transferred,* or based on your company's *reputation.* If you earned the client's trust, write down in a few words *how*: what results did you deliver that enabled her or him to Win in the past? If the credibility was transferred, write down the name of the person responsible. And if it was gained by reputation, write down those aspects of your company's track record—its Unique Strengths and/or history of performance—that made this potential buyer trust you.

Step 3: How did you build credibility? Now list the actions you took in the same sales call to build on and maintain your credibility. Refer to our "Earning Credibility" guidelines laid out earlier in the chapter, and write down short identifying comments to remind yourself of how you built trust. "Asked him very precise questions about quality control," for example, or "Let him know I wanted him to Win in spite of his rejection of original specs." What you're aiming for here is an overview of how the good sales call went, and what you did during it to maintain your trust position.

Step 4: List symptoms of "no credibility." Now move to the second sales call: the one where you *didn't* have credibility. Again, write down the name of the account and the name of the person(s) with whom you met. Then list the symptoms that made you convinced that this particular person did *not* trust you. Use the page 223 list again as a guide, and make your comments specific. "She fidgeted with her pen for half an hour." Or: "He constantly attacked my reliability: said we couldn't possibly perform as I said."

Step 5: What could I have done to gain trust? Now, for the same sales call, list actions that you could have taken to have turned the person's perception of you around. Refer to our "Earning Credibility" guidelines again, and pay particular attention to Item 5, where we explained how to earn credibility by staying Win-Win in a hostile situation. Perhaps "more specific questions" might have been a key, or "meeting objections in a calmer, less defensive manner." Whatever you write down, check that it is a potential action that would have verified *your eagerness to play Win-Win.* Because—to reiterate a point we made when we spoke about why people refuse Commitment—one of the central elements of getting a person to trust you is demonstrating that you don't want *him or her* to Lose, any more than you want yourself to.

Having reviewed your performance in these two sales calls, you should have a somewhat clearer notion of what it feels like—and what it means—both to have credibility and to lack it. We urge you to use that clearer understanding in managing every sales call in the future—in other words, in making our first selling prerequisite part of your tactical *planning* for every call.

But before you actually go into those calls, there is one

more observation to be made. It relates to the fact that credibility can be lost as well as gained. And one of the principal facets in the *maintenance* of any salesperson's credibility is that tricky commodity, timing.

Credibility and Timing

Everybody in sales has his or her favorite story about deals that fell through in spite of competent selling simply because "the timing was wrong." In selling, as in anything else, being in the right place at the right time is often a component of success, and being in the same right place at the wrong time can just as easily spell disaster.

We have no argument with the view that timing is critical to good selling. Where we differ from most "analysts" of the sales scene is in our conviction that you, the seller, can have far more *control* over timing than is usually imagined.

Most people tend to think of timing as something that just "happens" to them—and to think of themselves as the unwilling, passive victims of this "happening." Like the people who credit Lady Luck with their finding the dollar bill on the sidewalk, or who thank "fate" for the fact that they just missed the plane flight that crashed. That kind of reasoning may be valid when it comes to dollar bills or plane crashes, but it doesn't have anything to do with selling. Pointing to "bad timing" as the reason that a given sales call went badly is a cop-out. In Conceptual Selling, it's your job to *find out if the timing is right*, and to do that *each time you meet with a client.* If you don't do it every time, you're going to end up with a string of nonproductive meetings where you "just happened to hit him on a bad day." That isn't fate. It's bad planning.

The one way to avoid being the victim of bad timing, and to capitalize on good timing, is to be sensitive to the individual buy/sell situation from the beginning of the sales call. We'll give you two examples to illustrate this, one positive and one negative.

First, the negative example. Alex was an industrious and persistent salesman who, a few years ago, managed to set up an appointment with the CEO of a major trucking firm. It had taken him months to arrange the top-level meeting, and he prepared for it with great care. But when he walked into the CEO's office, he made one simple mistake. He failed to pick up on the fact that the man was nervous and distracted. Even though he had honored the meeting time, it was clear that his mind was somewhere else. Had Alex been sensitive to that fact, he would have asked if a different time would be better—and given himself the opportunity of making this important presentation when the CEO could give him better attention. Instead, Alex bulldogged his way through the call, and got nowhere. Later—too late to be useful—he found out that the CEO had been scheduled to undergo major surgery three days after their meeting. No wonder he had been distracted—and no wonder Alex had been ignored.

Now, maybe if he had allowed the preoccupied executive to reschedule, the eventual outcome would have been no better. But he would at least have had a fighting chance. As it was, by ignoring the signs of poor timing, Alex virtually ensured a bad call: as he told us after the fact, "I realized an hour after I left that the guy hadn't heard a word I said." That is a very common outcome of sales calls where, for reasons over which the seller has no control, the scheduled time is just wrong.

Here's the positive example. Kate is a top-level field rep for one of the big computer firms. She recently encountered a situation very similar to Alex's, but she handled it entirely differently. When *her* fidgety, obviously distracted potential customer started to look like his mind was in Tahiti, she stopped the interview cold. "Mr. Hoskins," she said, "it seems like you're preoccupied with something else. If this is a bad time for us to talk, maybe you'd like to reschedule the appointment."

Hoskins, Kate later told us, was "relieved, thankful, and impressed." "He said he appreciated my thoughtfulness in picking up on his distraction. It turned out he was due to run a seminar that afternoon on a new Management by Objectives training program, and he was having trouble understanding the material. Luckily, I knew that material, so I offered to give him a half-hour briefing on it in lieu of our scheduled interview. We didn't say two words about computers that day, but since then I've met with him four times, and his firm is my hottest account. We're solving their computer problems, of course, but what got him in my corner wasn't computers; it was just being sensitive to where he was—spotting the symptoms that my timing was off."

Testing the waters. What Kate did with her fidgety buyer illustrates more than mere "sensitivity." It illustrates the value, in every sales call, of "testing the waters" before you jump in. The credibility that Kate earned with her buyer was the direct result of such testing: before she got in over her head in the call, she tested where she was with a good question. In determining the rightness or wrongness of your timing, that is always a good model to follow.

We say that you should test the waters in this way as *early* in the sales call as possible. In fact, it's not out of place to *begin* most sales calls with a "timing question." Virtually every business call we make begins with an introductory confirmation that the timing for the call is all right. "Is this a good time for you to talk?" or "Am I interrupting anything right now?" or "May I have ten minutes now or would it be better for you if I called later?" By asking such a question—it's a special type of Confirmation Question—at the outset, you gain two immediate advantages:

1. You demonstrate by the courtesy of the question that you care about the client's needs and priorities. This signals the person that you are playing Win-Win—and instantly increases your credibility.
2. You give the client the opportunity to postpone or reschedule a call that is likely to end up as a Lose for you both, because one of you will not be really "there." Thus you save yourself, and the client, from wasting time.

The hidden point here is that your prospective customer has a set of priorities which may not be the same as yours. The best arranged sales call in the world can still be thrown off track because, since you made the appointment, your customer's needs have changed, or personal issues are occupying his attention, or any one of a thousand other things has happened to make the "right" timing wrong. Asking about timing up front lets you make the best use of your time by concentrating on those sales calls where you both have a good chance to Win.

The "courtesy" trap—and the reverse. Two "traps" you need to look out for. The first might be called the courtesy trap. It's what happens when a busy or preoccupied client, not wanting to offend you or foul up your schedule, goes ahead with a prearranged sales call even though the timing is wrong for him. Don't mistake courtesy like this for proper timing. If a buyer honors an appointment merely out of politeness, you stand a strong chance of making a presentation to someone who won't hear what you say. Therefore, even if Mr. Hoskins says, "Yeah, I guess this time is as good as any," if you have any suspicion that he's just "being nice" to you, give him a second option to back out. Be straight with him. "I appreciate that you're willing to go ahead at this time, Jim, but I think we'd get a lot more done if we could meet when it felt better for you. Are you sure you wouldn't prefer to reschedule?"

The second trap is the reverse of the first. It's mistaking a potential buyer's *current* uneasiness about meeting with you, or dealing with your proposal, with a *general* rejection of your business. If your proposal to Hoskins meets with nervousness, hostility or silence, it's not necessarily because he hates your company and everything you stand for. It may be simply that you hit him on a bad day. To find out whether he's reacting to you and your proposal, or merely to bad timing, follow the same course of action that you would when faced with the "courtesy trap": *ask* the necessary confirming questions.

When to Confirm and Reconfirm

We've said that checking your timing should be an ongoing procedure throughout the selling cycle. There are three times in particular when performing this check is important.

1. When you make, and confirm, the appointment. Nobody but a very disorganized person or a masochist will agree to meet you at a time that he knows is going to be bad for him or her. But people will agree to appointments that are set at "less than ideal" times. When you call to set up an appointment, make sure you get it as close to the prospect's "ideal time slot" as you possibly can—without, of course, fouling up your *own* schedule. If she agrees to Friday but seems uneasy about it, play it straight: "If there's a time for you that's better than Friday, tell me what the better time would be." If you typically confirm your appointments by telephoning a day or two in advance of the sales call, this "set up" call is another time when you should confirm the appropriateness of the timing. If you don't reconfirm your timing on such calls, it's very likely you will run into cases where a time slot that was great when you first made the appointment has in the meantime turned lousy.

2. At the beginning of the sales call. We've already stressed this earlier in the chapter, so we won't repeat ourselves here. One addition. It's often useful, when you confirm the appropriateness of your timing at the opening of a call, to set out the time *limits* also. "Is this still a convenient time for you to give me about half an hour?" If you don't confirm the parameters of the meeting in this way, you may find yourself just getting down to business when Hoskins cuts you off in midstream. If your appointment is for 3 P.M. and you expect to be with him until 4 P.M., state that clearly at the outset, so you won't be surprised by a 3:30 P.M. intruder.

3. Toward the end of the sales call. As said in the chapter on questioning, it is usually appropriate, before you end a sales call, to ask a Commitment Question—that is, a question designed to elicit from the customer a promise to *do* something to move the sale forward. You can tie in questions like this with questions about his or her timing. "Will you be able to show these specs to the committee by the 21st, Jan?" Or "We can begin the installation process in March. Will that be a good match to your schedule?" Asking timing questions like this helps to move the selling process forward by defining *future* timing requirements.

In short, by checking your timing throughout the selling process, you keep in constant touch with the client's inevitably changing priorities and needs. That does more than keep you alert to exactly where you are in the sales call, and in the selling process as a whole. By reminding the customer continually that you are concerned that the timing is right for *him or her,* you also enhance the Win-Win relationship, and thus reinforce your credibility.

· 12 ·

VALID BUSINESS REASON

The second prerequisite you need for each sales call is a reason to make the call in the first place. We don't mean *your* reason for wanting to make the call; we mean your potential *customer's* reason for wanting to see you. Any time an individual agrees to meet with you, he or she takes time out of a schedule that might have been spent on other priorities. Whenever you ask people to do that, they deserve to be told the reason why.

This sounds obvious enough, and yet most salespeople don't do it. Instead of giving their clients sound business reasons for spending time with them, they focus on nonproductive social calls and lunch dates. As a result, they run again and again into the professional seller's oldest difficulty: not being able to get a foot in the door.

Valid Business Reason: Key Ideas

A Valid Business Reason, as we define it, is something that gives the potential buyer a reason for wanting to spend some of his or her valuable time in meeting with you. It may reinforce your reasons for wanting to see the client, but it emphasizes his or her priorities, not yours. In general terms, a Valid Business Reason accomplishes two major purposes:

- First, it gives the potential customer *data* that he or she needs to understand exactly who you are and why you want to meet at this particular time.
- Second, it establishes a common *foundation* or departure point so that, when you do meet, you will be able to begin the questioning process most efficiently, by concentrating on the Concept Sale.

It should be clear, therefore, that a good Valid Business Reason—unlike the typical "social" reasons that salespeople often give for getting together—is extremely *precise*. It doesn't focus on the account in general, or your business in general, but on a specific upcoming sales call with an individual client. It defines why a particular customer or prospect should want to meet with *you* at this time—and for what particular *purpose*. For example, "I'd like to see you next week to discuss our new waste retrieval process because I believe we might help you reduce your scrap loss by about 15 percent."

His loss. His needs. The primary purpose of any good Valid Business Reason is to make the customer want to see you because it makes sense in terms of *his or her* business reality. But there are other purposes. We consider these the most important:

1. The Valid Business Reason precisely sets forth the *reason* for the sales call. When you use a Valid Business Reason as a way of getting in, there's no deception involved. The person knows clearly what you have in mind.

2. Stating a Valid Business Reason shows you have done some *preparation*: you've been thinking about his or her problems (or possible problems), and you've begun to do your homework toward solving them.

3. Setting out a Valid Business Reason minimizes your *calling time.* The Valid Business Reason is a kind of screening device that enables you to cut down on the number of calls you have to make, and to concentrate on those where there is a real chance for mutual success. We realize that, to those people who were trained to make as many calls as possible, this will sound heretical. But in Conceptual Selling you go for quality, not quantity. The *maximum* number of calls is not necessarily the *optimum* number, and we're showing you how to go for the optimum. Furthermore, stating a Valid Business Reason also eliminates wasted time once the call begins. When the client knows in advance why you're coming, you don't have to spend valuable time—either yours or his—defining the purpose of the meeting. You can get down to the business at hand immediately.

4. Stating a Valid Business Reason decodes, to the client, as "Time is valuable." In other words, it not only *saves* you both time; it lets him or her know that you consider it *important* to save this valuable time. To a potential customer whose time is always short (which means most people today), this puts you in an exceptionally good light. It says that you are both *courteous* and *efficient.* Even if the person is not interested in doing business with you at the current time, that perception may still help your future sales.

5. The Valid Business Reasons sets mutual *expectations* for the meeting. It lets clients know what you will be speaking about. But it also lets them know what you expect *them* to be *ready* to

talk about. If the client knows in advance why you're coming, he has time to double-check his own information, to clarify his understanding of his problem, to pull out the necessary data for you to see—so that, when you sit down with him, you both get what you expect.

6. Finally, stating the Valid Business Reason in advance gives the Buying Influence the *time* he or she needs to do just this kind of preparation. And it also gives him or her time to think out positions in advance. Remember that in Win-Win selling, both the buyer and the seller have a responsibility to participate in the sales call—to move the selling process forward so that it leads to mutual satisfaction. Your clients can only do that effectively if they understand *before* the call what will happen.

A summary of purposes appears on page 243. Let's move now to a fuller discussion of how to fulfill those purposes, by making sure that you have a Valid Business Reason on every call.

Valid Business Reason: Criteria

Before you can state your reasons for wanting to see anyone, you first have to determine, in your own mind, whether you really do have a Valid Business Reason for the meeting. You do that by focussing on five criteria. We outline them here in the form of questions that you should ask yourself well in advance of the prospective sales call.

1. *Will the client accept the reason I want to see him as having an impact on his Concept or "solution image"?* We assume, if you're committed to Win-Win selling and to the Joint Venture approach, that you intend to manage every sales call by relating your product or service to what the customer feels needs to get done. But it's not enough just to address your prospects' problems. They have to *know* that you're doing this. So, in stating a Valid Business Reason, make sure the client understands up front that his

PURPOSE

- Precisely sets forth the objective of the sales call.

- Shows you've been thinking (preparation).

- Minimizes calling time.

- Decodes as: "Time is valuable."

- Sets expectations for the meeting.

- Allows Buying Influence to think and prepare ahead of time

"solution image" is one of your primary concerns, and isn't just incidental to your making a sale.

2. *Does the Valid Business Reason I'm using tell the customer or prospect why he should place this call at the top of his priority list?* The issue here is urgency. Whenever you try to set up a sales call, you're competing with a hundred other priorities that the client may have: calls that your competition may want to set up, meetings within the buying organization, planes to catch, personal appointments—and on and on. Your Valid Business Reason must make the customer want to see you first, or at least soon. Therefore, reasons with the highest likelihood of getting you in will be those that focus on current, pressing business problems.

3. *Will this Valid Business Reason help him to make a decision, reinforce a decision he has already made, or give him data that will help in future decisions?* Potential buyers—especially those at high levels in major organizations—are constantly being asked to *decide,* and like most human beings they are often forced to decide on the basis of insufficient information. If your Valid Business Reason can help a client around this difficulty, and he knows it, he is very likely going to want to see you.

We've explained the three stages of the human decision-making process, and pointed out that the most fluid and productive sales calls permit the client to follow this process in the "ideal" sequence: that is, from Cognition to Divergent thinking to Convergent thinking. The same thing holds true even before the sales call begins, when you state your Valid Business Reason for making the appointment. The best Valid Business Reasons enhance the customer's sequential thinking about a problem the seller might address.

4. *Does the Valid Business Reason make it clear what's in the sales call for her or him?* The client already knows what's in the call for you, or he can figure it out easily enough: since you're trying to set up an appointment, he or she can safely assume that, somewhere down the line, you'll want an order sheet signed. But will there be any benefit to the client and his or her company in doing so? He's still in the dark about what matters the most to him. One function of a properly phrased Valid Business Reason is to get him out of the dark, by demonstrating that meeting you can help him Win.

This doesn't mean that you have to give the entire show away in stating your Valid Business Reason. Obviously, the real selling only begins when you're sitting down face to face with the client. But in order to get face to face at all, you have to show him he might *benefit* from the call.

5. *Is it clear that my Valid Business Reason relates to the customer's business, not just my own?* This is a subtly different point from the previous one. Naturally you want to meet your customers for reasons that will enhance *both* your business opportunities. But in stating a Valid Business Reason, it's the potential buyer's business that really counts—even at the temporary "expense" of your own. By helping your customers to Win in their *own* business, you're building credibility, a history of mutual success—and a foundation for future business.

Our five Valid Business Reason criteria are outlined here.

VALID BUSINESS REASON CRITERIA

- Will it be perceived as having impact on customer's Solution Image?

- Does it answer questions why should this call be at the top of customer's priority list?

- Will it help make a decision, reinforce decision or provide data?

- Is it clear what's in it for the Buying Influence (and the Buying Company) to see you?

- Is it related to **customer's** business (not necessarily your product)?

Beyond the "Cold Call"

Implicit in all these criteria is the assumption that, before you ever walk into your customer's or prospect's office, each time, you've already done some thinking about his business. In Conceptual Selling, there really isn't such a thing as a "cold call," because we urge all the professionals we work with to do tactical planning before every call—even the first visit on a new prospect. In fact, if you don't do this planning—if you don't give some thought to whom you'll be meeting, what his or her likely problems are, and how your product or service might relate to them—there's no way you can draft a Valid Business Reason at all. And you really will be selling "cold."

You don't have to know all the details of a potential customer's operation. Obviously, on a first call to a new prospect, you're going to know very little, and there's nothing wrong with that. But it's not an efficient use of anybody's time to set up appointments with people when you've done *no* preliminary research. It may be something as elementary as having read a newspaper article about the prospective client's industry which leads you to believe there's a potential match. Or you may have heard about a reorganization in the buying organization that could lead to new vendors (such as you) being considered. The type of information you have may be ultimately less important than the fact that you've thought enough about the prospect to be one step up on the cold caller.

Our research indicates conclusively that many sales calls are too general—too "preliminary" and unfocussed to be useful to either the buyer or the seller. Thinking about the specific client, and about his or her company, in advance is one way of bringing focus into the situation, so that when you go into the sales call, you know that you are *managing* and not gambling with your selling time.

Setting Appointment Expectations

There are three basic points in a selling cycle when the use of a Valid Business Reason can be valuable: at the time when you make the appointment, at the beginning of the meeting itself, and when you encounter "surprise guests" in a previously arranged sales call.

Using a Valid Business Reason to get an appointment in the first place is the most obvious use of a Valid Business Reason, and the place where the value of the tactic will probably be most obvious to the seller. But it's important to emphasize one thing. When you use a Valid Business Reason to gain entrance, it's necessary to *state the Valid Business Reason* clearly on the phone when you actually make the appointment, because, as we've already explained, it can clarify for both you and the client what is *expected to happen* in the call. Setting the stage in this way gives you an immediate feedback benefit: it *reduces your potential buyer's uncertainty level,* and thus makes it much easier for you to develop fluid communication, and achieve real progress.

In setting appointment expectations, we advise that you pay attention to the following guidelines:

- Clarify *your selling responsibilities* in the call. What are you going to be speaking about, which of the customer's areas of concern are you expected to address, and what specific information are you expected to bring her or him? The more of this you spell out on the phone, the less chance there will be that you will make a presentation he wasn't expecting, and/or didn't want, to hear.

- Clarify *his or her responsibilities.* This ties in with what we said about Commitment earlier in the book. In Joint Venture selling, you and the client *share* responsibility for moving the sales process forward. If on a previous call your client has promised to "comment on your proposal next time" or "get the Finance Department's response," be sure to verify that responsbilility on the phone.

- State the *purpose* of the meeting, in the form of a Valid Business Reason. Stating this when you make the appointment reconfirms your interest in the customer's needs, and also clarifies your mutual agenda. Since people's agendas are changing all the time, this brings clarity into a potentially uncertain situation.

- Identify the *people to be present.* The reason for identifying the players at the time of making the appointment is twofold. It allows the person on whom you're calling to make the necessary arrangements for getting everybody there at the right time; and it minimizes the chances that there will be either too many, or too few, people there when you arrive. If you're expecting to be talking to only one person, and in the meeting you're surrounded by six unknowns, that can throw off your timing, your credibility, and the entire momentum of the call. On the other hand, if two people are critical to the success of the meeting, and one of them doesn't get that message, you'll end up spending two meetings to do the work you could have done in one. Guard against these opposite traps by defining the "audience" on the phone.

- Itemize the *materials* needed. If to make your presentation properly you need a blackboard, an overhead projector, or a special room, be sure the client understands that when you set up the appointment. If it's his responsibility to provide those materials, make sure he understands that. If it's your responsibility, tell him that too, so he won't waste his valuable time hunting up a projector when you're bringing your own with you.

These guidelines are profiled on page 249. Just one more point. If you make an appointment well in advance, and you later call to confirm it, it's definitely not out of place to run through these guidelines *again*. It might sound like repetition, but that beats false assumptions every time.

Verifying the Meeting's Focus

It's also useful to state your Valid Business Reason again right at the start of the sales call meeting. The reasons for this are the same as those we just gave for stating a Valid Business Reason (and the other appointment guidelines) when you reconfirm an appointment. It's natural and easy to do this, by simply phrasing a Confirmation Question—which, as we've stressed before, is usually a good way to open a sales call in any case. There is no better or more logical opener than a confirmation of the purpose of the meeting: "We were going to address the circuitry problem this afternoon, correct?" Or: "Am I right in understanding, Jerry, that you wanted a rundown today of our service

APPOINTMENT EXPECTATIONS

- Valid Business Reason should be stated on phone when arranging appointment.

- Expectations should be set forth to reduce Buying Influence's uncertainty level.

- **Guidelines** for expectations:
  - (a) your responsibilities
  - (b) their responsibilities
  - (c) purpose
  - (d) people to be present
  - (e) materials needed (e.g., chart stand, blackboard, projector)

record in your industry?" Stating your reason for being there at the outset signals your listeners that you know exactly *what you're doing*—and invites them to confirm, before anyone's time gets wasted, that it's *what they still want done.*

Dealing with "Surprise Guests"

It's especially important to do this when you enter a meeting room and discover that you're not facing the person or persons you thought you'd be facing. We made a similar point with regard to Joint Venture selling, when we said that you should always find out who your listeners are *before* you start a presentation. One way of finding that out is to state your Valid Business Reason at the beginning so that the "audience" knows as well as you do that it's in the right place at the right time.

If you don't do this, you're asking for grief. An acquaintance of ours recently gave a presentation to a roomful of middle managers from a multinational corporation. He neglected to state the Valid Business Reason that had brought him there, and he was ten minutes into his spiel when a visibly confused manager in the front row got up from his seat, mumbled "This isn't my area at all, I must be at the wrong meeting," and left sheepishly. The manager felt lousy, his colleagues were distracted and embarrassed for him, and our friend had to spend valuable time regaining his own bearings and composure. "It threw my timing completely off," he told us. "I felt like a college professor who had been lecturing to a Greek class on Chemistry." And all of this confusion could have been avoided if he had stated the Valid Business Reason first.

Three Issues—and Our Responses

Virtually all of the professionals we work with see the value of having a Valid Business Reason on every call. But we do encounter occasional resistance, usually from people who were taught that "friendship" or "keeping in touch" can be an adequate reason to call on a client. Here's how we counter their objections.

Issue 1: "It can't be necessary on every call. There are still some calls where socializing is the only agenda, and where I don't really need a valid reason for meeting because I'm not doing business; I'm just keeping the fires warm."

Sure, there are scenarios like this. There are plenty of social situations where you just want to wine and dine a potential customer, for the simple reason that you like his or her company. *But you should not confuse these situations with sales calls.* In a real sales call, you are asking a potential business associate to give you his or her *professional time* so you can explore ways of benefiting each other. When you work together professionally in this way, no matter how close you are personally, you owe the person quality time in return. And the only way you can be sure of giving him quality time is to have a Valid Business Reason when you meet. Every time. If you don't, the best personal friend in the world is going to back off from doing business with you—he won't be able to afford not to. Remember that the classic case of the "socializing" salesman—the guy who didn't need a Valid Business Reason every time—was Willy Loman, the nice-guy loser in *Death of a Salesman*.

Issue 2: "*I don't want to come across as a hard-nose.* I don't want to be so rigid in insisting on the business side of the relationship that he thinks I don't care about him as a person. Miller-Heiman says I should seek ways to let all of my clients Win, personally. How can I do that if I never talk about anything but business?"

This issue also confuses the personal and professional aspects of a business relationship. If you're relaxing at the pool or on the golf course with Good Old Joe, fine: relax. But a sales call is a very special situation, with its own exacting requirements. Obviously, even in this exacting environment, you should avoid precipitous bluntness, as in statements like "Let's not waste each other's time" or "Hi, Joe, the purpose of this meeting is . . . " But this is a matter of style and of maintaining sensitivity to your individual clients. As we explained in our discussion of questioning, the pleasantries which open many sales calls are perfectly acceptable as ice-breakers. But don't kid yourself: they are *not part of the sales call proper.* When the two of you get down to business, that's exactly what you have to do: focus on your mutual business needs.

Far from being "inconsiderate" or "hard-nosed," defining a Valid Business Reason on every call is actually a *very* considerate way of doing business. It indicates to the potential buyer—whether you've known him twenty years or ten minutes—that you've given some thought to his current position, and that you're seeking ways to improve it.

Issue 3: "*I feel uncomfortable stating the reason out loud.* It seems too obvious, too direct, to come out blatantly and announce, 'We're meeting today for the following reason.'

And it seems almost insulting, as if the buyer can't figure that out for himself. I prefer to feel my way into the situation, rather than being so blunt."

Our response? Whenever you feel uncomfortable about stating the purpose of your meeting, it's a pretty clear sign that your "valid" reason is in some way inappropriate. Perhaps you've phrased it (to yourself or to the buyer) incorrectly; or perhaps you don't really understand, yourself, why the two of you are getting together. If the Valid Business Reason is correctly stated, it will *never* be "insulting" to the client—and it should never make you want to "feel your way." If you have some anxiety about saying out loud why you're there, reexamine what you feel to be the purpose of the meeting. You may find it helpful, in doing this, to rephrase the Valid Business Reason in the form of a Confirmation Question: "Am I correct in understanding that the purpose of this meeting is to . . . ?"

We've found that there are three basic scenarios possible when a seller is uneasy about stating a Valid Business Reason. Either a) he doesn't know the purpose of the meeting himself—in which case he's got no business being there. Or b) he's not sure that the customer's understanding of that purpose is the same as his, and he doesn't want to discover the discrepancy—in which case he's putting blinders on himself, and ruining his shot at a quality sale. Or c) he's afraid the buyer will jump down his throat for being "simple" and wasting his time. In this last scenario, the salesperson makes the implicit assumption that the customer is both *smarter* than he is, and so *impatient* that he cannot spare ten seconds to confirm why he's agreed to a meeting. If you meet a so-called "brilliant" ogre like this our advice is still the same. It's to stay Win-Win with the guy by stating the Valid Business Reason up front. If he wants to throw it back in your face, that should be evidence to you that he may not be willing to stay Win-Win. And that you may not belong in his office.

It all comes back to Win-Win. Clarifying your purpose with a Valid Business Reason is a straightforward and necessary tactic for enhancing clarity and good information flow. Any buyer who wants to play straight with you will welcome the opportunity of meeting with you on the basis of a stated Valid Business Reason. A person who rejects or mocks your stated purpose, or who thinks that the purpose is either "obvious" or "irrelevant"—that person is not going to bring you good business anyway. So why waste your time going after him?

The Long-Term Payback

In addition to the benefits of a Valid Business Reason that we've already described, there is one benefit that is so important and so unexpected that we need to highlight it specially. That benefit is the long-term payback you get in terms of *differentiation.*

We said in the chapter on Giving Information that customers decide by differentiating, and that it is one of your chief tasks in a sales call to help clients differentiate in your favor. The use of a Valid Business Reason is a perfect way for you to do that, for the simple reason that it is so rarely used. Most sales professionals still feel they have to manipulate their way into appointments by giving the client "social" or "nonthreatening" reasons for getting together. Like the pavement pounder who gets his foot in your door under the pretext that he's "taking a survey," or the corporate rep who pretends not to be interested in a client's business, and just wants to "take him to lunch." Against this kind of traditionally manipulative backdrop, the seller who announces a business interest up front, and who gives the client a Valid Business Reason for meeting—that seller stands way apart from the rest. He or she will be *remembered,* and *listened to,* as clearly differentiated from the competition.

One former Conceptual Selling participant makes the point well. "I can't tell you how many supposedly inaccessible people I've gotten in to see by stating a Valid Business Reason up front. The shock value of the tactic is terrific. People are so used to having sales reps try to weasel their way in, when I come out and say *why* I want to meet, it really clears the decks. Three or four clients have told me that nobody had ever done that with them before. So automatically I'm in a class by myself." *That's* differentiation. And it's credibility that you cannot buy, no matter how many lunch tabs you pick up.

Personal Workshop: Valid Business Reason

You can now perform a brief exercise to relate the concept of Valid Business Reason to your upcoming calls. Write the heading "Valid Business Reason" at the top of a notebook page. Then, for a call that you hope to make in the near future, but for which you haven't yet made an appointment, write down the name of the account, the name of the person you expect to meet, and what you hope to accomplish by meeting him. By "what you hope to accomplish" we mean here the *purpose,* as *you* see it, for the meeting.

Step 1: State your Valid Business Reason. You've just defined what you believe (or hope) to be the purpose of this upcoming meeting: you know why you want to meet this person. Now define a reason that *he or she* should want to meet *you.* Remember, for your reason to be a Valid Business Reason, it has to satisfy the client's requirements, not just yours. So review the Valid Business Reason criteria that we presented earlier, and ask yourself the following questions:

- What Valid Business Reason would have an impact—and be *perceived* as having an impact—on this customer's solution image?
- What Valid Business Reason would cause this person to put me at the top of his or her priority list?
- What Valid Business Reason would help him or her to make, reinforce, or plan a decision?

- What Valid Business Reason would make it clear that there's something in the meeting for him or her and for his or her company?
- What Valid Business Reason is clearly related to this person's business, not just mine?

Using these questions as a guide, write down a brief definition of your Valid Business Reason. It doesn't need to check out against all five of these criteria, but it should satisfy at least one or two. The Valid Business Reason you're defining here is the *real* reason that this customer will want to meet you.

Step 2: Test this reason. As a preliminary test of validity, we suggest you try out your stated Valid Business Reason on your colleagues. Ask your peers and your sales manager whether or not your reason for arranging the call makes good business sense to them. Ask them to put themselves in your potential buyer's place, and imagine that your are asking for an appointment. Does your Valid Business Reason seem to them a good enough reason for a client to spend time with you? If they're not sure of its validity, you may not really have a Valid Business Reason—and you may want to think further about the meeting's purpose.

Step 3: What actions can I take next? Finally, define the specific actions that you can take, now, to better define and present your Valid Business Reason. Maybe you need to do more reading about the client's general field of business. Maybe you need some good coaching, either from someone within the buying organization, or from someone in yours, or from a person not associated with either company. Maybe your currently stated Valid Business Reason is already solid—maybe it already passes the criteria and the "peer review" tests—and the next action you should take is to call your client to state the Valid Business Reason. Whatever actions you decide on to move you closer to a good meeting with this person, be sure they improve your understanding of *his or her* situation. Remember, your ultimate purpose in stating the Valid Business Reason is to demonstrate to the person that you, and your company, can help him *Win*.

Once you've completed this exercise, not only should you have a better understanding of our second prerequisite to the sales call. You should also have one more tactical element in hand that can help you manage each sales call most effectively from the moment it begins. There's only one more element to introduce before we show you how to put this all together: that's to be able to define, in a very specific and very realistic manner, the *target* you should aim for in each call.

▸ 13 ◂

YOUR SALES CALL TARGET

The third prerequisite you need before you enter a sales call is a clear, precise understanding of what you want to have achieved by the end of the call: in other words, a definition of your *sales call target* as it relates to this client or prospect in this place at this time. We've mentioned frequently that you should approach each of your accounts with a single sales objective in mind: you should be able to define at any given point in the selling cycle what you want to see happen in the account that isn't already happening. The concept of a predetermined sales call target brings that requirement down to the specific level of the individual meeting. If you're meeting Jeffries from 3 P.M. to 4 P.M. this Tuesday, having a specific sales call target means defining what the sales picture will look like to you not this Friday or next week or next month, but at 4 P.M. on Tuesday afternoon.

It may seem obvious to you that a seller ought to have a

target in mind before he or she enters the call. After all, salespeople are very "results-oriented"; they're constantly setting levels of achievement for themselves that will make them the top producers of this quarter or the branch commission leaders or Salesperson of the Year. In alliance with marketing departments and their own sales managers, most professional salespeople constantly have their eyes on *some* target. But our research shows that, in spite of this results-oriented attitude, *most* professionals in sales fail to set clear and realistic targets for themselves from one sales call to another. Even among highly experienced sellers, the annual objectives and the career goals are clear, but the target for Tuesday afternoon remains uncertain.

The Traditional "Target"

When we introduce the sales target prerequisite in our Conceptual Selling programs, we ask the participants to identify and describe success measurements they set for themselves at the outset of several recent sales calls. These are highly experienced professionals. Yet we find over and over that even they have difficulty in pinning down specifically what they were after when they made those calls. Typically, we find three related problems with their "targets": they are too general, they are unrealistic, and they are almost always "salesperson-driven" rather than "customer-driven."

1. Too general. Unless a sales call target is specific, tangible, and measurable, it's very easy for the seller to leave the call not knowing whether or not it's been achieved. A good sales target is a benchmark, and if that benchmark is something as vague as "moving the process forward," it's easy to leave the sales call uncertain about how far, or in what direction, you've come. Good sales call management tells you exactly where you are in the call, and what still needs to be done to move the selling process toward Win-Win. The more precisely stated your sales target, the better you can perform that management. With a specific target, you can see the bulls-eye, every time; with a non-specific "target"—one that sees *any* motion forward as "progress"—you're just shooting into the wind.

2. *Unrealistic.* Ask any ten salespeople what they want to get out of the next sales call they're going to make, and we bet you nine will say "the order." In certain types of selling, of course—such as retail floor selling or selling where the typical sticker price is low—that's not always an unreasonable expectation. But in most kinds of selling it is. In most corporate selling, for example, where the typical selling cycle may involve five or ten calls on several diffcrcnt Buying Influences, "getting the order" is rarely a realistic sales call target. Yet, in an impatient world, where the glamor of an end result often obscures the process that it took us to achieve it, "getting the order" remains a commonly stated sales target—even though a very small percentage of sales calls are ever managed to this happy outcome.

It is the function of our "sales target" prerequisite to bring reality into this situation, by showing you how to set targets that *can* be achieved on each call. A good target can bring a sense of *direction* into your selling that no wishful thinking or "supersales" techniques can even bring. It can help you avoid the misery of those "rudderless" calls that wander aimlessly from one point to another, but that never seem to *get* you anywhere. Every seller we know has experienced "sales drift" of this sort. We like to think of the "sales target" concept as a kind of navigational tool, by which you can spot and correct that drift as you go—*before* you hit the rock.

3. *"Salesperson-driven."* When our program participants state their sales targets, most of them focus exclusively on what they will do, rather than on what the potential customer must do. This is natural, because most sales professionals are still being told that they should stay constantly in "control" of the sale, and never let it fall into the customer's (that is, the enemy's) hands. So they set "targets" like "lay out all the packaging specs" or "highlight our great service record."

Targets like these fail to take into account two fundamental lessons of Conceptual Selling.

The first lesson is that sales are necessarily "customer-driven," not "salesperson-driven." Since everything begins with what's in the customer's mind, you cannot manage a sales call properly if you focus exclusively on what *you* are thinking and doing. In addition, when your sales target involves you alone, it's very easy to let yourself off the hook when you come out of the meeting with empty hands. You can say, "I did my job. I did everything I was supposed to do. So it's not my fault it went nowhere."

The second lesson is that all good sales depend not just on mutual satisfaction, but on mutual *commitment*. A good sales target by definition *must* involve the customer in commitment.

Commitment Revisited

In the chapter on Getting Commitment, we said that every good sales call interview should end on *what the client is going to do.* In Win-Win selling, you and your various clients and prospects are partners in a Joint Venture process, and as partners you both have responsibilities as well as needs to be met. It's the fundamental conviction underlying Win-Win that the only truly sound business relationships, long term, are those in which *both* parties accept their responsibility, and are committed to each other's satisfaction. That's why we insist that *every* sales call must conclude with a specific, action-oriented Commitment by the customer. That Commitment signals you, the seller, that you aren't selling alone. It lets you know that the potential customer knows you are not peddling a free lunch.

As you know, we are very exacting in our definition of customer Commitment. We say it's never enough for a potential buyer to "think about it" for a few weeks, or to "get back to you" at his or her convenience. Commitment, when it's real, involves the buyer giving up some of his or her time to *do something concrete for the sale.* It's got to be action, not just words. For this reason, when we introduce the notion of setting sales call targets in our programs, we often speak not just of Commitment, but of *Action Commitment.*

In linking realism, your customer's Action Commitment, and your sales targets, we speak of two levels of Commitment that you can ask for on a given sales call. Together these two levels define the parameters of Commitment possibility, between on the one hand the *most* that you should hope for and, on the other, the *least* that you should accept.

Let's look first at the more desirable of these two commitment levels. We call it Best Action Commitment.

Best Action Commitment

As the name implies, the Best Action Commitment is the high end of the Commitment scale. It's the best level of Commitment you can realistically expect your Buying Influence to make as a result of this particular sales call. The ultimate Best Action Commitment would be for the order to be signed, but as we've already emphasized, that's seldom a realistic target. For most sales calls—and for all but the last call in a drawn-out, multi-call process—you'll have to aim for something less than the order.

We spoke in Chapter 7 about getting *incremental* levels of Commitment, and that's an important point to remember in defining your Best Action Commitment sales target. "Get him to set the date for giving me the final review committee report" might be a reasonable Best Action toward the end of a complex selling cycle; toward the beginning of that same cycle, it could be highly unrealistic. The idea in setting Best Action targets is to be sure that the action you want is *appropriate to where you are in the selling process*—that it builds on the client's past Commitment, and that it looks toward firmer, future Commitment.

Take a hypothetical scenario. You're trying to sell a large manufacturer a solution that will increase its production efficiency. You have a sales call coming up with Jim Jeffries, the division head of operations, and he's already committed to your proposal. You're in a comfortable, Win-Win situation with him, but you know that he cannot give final approval for this deal. And you don't know who can. One Best Action Commitment for the upcoming sales call might be: "Get him to agree to identify and introduce me to the person with final authority to approve." That would *build* on your already good relationship by continuing to involve him in the selling process, and it would look *forward* by putting you in touch with another crucial Buying Influence. That's incremental Commitment.

There are any number of other Best Actions you might set as sales call targets in this scenario. There's no single, "ideal" Best Action that exists objectively in any call, but only a range of good actions from which you, the "managing" seller, have to select *your* Best. Because you know your sales much better than anyone else, we can't define what would be best for you. But we can give you some guidelines to be sure that you are focussing on actions that really do tie in with Commitment. In selecting a Best Action Commitment for a given sales call, we suggest you ask yourself the following questions:

1. *Is this Action Commitment specific?* Does it define the who, what, where, and when of the action? In asking your clients for Commitment, you have to be attentive to specifics, and especially to the specific *timing,* because the "when" of a Commitment is often the most difficult to pin down. But it's got to be pinned down, or you're going to be spinning your wheels. It's great for Jeffries to agree to introduce you to the division manager, but if he won't give you a time frame for that Commitment, you may be waiting around for six months on the basis of a promise. So, in this scenario, we'd recommend, "Get him to introduce me within thirty days" (or whatever time frame is realistic in terms of your type of business).

2. *Does it focus on what he or she will do?* Remember: it's mutual Commitment or it's worth nothing at all. So be sure your Best Action Commitment puts the burden on the client to expend some energy in your behalf—in your *mutual* behalf. And be aware of one potential problem. You've got to be sure that the action Jeffries is commiting to is not only something he *wants* to do, but something that he *can* do. Many salesmen make the mistake of getting Mack to agree to do something that involves Janice as well, in situations where Mack does not have the authority to get Janice involved. In our scenario, it's reasonable to assume that Jeffries, as head of operations, can get you in to see the division manager; but if Jeffries were a line operator or dispatcher, that probably wouldn't be a reasonable assumption. Sensitivity to your individual buyers' responsibilities and authority, as well as their business needs, can go a long way toward helping you define what they can and can't do.

3. *Is the statement of Best Action measurable?* We mean measurable by you, the sales representative. In other words, once Jeffries performs the Best Action you're asking of him, is there a way that you'll *know* it? You know as well as we do that people don't always say what they do or do what they say. When you ask for Action Commitment, therefore, don't be afraid to ask for the evidence later. If the Commitment is an appointment with the division manager, the evidence might be a confirmation phone call to his secretary. If the Best Action was to send your report to a review committee, the evidence would be the committee's response. We don't mean you should be sneaking around "checking up" on your buyers. But you're expending your time, and you have a right to know what Commitment you're getting in return. Commitment means something was done. If in fact it *was* done, then you ought to know what resulted.

4. *Is this Best Action realistic?* This is always the final, last-cut test, and it's really a summary of the other three. A realistic Best Action sales target is specific, it focuses on what the customer can and will do, and it can be measured by you when it's done. If Jeffries's meeting between you and the division manager is set at some vague point in the future, if you're not sure he even knows the salesperson, and/or if there's no way for you to check that the meeting will actually come off—then by definition your Best Action is not realistic.

Realism is the basis of getting any solid Commitment, but you wouldn't know that from the way many sales trainers talk. With their emphasis on "positive thinking" and the "Go get 'em!" attitude, they often seem to be saying that the facts of the situation are less important than the way you look at them: there are "no problems, only opportunities." We criticized this simple-minded, "mind over matter" view of selling back in Chapter 1, and we reiterate our criticism here. Always start with reality. Not pessimism or negative thinking, but *reality.* If you sell with your eyes open, you know what reality is. You know what Jeffries can reasonably be expected to do for you, and what he cannot. We urge you to set Best Action targets for yourself that start, every time, from that baseline.

If you really don't know what's realistic in a given situation, you have one sound way of finding out. *Ask.* On this call, and the next, and on every call in the future, use the questioning process we explained earlier to help you clarify your view of Jeffries's reality, so that you *do* know what he can and can't do, as well as what he will or won't do. The more you do that, over time, the quicker you will be able to assess, on any given sales call, the *real* Best Action you should ask for.

As realistic as you try to be, however, you're not going to get your Best Action every time. Sometimes this will be because you've misinterpreted the possibilities. Sometimes it will be because the situation has changed since you saw Jeffries last. Or it may be that, for any one of a thousand reasons, the buyer just doesn't see the situation the way that you hoped he would see it. That is why, when you're setting a sales call target for yourself, you have to define a low end of the scale as well. We call this low end the Minimum Acceptable Action.

Minimum Acceptable Action

The Minimum Acceptable Action is just what it says: the minimum that your potential buyer must do so that you find the outcome of the sales call acceptable. It's the *least* Commitment that you will settle for, because it's the least he or she can do to indicate to you that there's still a mutual interest in carrying the sale forward.

Mutual interest again. Remember the $500 figure we mentioned in the chapter on Commitment. That's how much you're spending every time you make another call on the prospect. Minimum Acceptable defines the lowest exchange you will take for that $500 investment of your time and energy. If you don't get at least that, then you're not coming back.

In defining a Minimum Acceptable Action, you should remember the same guidelines that we laid out with regard to Best Action. Each Minimum Acceptable Action—even though it's at the low end of the scale—should still be *specific;* it should still focus on what the *customer* will (and can) do; the outcome of the Action should still be *measurable* by you, the seller; and it should still be *realistic.*

But one more thing. The Minimum Acceptable Action for a given sales call should also be *related* to your Best Action outcome for that call. Relating the high and low ends of the "acceptability scale" helps to keep you focussed on your overall selling objectives, and saves you from the kind of "sales drift" that can happen when you don't go in with a clear focus. Tying Best Action and Minimum Acceptable together makes it clear to you that, even if you don't get the Best Action on this call, you will still get something that's moving you in that *direction*. You won't be in the sorry situation of the person who sees *any* positive response, any time, as acceptable—and so ends up with bones from the table.

Take the Jeffries example. Your hypothetical Best Action on that call is to get him to identify and introduce you to the person who makes the final decision—the person who can release the money. The Minimum Acceptable Action you choose for this call should point, directly or indirectly, to that same final decision-maker. Maybe Jeffries will agree to explain to you in detail how decisions are made in his company for a proposal of your type. Maybe he can agree to bring your proposal to the head honcho himself. Whatever you determine to be minimum—the minimum return for your $500 investment—the action that Jeffries will perform must move you closer to Best Action, and it must verify his incremental Commitment.

Best Action and Minimum Acceptable Action are summarized in the box on page 267.

What If You Can't Get the Minimum?

We're asked this question all the time. Sales professionals seem to have little difficulty understanding the concept of Best Action, but the idea of having a "floor" under which you won't go—that seems unrealistic to some, and threatening to others. "If I walked away every time I failed to get the least I wanted," we sometimes hear, "I'd be out of business tomorrow. It puts too much pressure on everybody to demand an outcome like this. Sometimes you just have to settle for nothing, and come back to fight another day."

That argument is superficially convincing—it sounds solid and realistic and flexible—but it can easily serve as a cop-out: an excuse for letting both buyer and seller off the hook. It can be a disguised way of saying, "I haven't done

---

BEST ACTION COMMITMENT

Realistically, "What is the best commitment to action I can expect this Buying Influence to make as a result of this sales call?"

MINIMUM ACCEPTABLE ACTION

Answers, "What is the minimum action from the Buyer acceptable to me as a result of this sales call?" (Emphasis is always on what the customer agrees to do, **not** on what you will do.)

GUIDELINES

- Is it specific?
- Does it focus on Customer's action?
- Is the statement measurable (by sales representative)?
- Is it realistic?

---

my homework on this one, and I'm afraid to be turned down, so let's let it slide and hope he feels better next time." Which he seldom does. Because unless he cannot live without your product, when you shirk your responsibilities for moving the sale forward, your buyer's natural tendency is to follow suit. And "sales drift" soon sets in.

One thing should be made clear. We assume that you are going for Win-Win, long-term relationships, in which you get the *best possible results from every sales call,* every time, and where—when those results aren't happening— you're willing to say "This isn't Win-Win" and bow out. We don't introduce the idea of Minimum Acceptable Commitment to browbeat or intimidate anyone—and certainly not as part of a pop-psych, upbeat, "You can do it!" philosophy. We introduce it because it gives you a handle on where progress is being made in the sale, and where it isn't. If your customer is unwilling to meet your *lowest* expectations for the sales call, there's something seriously wrong with the selling process. When that's the case, you need to immediately find out and confront why he's moving at a snail's pace, or not moving at all.

Whenever the client won't help you move things forward, you need to ask yourself first of all whether or not there's real potential here for a match between his Concept and your product. If there *is* a potential match, and you can't get even Minimum Acceptable on a call, there are really only three things you can do. You can 1) ask Basic Issue questions to uncover the reason for the client's lack of Commitment. You can 2) revise your Minimum Acceptable Action downward in response to what's happening (or not happening) in the sale. Or, if these two tactics don't help, you can 3) shut your briefcase quietly and walk out. Let's examine these three options.

1. Asking Basic Issue questions. We've discussed this in the chapter on Commitment. It's important to ask Basic Issue questions when a sale is stalled because such questions help cut through the garbage. They can get around the patent excuses and forced objections that a buyer who feels he's Losing will throw up as a smokescreen, and allow you to focus on the *cause* of his resistance. If you're getting to the end of your thirty minutes with Jeffries and it's clear he's not even going to tell you who can give you final approval, then it's time to ask a Basic Issue question: "You seem concerned about me meeting this guy, Jim. Could you explain to me why that's a problem?"

2. Revising downward. Revising the Minimum Acceptable goal downward is not something we heartily recommend, since it's a tactic that can obviously be abused— until you end up, on every successive sales call, with less and less. But there are situations where it may be warranted. Generally, you should consider revising downward when you walk into a meeting and you find that the situation is *significantly different* from what you had thought it to be. If as you walk in the door you discover that Jeffries has just been promoted (or demoted), then obviously it's time to rethink your tactics—including your definition of Best Action and Minimum Acceptable. Any surprises or change of condition, since the last time you saw the Buying Influence, means that your information is not up to date. It's hazardous to proceed "as planned" in this kind of situation until you've gotten the new facts straight.

One specific clue that it may be time to revise either, or both, of your sales targets is when you get an unexpected answer to a Confirmation Question. For example. Suppose you walk into Jeffries's office a month after your last meeting and announce, "We were going to discuss delivery schedules today, correct?" Instead of nodding Yes, Jeffries snaps back, "Hell, no, we're nowhere near that stage yet!" Obviously it's time to revise. If your Minimum Acceptable Action going into that call had been "Get him to set trial delivery schedule," the new information should now point you toward a more modest goal. Perhaps the *Best* you could hope for in this situation would be for him to set the trial schedule; the Minimum Acceptable Commitment might become "Get him to agree to a survey so we can set a delivery schedule in two weeks."

So Best Action and Minimum Acceptable are not meant to be taken as rigid, "Do or die" propositions. Yes, when the situation warrants it, you can revise either one. But it's important not to do this frivolously, or in response to a mere "difficult" customer. If you're willing to lower your minimum every time you experience *any* difficulty, there's no point in having a minimum at all.

3. *Walking.* Walking out is a last-resort action, but it's not one you should avoid at all costs; because if you set your Minimum Acceptable targets realistically, and in accord with the guidelines we've laid out, there should be very few sales calls where the customer will balk at the "floor." If he does, is he really committed? Does he really want to play Win-Win? If you can't answer Yes to those questions, you may be wasting both your times by pursuing him.

Sometimes we are asked by skeptical salespeople, "Do you *really* not come back if you don't get the Minimum Acceptable?" With the rare exceptions we've just discussed, our answer is a very firm Yes. We look at it this way. We set our Minimum Acceptable Actions based on the *least* we need to obtain to make spending any more *time* on this sale worthwhile. If we don't get that least, then we walk. Anything else is selling ourselves short. And it's saying to the no-Commitment client: "My time isn't as valuable as yours. I'd rather wait for the crumbs you throw me than go out and hunt up real business." A client who gets that indirect message will have no qualms about playing you for a fool. You've given him carte blanche to do so.

Two related provisos. One, we don't advise anyone to walk as an excuse for not selling, and selling hard. Be straight with yourself as well as with your client. If you didn't do your homework, or didn't answer his questions, or in any way didn't manage the sales call properly, you shouldn't expect to get a Commitment—even a Minimum Acceptable one. But if you've done your job right and you still can't get the minimum, it's time to start thinking about the door.

The second proviso is common sense. If you're considering walking, it's reasonable to discuss your decision first with your manager. For every call you've made on the no-Commitment prospect, remember, you've spent $500 of your company's money. Before you write that off as a bad investment, it makes sense to discuss the account with someone else: your manager may have some insight as to whether another call is worth your while.

"Trading Up"

One more useful tactic for setting Commitment targets was suggested by one of our Conceptual Selling program participants. In many cases, sales professionals find it easier to define Best Action—after all, that's what they really want—than to define a good Minimum Acceptable Action. If you have difficulty here, we suggest you try the "trading up" technique.

In "trading up," when you know the Best that you want but not the Minimum, you make that Best serve as the Minimum, and "trade up" for a new Best. For example, suppose the Best Action you can imagine actually happening is for Jeffries to set up a preliminary survey; at this stage in the selling cycle, you would take that as a real coup. But you cannot imagine a lesser Commitment that would sustain your level of satisfaction: so "set up survey" comes to stand as both Best and Minimum Acceptable. All right. Call that Commitment outcome your Minimum Acceptable, and set your sights on a higher level of Commitment to define a *new* Best Action. "Get him to introduce me to the final approval authority," perhaps, or "Get promise for division manager's review by month's end."

The danger in trading up, of course, is that you will price yourself out of the running, by setting the new Best Action too high. If you began by thinking of "final approval explanation" as the best of all possible worlds, then don't jump from that to "get the order" when you set your new top sight. The watchword, as always, is realism.

Personal Workshop: Action Commitment

Now, to apply the principles of our third prerequisite to your own upcoming sales calls, write the heading "Action Commitment" at the top of a notebook page. Under the heading write the name of an account that you're managing and the name of a specific person that you'll be calling on soon in that account. For this exercise you should choose a person on whom you've called once or twice before.

Step 1: Current level of Action Commitment. Start by getting a fix on the person's current level of Commitment. Write down in a sentence or two the specific actions that this individual has performed for you in the past in order to move the selling process forward. This can range from "Set up a survey" to "Sent my proposal to CEO with his positive recommendation." Be sure, as you're writing down these notes, that you include an identification of the *last* action the client performed, or was supposed to perform. If he's agreed to do something by the time of your next meeting, put that down. If he's never done anything for you up to now, put that down also.

Step 2: Your current Commitment. Now list the actions that *you* have performed for the client as a way of moving things forward. Anything from drafting proposals to making presentations to simply giving him or her your time on an initial or subsequent sales call. Remember that, for every time you have met with this client or prospect, you have expended an estimated $500. You might want to add up the estimated money here, and write down the ballpark figure.

Step 3: Are you sharing Commitment? Now look at the two lists you have—the indications of the client's Commitment and the indications of yours—and compare them. Are you *both* making a Commitment to the selling process, or is one or the other of you falling behind? If the Commitment is unequal and you're the one who's holding back, you need to ask yourself what you can do, on this upcoming sales call, to better demonstrate your Commitment. If it's the client who's been holding back, you need to ask yourself these questions:

- What specific actions could he or she have performed for me by now that have not been performed?
- What Basic Issue questions have I asked in the past to find out why this person is holding back?
- What Basic Issue questions should I ask on *this* call to uncover the reasons for his or her lack of Commitment?

And write those questions down. If you need help in

phrasing Basic Issue questions, refer to our discussion in Chapter 7.

Step 4: Set your Best Action target. With the customer's current level of Commitment in mind, and with an understanding of the specific action (if any) he has promised to do for you by your next meeting, set out your Best Action target. In other words, define the *best* thing that, during the call, he could agree to do by the *following* meeting. Remember that whatever he agrees to do has to indicate a higher (incremental) level of Commitment than what he has already agreed to do. And remember also that every Action Commitment target has to be *specific;* has to focus on what the *customer,* not you, will do; has to be *measurable* after it's done; and has to be *realistic.*

Step 5: Set your Minimum Acceptable Action. Finally, define the low end of your acceptability scale by stating the *least* you will settle for. In other words, when you next sit down with this person, what is the minimum commitment you will accept at that time for him or her to perform for the *following* call? Again remember incremental Commitment and our four guidelines. And, if you have trouble defining a minimum, recall the "trading up" technique that we described just before this Personal Workshop. Be sure, finally, that the Minimum Acceptable Action you will require from the person you're meeting is related to the Best Action. Define your Minimum Acceptable in a sentence, and write it down in your notebook.

You now have an articulate overview of the specific sales call to come, with the Best case and the Minimum Acceptable case serving as brackets for the possible outcomes. What will happen in the actual call will depend on how well you *manage* the buy/sell encounter, with regard not only to the principles in this chapter, but also to those in all the rest of this book. In the final Part of the book, we're going to show you how to put it all together, as we take Conceptual Selling into Zero Hour.

ZERO HOUR

· 14 ·

REHEARSING

Every professional whose work involves public presentation knows the importance of rehearsing. Public speakers, actors, athletes—all of them spend time practicing their performances over and over without the audience so that, when it's time to go on, the work becomes almost automatic. Success in these fields, very often, comes not to the person who puts in the most effort *during* the performance, but to the person who has already put so much into rehearsing that he or she can manage the performance as if by instinct.

Since selling is also an art of public presentation, the same thing is true here too. But with one important proviso. We've emphasized throughout this book that selling should never be an song and dance that you "put on" for your potential buyers. Yes, a good sales call is a kind of performance. But it's a performance in which you and the customer are equally significant to the outcome—

one in which his or her "lines" are as much a part of the "script" as anything in "your" presentation. In fact, the whole point of Conceptual Selling is to *interact* with each of your customers, rather than to "act" to, at, or in spite of them. The whole thrust of tactical planning, as we've been explaining it, is to allow you to manage each interaction intelligently rather than to impress or dazzle your "audience." In Conceptual Selling, unlike acting or public speaking, you are not simply on stage; indeed, success comes from breaking down the distinction between "performer" and "audience," so that a positive flow of information is created and sustained, both ways.

This doesn't mean that rehearsing is unimportant to the sales professional. It's extremely important. In fact, running through the possible "lines" of a sales call can be a very productive exercise for you to perform just before you hit Zero Hour, and are ready to sit down with the client. In this chapter we're going to walk you through just such an exercise, by pulling together all the tactical planning we've introduced so far, and showing you how to apply it, in a coordinated fashion, as a last-minute "dress rehearsal." The difference between this rehearsal and those of an actor or speaker is that you will be rehearsing an *interactive* "performance"—in other words, a conversation—rather than a cut-and-dried, show-and-tell delivery.

The first step in the rehearsal format is for you to pick the specific sales call that you will be rehearsing. Since this chapter will be both a review of the tactical planning principles we've already introduced, and a practical application of those principles, we suggest that you select one of the sales calls that you've worked with throughout this book—a "model" call that you chose in the Personal Workshop in Chapter 2. If your own selling situation has changed since you chose that call, and you're now more eager to have solid tactical help for another call, fine: choose the upcoming sales encounter that is, right now, most important to you.

Since this is a last-minute "dress rehearsal," you can choose an encounter that is going to happen very soon.

The process we'll develop in this chapter, in fact, is most effective when applied only a day or two in advance of the sales call.

The Sales Call Guide

Once you've chosen the call, open your notebook flat, so that you have a two-page spread before you. If you prefer, use a single sheet of large paper laid out with the long side horizontal. You're going to be constructing a sales tool, the "Sales Call Guide," which involves a little more space than the Personal Workshop notes you've done before. Across the top of the page or pages write the heading "Sales Call Guide." At the top left hand corner of the Guide, write in the name of the account you'll be calling on, the name of the person you'll be contacting, and a statement of your *single sales objective*. Remember that a good single sales objective defines what you want to have happen in the account that isn't happening right now, and that it is always specific: it tells you *what* you want to be selling, *how much* of it you want to be selling, and by *what date*.

Now you can construct the Sales Call Guide by following the format we've laid out on page 280. You'll see that the left-hand half of the Guide is divided into four equal boxes, and the right-hand half is divided into three equal horizontal segments. Make those line divisions on your Guide, and fill in the subheadings and questions as we have filled them in on the sample.

Now, with your single upcoming sales call in mind, you can rehearse your "lines" for the encounter by pulling together the information you generated in the Personal Workshops, and organizing it into one concise tactical tool. We'll walk you through this trial "rehearsal" by taking each of the sections of the Sales Call Guide in turn.

Credibility. Begin at the upper left, with Credibility. Turn in your notebook to the "Credibility" exercise, and transfer the following information to the Guide:

Sales Call Guide

Account: _____
Prospect / customer: _____
Single sales objective: _____

Credibility

- Strong, weak or unknown:

- Earned, transferred, or reputation:

Valid Business Reason

- Valid Business Reason/ purpose of call:

- When stated:

Win-Win Matrix

- Current Win-Win Matrix position:

- Actions on this call:

Planning Matrix

- Present Planning Matrix quadrant:

- Where to go now:

- Actions to get there:

Getting Information

- Confirmation Questions:
- New Information Questions:
- Attitude Questions:
- Commitment Questions:

Giving Information

- Unique Strengths:

- So what?
- Prove it!

Getting Commitment

- Commitment levels: Best Action
  Minimum Acceptable

- Possible Basic Issues:

- Basic Issue Questions:

- First, is your current level of Credibility with this prospect or client strong, weak, or unknown? If it's weak or unknown, remember that you need to strengthen it on this call, with the guidelines given in Chapter 11.

- Second, was your Credibility earned, transferred, or gotten by reputation? If it was transferred or gotten by reputation, note how this was done. And remember that, eventually, *all* Credibility has to be earned.

Valid Business Reason. Now, with reference to the Valid Business Reason Personal Workshop in Chapter 12, transfer the following data into the lower left-hand box of the Sales Call Guide:

- State the Valid Business Reason that you have for meeting with *this* client on *this* call. Remember that this is the purpose of the meeting, and that it must be a purpose that makes sense to *him or her.*

- Put down *when* you last stated this Valid Business Reason: at the time of making the appointment or at the time of confirming it. Whether or not you have already made this Valid Business Reason known to the client, note that you must state the purpose of the call at the beginning of the upcoming meeting.

Win-Win Matrix. Now turn to the Personal Workshop notes that you made in Chapter 8. Transfer onto the Sales Call Guide these two pieces of tactical information:

- What is your *current* Win-Win position with this prospect or client? You can identify this position best by remembering which of the four quadrants of the Win-Win Matrix you were in when you ended the previous sales call on this person.

- Now put down the specific Win-Win actions you can take on the upcoming call to move you toward the Win-Win quadrant. Remember that appropriate actions to accomplish this will be realistic, personal (that is, something *you* can do), and concrete. And remember that well-phrased *questions* can also qualify as "actions."

The Planning Matrix. Moving down to the fourth box in the left-hand side of the Guide, and referring to the Personal Workshop at the end of Chapter 10, write down the following data:

- What is your present quadrant? That is, in which quadrant of the Planning Matrix did you and your client spend most of your time in the previous sales call: Joint Venture/Concept; Unilateral/Concept; Joint Venture/Product; or Unilateral/Product?

- Where do you need to go now? What quadrant do you need to concentrate on in the upcoming sales call?

- How do you get there? What specific actions can you take in the upcoming call to move you toward the most productive quadrant of the Planning Matrix? Remember that good questioning is a key factor here, and that it is your responsibility to *manage* each selling encounter so that it moves the selling process toward Win-Win.

Getting Information. Now move to the top of the right-hand side of the Sales Call Guide, and organize the data you have collected about the three basic phases of the sales call. Start at the top with Getting Information. Refer to the Personal Workshop on questioning, and to the Question Grid that you constructed in Chapter 4, and write in the following information:

- At least one good Confirmation Question: a question that will validate or invalidate information you think you already have.

- At least one good New Information Question: one that will help you to update information, fill in your information gaps, resolve discrepancies, and/or get further information about this person's desired results.

- At least one good Attitude Question: one that will clarify your understanding of this person's individual values and attitudes.

- At least one good Commitment Question: a question that will tell you where you are in the selling process, and what still needs to be done to move you closer to a Win-Win outcome.

Giving Information. Move down to the middle section of the right-hand side, and refer back to the Personal Workshop in Chapter 6. Then fill in the following points:

- Referring to your "Unique Strengths" chart, identify your Unique Strengths in this selling scenario with this particular customer. Be sure to avoid "strengths" that are merely "me too" strengths; and remember that difference in *degree* can also be seen as "unique."

- So what? Test the validity of your supposed "uniqueness" by answering the question "So what?" Remember that the answer or answers you give must be relevant to *this* person right *now*.

- Prove it! Finally, write down the "proof" that you're unique by answering the questions we gave in Step 4 of the Personal Workshop: "We are the only ones who_____" and/or "We are different because_____." Be sure that each answer you give here effectively links your product or service to this particular customer's Concept.

Getting Commitment. To plan the "third phase" of the upcoming sales call, move to the bottom right section of the Sales Call Guide, and refer back to two previous Personal Workshops: the one on Basic Issues in Chapter 7, and the one on Action Commitment in Chapter 13. Fill in the following information:

- Set the levels of Commitment required, on this sales call, from this customer, to make another call worth your while. Define briefly the Best Action Commitment and the Minimum Acceptable Action you will settle for. Remember that both of these have to be *incremental* in terms of this person's previous Commitment. And remember that every definition of Commitment means something that the *client,* not you, will *do.*

- What are the possible Basic Issues that might impede Commitment on the upcoming call? Remember that a Basic Issue is the root cause of an "objection" being raised; it has to do with the prospective buyer's feeling that he or she is going to Lose.

- What Basic Issue Questions should you ask? To uncover and address the customer's "Lose" perception, you need to ask Basic Issue Questions. Remember that the most effective Basic Issue Questions are positively stated, and that they seek to identify the client's areas of uncertainty or concern. Write down the question(s) you need to ask in order to do that.

Once you've collated all the available information you have onto the Sales Call Guide, you have a concise, organized planning tool that focusses on what is actually going to happen in the call, based on your past experience with this buyer. That's a necessary baseline for rehearsal, but it's still only a baseline. It's approximately equivalent to what an actor has when he or she has learned the lines cold. In order to put those "lines" into operation, you can still profit from a "dry" performance, and that's exactly what we suggest as the next step in the rehearsal exercise.

"No Risk" Rehearsal

In our Conceptual Selling programs, we split our participants up into pairs at this point, and ask them to practice the principles we've introduced in "trial" exchanges. In these exchanges, the person who is actually going to make the sales call rehearses himself or herself, and the partner that he or she is working with rehearses the part of the prospect or customer. We have found that this kind of exercise, where people are allowed to run through the basics of a call in a low-stress, "no risk" environment, enables them to become comfortable with the Conceptual Selling process much more readily than could if they just jumped into the call feet first. So we ask you to consider doing the same exercise.

Select a friend, fellow seller, or family member to be your client for you. Take about five or ten minutes to brief that person on the selling situation, so he or she can be your key buyer more effectively. The briefing you give the person will, of course, vary depending on the particular situation, but you will at least want to fill your rehearsal partner in on the following:

- The role the Buying Influence currently plays in the buying organization;
- What business you've done with the person in the past, and the Win-Win history of that business;
- Your specific sales objective for this sale, as well as the sales target you've set for yourself in this particular sales call;
- A rundown of this person's current responsiveness to your proposal—both in terms of the results he or she wants, and in terms of his or her personal feelings about the sale;
- Anything else that is relevant to the way the person is likely to respond to you in the sales call.

Once you've briefed the person you'll be "trying out" the call on, take just ten or fifteen minutes to go through the "dress rehearsal." Encourage your partner to be as resistant and "difficult" as necessary to reflect the real responsiveness level of your particular target client. He will only be able to do so, of course, if you have briefed him properly beforehand.

We realize that the exercise we're suggesting here may not always turn out as realistically as you would like. Your partner may not be as perceptive or demanding as your real customer will be—and he or she certainly won't be as personally involved in the possible sales transaction. We don't say that rehearsal is the same thing as making the call. There's no way to "copy" a reality that's still in the future. Rehearsal is only an approximation of what will happen when you sit down face to face with the client.

Yet even such an approximation can bring you enormous benefits. The reason is that, even in an artificial setting, you seem to lay down a preliminary but still useful "map" that you can follow, with the necessary adjustments, in the call. Athletes sometimes speak of mentally going over and over a given motion or technique until it becomes second nature, and they don't have to think about it in performance. Rehearsing a sales call with a friend seems to have somewhat the same function: it burns a basic path in your thinking that you can start from when you're actually in the call.

Now, in order to be as sure as possible even before the call that this path is an appropriate one, we suggest that you perform one more exercise before the call. Check the fluidity and effectiveness of the path you've laid down by getting some *feedback* on the rehearsal.

Pre-Call Feedback

In our two-day programs our participants get this feedback from a third party whom we call an "observer"—someone who observes the rehearsal of the call and gives constructive criticism afterward. You can use this same format yourself, or you can simply get feedback from talking to your partner about how the call went. In either case, what you should look for are areas where your interaction was effective, and areas where it was defective. In focussing on these areas, we have found the following checklist to be helpful. After the "dry run" call is over, ask yourself these questions:

1. Did I clearly state the Valid Business Reason at the outset?

2. Did I lead off with a good Confirmation Question?
3. Did I ask at least one good Attitude Question?
4. Did I ask at least one good Commitment Question that invited incremental Commitment?
5. Was the order of my questioning logical?
6. Were the questions phrased properly—that is, did they use the appropriate key words?
7. Did I fill in the client's Cognition gaps (and my own) before moving on to suggest Divergent alternatives?
8. Did the information I gave the client clearly highlight my Unique Strengths?
9. Did I practice Golden Silence I and Golden Silence II?
10. Did I avoid using dangerous verbal signals?
11. Did I use Joint Venture selling; or, if I used Unilateral selling, was this in response to the client's specific request for Unilateral information?
12. Did I check my Credibility with this client before and/or during the sales call?
13. Did I strive to keep the call Win-Win—and did I make sure that the customer knew that?

As we'll explain in the next chapter, you'll only really be able to answer these questions after you've gone through the actual sales call, and have feedback from your real client. But running this preliminary check on your selling often proves to be valuable. It's a way of highlighting problem areas in your presentation, and therefore of being able to correct them before Zero Hour.

If your partner, for example, has the impression that you were rushing too quickly toward the close, then the chances are good that your real customer might have the same feeling. Or if your partner doesn't recall your asking a Confirmation Question toward the beginning of the call, you can make a note to yourself not to neglect this factor in the real call. Getting this pre-call feedback is like getting last-minute instructions from a drama coach: it gives you the opportunity of smoothing off the burrs of your presentation before they have a chance to disrupt your selling in the actual "performance."

The "Unrehearsable" Call

This kind of exercise, we've found, can be a sound learning technique even for so-called unrehearsable sales calls—the kind of "calls" you might make, for example, if you are selling over a counter or on a floor, where potential customers come to you.

If you're involved in this type of selling, obviously you can't use all the rehearsal principles that we've been talking about. A Sales Call Guide will be of limited use to someone who typically meets a customer once, sells or does not sell, and often never sees the person again. In addition, when you sell in this manner, you can't really state a Valid Business Reason or ask an initial Confirmation Question: so items 1 and 2 on our "pre-call feedback" list will not be relevant to your situation.

But the technique of rehearsal *can* be valuable to sales professionals who must wait for the customer to come to them. If you're a floor salesperson or involved in over-the-counter sales, we urge you too to try out your tactical skills on a friend or fellow salesperson. By getting a friend to be the "just browsing" customer or the person who isn't sure what he wants, you can construct your own type of "maps" for dealing with a variety of situations. You'll be surprised at how well this helps you to hone your interactive selling skills.

The watchword here is the same one that applies in "call" situations: *Always start with the Concept.* Remember the story we told in Chapter 2 about the friend who entered a clothing store intending to buy one blazer, and ended up carting home half the stock because a salesperson had focussed on his Concept. That's the first and most important lesson that anybody in selling can learn, whatever the type of transaction.

Secondly, we urge you to perform the same "pre-call feedback" on your rehearsal interactions that we have described above. It's true you can't very well check out your Valid Business Reason or Confirmation Questions. But the ten remaining items on the checklist *are* relevant to your type of selling—they're relevant to *any* type of selling—and we encourage you to apply them to your situations.

How Much Rehearsal?

Ideally, you should plan tactics for every sales call with the same diligence and comprehensiveness that you have put in to the Personal Workshops here. Ideally, you should have a Sales Call Guide, with all the questions answered and all the boxes filled in, for every meeting you walk into. And ideally, you should rehearse every face-to-face interaction as we've asked you to rehearse this one. If you did these things before every call, there's no question that the quality of your calls would shoot up 100 percent.

But you live in the real world, not an ideal one. And you know that if you performed this kind of extensive analytical labor on every sales call you had coming up, you'd never have time to do the selling. Because we understand that, we don't advise you to be as extensive in your sales call analysis, every time, as you have been for your model calls in this book. What we've laid out in this book is, we believe, the most complete and comprehensive planning format that you can possibly apply to your sales calls. On the *most* important, *most* urgent, or *most* complicated calls, you may want to run through the whole format: you may want to use every one of our Personal Workshops, to organize the information you get from them into a new, specific Sales Call Guide, and to spend time rehearsing the call as well. But not all calls will demand that extensive treatment.

As you use the principles of Conceptual Selling over time, it will gradually become clearer to you which calls do deserve the full treatment, and which ones can be appropriately managed with something less. But the basic guidelines here are simple ones:

- The more *money* involved in the potential sale, the more attention you want to pay to how each individual sales call is managed.

- The more *time* you have already invested in the sale, in terms of sales calls already made, the more important the planning. We say this not only because more calls mean more investment, but also because, as any sale approaches the close, it becomes notoriously prone to inertia, laziness on the seller's part, and possible dissolution.

- The better chance you have with an individual Buying Influence for establishing a *long-term* Win-Win relationship, the more sense it makes for you to manage every sales call to that person in a highly organized manner.

Thus the last word here, as in most aspects of Conceptual Selling, is that ultimate sales success depends on looking to the future. It depends on managing each individual sales call not only so it's a success in itself, but also so that it fits into a larger pattern. The amount of rehearsal you should do for an individual sales call, ultimately, is the amount that will best reinforce your *career* relationship with this customer. You start with the individual sales call, but you never forget the big picture.

As a way of helping you to keep that big picture in mind, and of moving your sales calls continually forward, we'll move now to the final element of tactical planning: the evaluation of what Zero Hour has brought you, and how to use it in managing the future.

⁍ 15 ⁌

EVALUATION

The last element in our tactical planning system is put into place only after the sales call is made. That element is Evaluation, and even though it follows the "real" business of the sales call, it is by no means optional or merely an "afterthought." Just as an actor uses the responses of his or her audience to adjust and fine tune future performances, and just as an athlete watches game films, the Conceptual Selling professional analyzes the dynamics of each individual sales call in retrospect as a way of sharpening the management of future calls. Immediate post-call Evaluation, then, is a critical factor in ongoing success.

There are basically two reasons that it is valuable for the salesman to perform an Evaluation after each call:

1. Evaluation helps you to assess the actual "hard" data of the call—that is, to understand *what information* has been successfully exchanged, and what still needs to be exchanged.

2. Evaluation helps you to assess the "soft," interpersonal data of the call—to see better *how you interacted* with the customer, and how you should alter your interaction in the future.

It is to help you gain these two tactical benefits—an understanding of the *what* and an understanding of the *how*—that we introduce the element of Evaluation.

To use this element effectively, you need to sit down as soon as possible after the sales call, take out a notebook and pencil, and run through three distinct but interrelated processes of Evaluation. You'll have the opportunity in this chapter to run through those three processes with regard to your model sales call. If you haven't yet made that sales call, we suggest that you wait before reading further. After you have made the call, begin your reading again here.

First Process: Review

Typically, when sales professionals come out of a sales encounter, they have no more than a vague sense of how things went in the call. We ask field reps all the time to give us a "reading" on their calls. Unless they've actually nailed down the order or been thrown out on their tails, their responses tend to be nonspecific: "I think it went all right." "He seems to be really interested." Or: "It's hard to say what, but something's wrong."

The purpose of the review process in Evaluation is to make better sense out of these vague feelings. It's to look more closely at specific elements of the sales call to understand *why* you feel "OK" or "pretty good" or "not sure."

Which elements? Well, the basic elements you want to check in the Evaluation stage are those that we identified in the "Pre-Call Feedback" list in the previous chapter. (See page 286.) We emphasized the importance of getting feedback from your partner in the Rehearsal stage, and/or from a third-party "observer." It's unlikely that you'll be able to get the same kind of feedback from your actual client, or from someone looking over your shoulder in the actual call. But you can get the feedback from *yourself,* by asking yourself these same "pre-call" questions. Do that now, and write the answers in your notebook.

These answers should help you to get a better handle on the reasons for your comfortable or uncomfortable feelings about the call; and they should help you to modify your tactics for future calls on this and other customers. For example, if in reviewing the situation, you realize that you used too many dangerous verbal signals ("Think about it," "Right?" and so on), then that might partially account for the resistance of your potential client. Or, if you realize that you failed to check your Credibility with this person on this call, that may help to explain why he or she was reluctant to open up to you. Whether the answers to your feedback questions are "favorable" or "unfavorable," they will still clarify your understanding—and that is *always* favorable.

In addition to the pre-call feedback questions, there are three other questions you should ask yourself in the review process of Evaluation. These relate to the three phases of the sales call that we discussed in Part II of the book.

1. What is the current information level? That is, what information did you actually receive in the sales encounter, and how does that information relate to the information you knew you needed when you went into the call? Remember that in the Getting Information phase of any sales call, you should be concentrating on the information you need to understand the prospective customer's Concept. If you've just come out of a meeting with Mr. Harrigan and you're still uncertain about his Concept, mark that down as an area of missing information. And start drafting good questions for the *next* call that will get you that information.

In focussing on the information you need to understand the client's Concept, we suggest that you turn back to the Question Grid that you constructed in Chapter 4, and review the seven typical "information poor" areas. To find out why the sales call went the way it did, ask yourself, with regard to each one of those areas, what information you wanted when you entered the call—and what information you still have to obtain.

This kind of review process can tell you a number of important things about the selling process so far:

- It can tell you that you have *less* information than you thought you had. Reviewing the information-poor area of "Competition," for example, you may discover that you ignored that area entirely in the call, and *still* don't know anything about the competition's new line. So you'll have to highlight that area in your questioning next time.

- It can tell you that you have *more* (or different) information than you thought you had. Focussing on your prospect's confusing "Resistance," for example, you may discover that in the call he admitted a fear of losing organizational responsibility. That might have been something you hadn't even thought of before the last call. Now you know that you'll have to address it in the future.

- It can underline the effectiveness, or lack of effectiveness, of your *communication process*. If in reviewing the last call you discover that you still have the same information gaps that you had going in to the call, then you know there's something wrong with the information flow. Knowing that, you can fine tune your questioning for next time.

The underlying point we're making here is that good information flow is not static. It's part of a dynamic, constantly changing system of interpersonal exchange that only works to full effect when you remain alert to your *current* information level, and work continually to raise it.

2. What's the current level of differentiation? In the Giving Information phase of the sales call, you deliver data to your prospects that will enable them to differentiate in your favor. In reviewing this second phase of your last call, you want to find out how successful you were in giving that specialized kind of information.

In doing that, you should focus on statements that the client made in the sales call regarding your specific proposal, your competition's possible proposals, and the current status quo. (Remember that one of your chief competitors in any selling situation is the way the client is doing things right now.) If he made comments indicating that you're the "only supplier" with a given capability, or that you're "different from the rest of the field" in some significant way, then your level of differentiation is probably high. But if he claimed he can get "the same solution, only cheaper" somewhere else, or if he's "not ready for this type of change yet," then you obviously have more work to do in this area.

There's only one way that a customer will differentiate in your favor. That's if he or she sees a Unique Strength in your solution to his or her particular problem. If the review process reveals that you are less clearly differentiated than you want to be, you need to ask yourself some questions. For example:

- Do I really *have* a Unique Strength in this situation? That is, can I really offer this customer a solution that is different (and better) to a significant degree than what anyone else is offering? If you're not sure about this, you should consider the possibility that there's not a real match here between your product or service and the Concept—and you should consider holding off on this sale.

- Have I made my uniqueness, and my strength, *clear?* If you're sure there's a good match, but the customer is still balking on price, or still "unclear" about your solution, you may not have highlighted your Unique Strength(s) properly. If review uncovers this possibility, you need to start thinking about tactics for the next call that will clearly *relate* your product or service to *his or her* Concept.

- Have I been helping, or hindering, the *decision-making process?* One reason that customers may be reluctant to acknowledge your Unique Strengths is that they have been rushed too quickly into Divergent thinking, and have not been given sufficient time for Cognition. You can use your evaluation of this possibility to set a tactical plan for the next call that focusses on Cognition, and on the client's personal "solution image."

Again, the point here is to begin with what's in the customer's mind. One of the principal advantages of reviewing the differentiation level reached on the last call is that it can alert you to the possibility that you have been falling into the "seller-driven" trap. Identifying an insufficient level of differentiation gives you the knowledge and the opportunity to move the next call into a more productive, "customer-driven" mode.

3. *What's the current level of Action Commitment?* This is a relatively easy question to answer, because it involves hard facts, not impressions. In evaluating Action Commitment, there are two such facts you need to note. First, when you walked into the call, had your client already performed the Action that he or she promised to perform by that date? That is, had he or she actually done what was supposed to have been done by the time of the meeting? Second, before you left the call, did he or she give you another, *incremental* level of Commitment for the next time? And was that incremental level of Commitment equivalent to your Best Action Commitment, or at least to your Minimum Acceptable?

If on this last call, your client had done what was promised, and if you got your Best Action Commitment besides, great: the selling process is obviously moving in the right direction. But if he had not come through for you, or if he was unwilling to give you a further, incremental Commitment, then you may have some rethinking to do. And if on this past call you were unable to get even your Minimum Acceptable Commitment for the following call, then you're going to have to make a decision.

We've been saying that review and Evaluation help you assess the effectiveness of each sales call as you go, so that you can fine tune your tactics for the next call. But if you haven't gotten even your Minimum Acceptable Commitment on this past call, then you have to consider the possibility that it may not be worth the effort to do any more fine tuning for this customer, at least not at this time. It may be necessary, to paraphrase Sam Goldwyn, to "include him out."

But we recommend that you take this drastic step only after performing the second Evaluation process: sorting.

Second Process: Sorting

We've said that when you don't get your Minimum Acceptable Action from a sales call, you should forget about coming back. Essentially true. But because we know how difficult it is for salespeople to walk away from potential business, and because we believe that you should always give your prospects a reasonable number of opportunities to stay Win-Win with you, we'll add a small rider to that advice. The second Evaluation process, sorting, enables you to perform a last-ditch check on difficult customers, to be sure you're not just letting yourself off easy by backing away from their business.

To sort your potential clients into those with real potential and those without it, recall the Getting Commitment phase of the sales call, and identify what we call the "Three Rs" of possible Basic Issues. Remember that the root cause of every blocked Commitment is a Basic Issue—the client's feeling that he or she will Lose by allowing you to continue the selling process. We ask you here to identify Basic Issues that were *raised, resolved,* and *remaining* on the last call. Before doing this, you may want to refer back to the Personal Workshop on Basic Issues that you did in Chapter 7.

1. What Basic Issues were raised? Remember that Basic Issues can be either known or unknown. In the Personal Workshop, you identified which Basic Issues for this customer fell into each of those categories, and in the sales call to this person you should have worked to raise and confront those Basic Issues that you had not previously been able to identify. Recall now what Basic Issues—what "Lose" perceptions—were actually discussed in your last meeting with this person. And ask yourself: Is it possible that there are still Basic Issues contributing to the lack of Commitment that I have *not* identified? If the answer to that is even a provisional Yes, then you may want to give him or her one more shot, to try to bring to the surface his or her personal reasons for withholding Commitment.

2. *What Basic Issues were resolved?* If you identified and confronted the customer's Basic Issue concerns on the last sales call, how were these concerns resolved? Are you sure that your reactions to his or her concerns laid the uncertainties to rest? Are you sure you didn't simply dismiss the client's worries as "unimportant" or "irrelevant" to the situation, rather than working with the person to demonstrate the potential Win-Win outcome? If you're not certain that you adequately resolved his or her "Lose" perception—and if you think that one more call might accomplish that—then maybe you shouldn't include this customer out just yet.

3. *What Basic Issues are remaining?* Finally, what Basic Issues might still remain in the buy/sell scenario? Are there concerns that the customer raised but that you could not resolve? Did you promise resolution in the past that you haven't yet delivered? And is it possible that this person harbors worries about doing business with you that you haven't yet even identified? Are there, in other words, any possible *hidden* issues remaining? If the answer to any of these questions is Yes, then it may be reasonable for the person to be refusing Action Commitment. And it may be reasonable for you to call on him or her one more time, to see if the Lose perception can still be turned into a Win.

But what if the answer to all these questions is No? What if, no matter what you've done on previous sales calls and no matter what you can imagine doing on future calls, you feel that this buyer will not budge. What if, in spite of the salesperson's standard-issue attitude of "Hope springs eternal," when you look at the situation honestly, you realize your chances are like a snowball's in Hell.

If that's the case, it's time to sort this person out, and to spend your time on potentially more profitable business. Face it. There are always going to be sales situations that you cannot make come out Win-Win. Some of these will be situations where, try as you might, there just is not a solid match between what you have and what the customer needs; in these cases, "hanging in there" is *never* an acceptable way to sell. In other cases, with the best match in the world, the individual client just won't see it, because he's not interested in staying Win-Win with you; in these Lose-Win cases, you always lose less by leaving than you would by toughing it out.

In short, when the selling process becomes a *battle,* you can be pretty sure it's time to cut out. We've stressed throughout Conceptual Selling that you should never consider your customer an "enemy" to be "beaten." It's just as true that you should never allow a prospect or client to think of *you* in this way. If you're playing any game but Win-Win, consider not playing at all. Selling should be *fun,* after all; even though it's very hard work, you should get a kick out of it, or what's the point? So if you're not *enjoying* your work with a given customer—if you're both not feeling satisfied most of the time—it may be time to sort this prospect out, and retire gracefully.

Not necessarily forever. Many times, you'll find that a selling process that founders in March runs along smoothly in July, because the situation has changed, and there is now a clear match between product and need. So, sometimes not only is discretion the better part of valor, but discretion can be extended to the future. The best sales professionals we know, when they are forced to sort a no-Win client out of their possible business, still keep one eye on the situation, for months or even years down the line. Timing, as we said in Chapter 11, is a critical aspect of Credibility. Sometimes waiting for good timing can be the critical difference between butting your head against a wall and building a solid structure together.

Third Process: "Feedforward"

The third and final process of Evaluation is to input all the information you now have into the *next* stage of your tactical planning. You've just reviewed and analyzed all the data that went into the outcome of the last sales call. Unless that was absolutely the final time you are ever going to sit down with that customer, then it is imperative to use the information to make the next call on this person an improvement. In other words, you've gotten the "feedback" you need to understand how things just went. You now have the chance to "feedforward," so that you don't make the same mistakes again—and so that, in that next call, you are able to build toward greater Commitment.

The bare minimum for doing that is to write down the *who, what, when,* and *where* of your next meeting regarding this account. But don't stop there. You should also identify, while it's still fresh in your mind, what specific Commitments both you and the client have agreed to perform before the date of your next meeting. Win-Win means *sharing* Commitment. So be very clear in your thinking about what specifically you've promised to do—and what the customer has promised in return.

We encourage you to write these Commitments down, as one essential feature of a new tactical plan. It's not too early, in fact, to begin laying out that plan now. And, since mutual Commitment is what is going to move the process forward, you should start by specifying Commitments. Not just the two that you've identified as being "due" by the beginning of the next call. Write down also the parameters of the client's Commitment that you will want by the *end* of that call: the Best Action you can hope for, and the Minimum Acceptable you will settle for.

Once you've done that, we suggest you go through all the other pieces of the Evaluation process that we've outlined in this chapter, and pick out those tactical "lessons" that can help you improve your interaction next time. If you were deficient on this last call in practicing Golden Silence, put that down in your notebook, and "dry run" the technique with a friend before you meet this customer again. If you've been in a selling process with this person for three or four calls and you still don't know who can give financial approval for your proposal, draft a good New Information Question to find that out on the next call. If you were so wrapped up in product specs last time that you lost sight of the customer's Concept, make it a priority of your new tactical plan to shift from a Unilateral to a Joint Venture method.

We could multiply such examples forever, but you see our point. The purpose of the Evaluation process is not simply to tell you where you've *been;* it's to show you how to get where you're going with more clarity and efficiency, and with a maximum of cooperation from your clients. Conceptual Selling always looks forward. With the application of "feedforward" after every call, you are able to manage the present *and* the future. The result is that, whether you are in the first stages of a long selling process or twenty minutes from signing a contract, you retain an essential tactical grip on the situation: you always know exactly *where you are* in each call, and you always know *what still needs to be done* to move the selling process toward a mutually satisfying, Win-Win conclusion.

And not just for *this* selling encounter. Conceptual Selling means continual reassessment and Evaluation. It means you manage each single encounter effectively—but not just for the immediate payback. When you develop a *pattern* of constant fine tuning, you gain much more than a string of individual "good deals." You gain a corresponding pattern of expanding success, where each Win-Win outcome you manage feeds into a broad network of further sales. Ultimately that is the most important sense in which feedback leads to "feedforward."

CONCLUSION: SELLING BEYOND THE CLOSE

The close is not the close.

We said it at the beginning of this book and there is no better advice we can leave you at the end. In today's superheated selling environment, with its countless savvy competitors and its equally savvy customers, going for the order alone is no longer enough. Any salesman or saleswoman who relies on the old "close him and run" philosophy is soon going to be left in the dust. The future belongs to the sales professionals who know how to sell *beyond* the close.

The reason is simple. We're in a computer-rich, highly literate, and heavily interactive selling environment, where whatever you do for a customer—good or bad—is going to hit the electronic grapevine sooner or later. In the Old West, where snake-oil drummers were the order of the day, a shifty, Win-Lose operator could stick it to any number of customers and still manage to hide from the consequences:

there was all that open space, and no telephones. Nobody can do that today. Whether or not you believe that McLuhan's "global village" is a reality, it's undeniably true that word gets around faster these days than it has ever before in history. Hiding from the consequences has become impossible. Burn the buyer, and, sooner or later, you'll have your own feet to the fire. Fail to pay attention to the long-term effects of your selling, and eventually you'll be paying the price in dissatisfied customers, lousy referrals, and lost sales.

An IBM marketing executive, quoted in Peters and Waterman's *In Search of Excellence,* makes the point exceptionally well. "Getting the order," he says, "is the *easiest* step; after-sales service is what counts."

The reference to service is particularly apt considering IBM's record in this area. But the same lesson applies to any business, whether or not it has superb service response, and whether or not it has an IBM-level reputation to maintain. If you're involved in long-term selling of any kind, you have to attend to what will happen *after* you've written the order. Or you'll soon have no business to attend to.

We don't mean that you have to scoot out in subzero weather when one of your customers has a maintenance problem. That's a service or follow-up responsibility, which may or may not be part of your job. And we don't mean you should "follow up" on your orders by obsessively sending out Christmas cards, or by remembering your client's favorite Scotch. That kind of "relationship selling" is fast becoming a relic of the past. There's nothing wrong with it per se—but it won't by itself ensure solid business.

What we do mean is that, every time you enter a sales call, you have to keep in mind that this call is only one step in a long-term, indeed a *career,* relationship. More than that: Once you pull down the order and a fat commission, you have to think of that order too as only part of a much longer process. That's what we mean by "selling beyond the close": constant attention to that developing process.

The key to managing that process effectively has nothing to do with face-to-face gimmicks, and almost nothing to do with this quarter's sales commission figures. It has to do with understanding two related ideas. First, your long-term success is intimately dependent on your various clients' success. And second, all good selling, like all good buying, begins in the *customer's* mind. It's only after you've determined what's in the customer's mind that you have any real chance of making a sale that will be good for you both.

To be more precise: All good selling begins ultimately with what the customer *believes that he or she needs.* We've called the client's "need perception" his or her Concept. Focussing on the customer's Concept is the only reliable way, eventually, to sell to "customer need."

Unfortunately, for many sales professionals, this is still a "radical" view. Commonly, when sellers speak of "need," they mean their own need to sell. Selling, in the traditional view, means *convincing* the potential buyer—whatever the business requirements or personal feelings—that he or she needs what the salesperson has to offer. So the goal of the traditionally trained salesman often gets dangerously close to the goal of the typical drug-pusher: it's to *create a need* that doesn't already exist. Refrigerators to Eskimos again.

We take the opposite approach. We believe that the customer or client usually knows at least as well as you—and probably much better than you—the nature of the problems he is facing. But he or she may not know the best possible solutions, and that's where you come in. We believe that if you encourage your clients to explore solutions with you, you have a far better chance of making a quality sale than you have if you simply push your product, and try to hypnotize them into "needing" it.

The "down side" of this philosophy is that sometimes you have to back off. Sometimes you have to acknowledge—even when the customer doesn't see it—that there isn't a good match here, and that, even if you manage to "sell" him, he won't be buying—and so he won't stay sold on your solution. When you realize a client can't *stay* sold, sometimes you have to say No. And lose business. When you're selling beyond the close, that's unavoidable.

But we say it's worth the temporary loss. We say it's a far better strategy in the long run to let the "sure thing" sale go to someone else if you can only make the sale through a Lose.

We mean *your* Lose too, not just the buyer's. We are not advising you to think more about your customers and forget yourself. On the contrary. We've stressed the sales professional's *dual* responsibility. You've got to ensure that your clients feel good about your business relationship, and that you feel good about it yourself. Without that balance, somebody always Loses. And there's nothing professional about that.

Ultimately, the "secret" of our system is just that simple. Conceptual Selling makes things easier and more productive for both you *and* your clients, because it's built on the new selling reality. Conceptual Selling says that every good close today must be a step toward the future. It says that real Winning, today, must be mutual. It says, finally, that success is the result of a logical process—a process where you work *with* your buyers, not against them, to develop solutions that both of you can own. To the professional, these are the only solutions worth delivering, because they are the only ones that build solid, dynamic business.

Business that can last beyond the close.

Miller Heiman, Inc.

Miller-Heiman, Inc. is a San Francisco-based service organization that delivers high-quality, individualized selling systems to experienced sales professionals and their management. It was founded in 1978 by Robert B. Miller and Stephen E. Heiman, the authors of this book, who between them have over fifty years of experience in sales, general management, and consulting.

Miller Heiman professionals deliver the lessons of our selling systems in a series of interactive programs attended by fifteen to twenty-five participants each. Every program's focus is pragmatic workshops. We use no canned case studies, but instead customize the individual programs to the participants' own needs and selling situations. We currently offer five programs.

- *Strategic Selling,* a two-day program, allows participants to set immediately applicable account strategies for their most important accounts and prospects.

- *Conceptual Selling,* also a two-day program, focusses on sales call tactics. Participants plan and rehearse interactions for specific sales calls on specific clients.

- Our *Managers Coaching* programs serve as follow-up support programs for both Strategic Selling and Conceptual Selling. The two coaching programs are half-day intensive workshops for first-line and senior sales managers.

- Our *Large Account Management Program* (LAMP) is a longterm consultative program for sales and support personnel that focusses on setting longterm strategies for a selling organization's largest and most important accounts.

If you would like more information about Miller Heiman, and about how we can help your company reach its full sales potential, please call or write for a fuller description of our programs.

Miller-Heiman, Inc.
375 N. Wiget Lane
Walnut Creek, CA 94598
(800) 526-6400

INDEX

Subjectivity of buying reasons, 40, 42
Success, elements of, 159–60, 304.
    See also Win-Win scenario
Success stories
    See also Chicago food service
        contract examples
    avoidance of bad sales as, 53–54
    carpentry work, 197–98, 225–26
    clothing sale, 47–48, 288
    General Instruments, 31–32
    IBM Unique Strengths, 125–26
    Shade Information Systems, 15
    of timing and credibility, 234–35
Superb Communication Process, 35
    definition of, 106
    Golden Silence, 109–15
    Question Shock, 106–9
    sales call sequence for, 132–33
"Surprise guests", dealing with,
    249–50

Tactical planning. *See* Planning
Tactics, definition of, 11
Tags, as dangerous verbal signal,
    118–19
Talking, listening vs., 65–69
Target. *See* Sales call target
Teaching, selling compared to, 156
"Think about it", as dangerous
    verbal signal, 115–16
Thinking
    natural order of, 188
    three types of, 182–87. *See also*
        specific types
    upside-down, 188–90
Thinking process
    insights into, 198–200
    in Joint Venture selling, 192,
        194–95
    Valid Business Reason enhances,
        244
Time, value of, 138
Timing
    of Action Commitment, 262
    audience change and, 249–50
    sales call success and, 233–38
    Valid Business Reason and, 241
    walking alternative and, 299
Track selling
    Concept Sale neglected in, 50

as myth, 30–31
    sequential thinking fallacy in, 95,
        104
"Trading up", 270–71
Transferred credibility, 225, 226, 227
Trust, importance of, 218–19. *See also*
    Credibility

Uncertainties, on Question Grid,
    99–102
Understanding, Cognition thinking
    for, 183–85
Uneasiness, as unknown Basic Issues
    signal, 152
Unilateral selling
    appropriateness of, 205–6
    in Concept Sale, 202, 205–6
    fallacy of, 191
    hazards of, 195–96
    Joint Venture selling vs., 196
    moving to Joint Venture from,
        209–10
    in Product Sale, 202, 206–9
Unique Strengths, 123–27
    areas of, 126–27
    Basic Issues resolution with, 150,
        151
    Concept determines emphasis of,
        127, 130–32
    definition of, 123–24
    features and benefits selling vs.,
        124–25
    Personal Workshop on, 127–33
    in Planning Matrix, 204
    post-call review of, 295
    in Product/Joint Venture quadrant,
        204
    proving value of, 131–32
    "relative uniqueness", 124, 130
    in Sales Call Guide, 280, 283
    validity testing for, 130–31
"Unstuck" sale, 146–48
Upside-down selling, 188–90, 191
Urgency, as Valid Business Reason
    criterion, 243
Urgency of buyer, sales success and,
    218

Valid Business Reason, 239–56
    cold call vs., 245–46